APPROACHING
HOLY
GROUND

SISTER MARY MARGARET DROEGE, SND

THE SISTERS OF NOTRE DAME UGANDA MISSION

APPROACHING HOLY GROUND
Sister Mary Margaret Droege, SND

Copyright © 2020

Published by Cincinnati Book Publishing, Cincinnati, Ohio

Anthony W. Brunsman, president
Sue Ann Painter, executive editor
Alaina Stellwagen, copy editor
Kara Thompson, assistant editor
Sarah Kaleem, assistant editor
Greg Eckel, design

www.cincybooks.com

Soft Bound ISBN: 978-1-7327493-9-9
Hard Bound ISBN: 978-0-9910077-2-1
Library of Congress Control Number: 2020934299

First Edition, 2020

To make a donation to the Uganda Mission, Mail a check payable to "Sisters of Notre Dame" to 1601 Dixie Highway, Covington, KY 41011 or give online at *www.sndky.org*. Indicate "Uganda."

PREFACE

This is not—strictly speaking—a history book. I have deliberately chosen not to include numerous facts about the history, culture, or politics. Such details are included only when the information is needed to explain the situation or background for the story.

This book has been long in coming. I began over fifteen years ago, researching and writing in the summers when school was not in session. This is absolutely the worst way to write a book such as this. Two incidents gave a good impetus to my working more seriously: First, I retired from teaching; and—most importantly—in 2015, the mission in Uganda became part of the East Africa Delegation, a perfect ending for the story. Until 2015, the mission in Uganda was sponsored by the Covington, Kentucky, and Thousand Oaks, California, provinces of the Sisters of Notre Dame. In becoming a member of the delegation, Uganda joined with other countries to work together, to share a common formation program for new members, and to be united under a common governing body. The East Africa Delegation includes the Uganda mission and the missions in Tanzania and Kenya sponsored by the Sisters of Notre Dame in India.

I have been to Uganda for brief visits, but I have never been missioned to Uganda. But as I heard the missionaries tell stories, and as I read their letters, I knew the Uganda mission story had to be preserved, and not just in the drawers of the archives. I wanted to preserve and to share the story with its challenges, its successes, its frustrations, and its touching moments. I wanted others to meet these amazing women who left the security of the United States or Germany to walk on what we called "holy ground," an area which had no electricity, no running water, no means of communication or transportation, and initially—very little food. Of course, these sisters had no idea that things would be so difficult, but they were ready to give it their best. With absolute trust in the good God, they set out to approach "holy ground."

The stories, quotes, and other references are primarily from the viewpoint of sisters from Covington due to the fact that almost all the materials were drawn from the archives of the Covington, Kentucky, province.

My name is Sr. Mary Margaret Droege, and I am listed as the author of this book, but in fact, since the writing is based on letters and reports, there are many authors. There is Bishop Deogratias Byabazaire, the Bishop of Hoima, Uganda; Sr. Mary Joell Overman, Sr. Mary Sujita Kallupurakkathu, and Sr. Mary Kristin Battles, who each served as superior general during these years; Sr. Mary Shauna Bankemper, Sr. Marla Monahan, and Sr. Mary Ethel Parrott, provincial superiors, who penned numerous letters. But the primary sources are the missionaries who wrote to family, friends, and the sisters with stories of the people as well as their own adventures. Among the sources are reports the sisters submitted that had more the character of a friendly letter than a dry, statistical account. In some cases, I quote from them directly. Thus, this book has a cluster of authors.

The sisters who were missioned to Uganda, discovered a country that had beautiful scenery, dangerous roads, and a generally pleasant climate despite its location on the equator. But more importantly, the sisters found a people who were so welcoming, so willing to share the little they had, and a people who smiled and lived their Catholic faith. Much of this can be explained with the words of Sr. Mary Annete Adams who arrived in Uganda a few years after the original four.

> My welcome by the parish was very touching and truly filled with an African flavor: speeches, traditional songs, dances, and gifts. I could only feel the joy and happiness of the people as they gathered to celebrate. I know they were also anxious to find out who this new sister was. *Bbooli* they came to call me: gentle, tender, humble.
>
> After unpacking and resting, each sister had a piece of Africa and our ministry to share with me. I will never have the same experiences they have had in being our first pioneer missionaries, but together we are already having new experiences as we open our new school!

As I visited a few villages I noticed the poverty of what is called "home." These are people who can only live in the present because that is what is before them. They "survive" the day and wake to a new one. There aren't calendars to follow, clocks that make one hurry from one place to another. Rather, there is the sun that shines on the land, the rain that waters the crops, the sounds of birds everywhere, the beat of the drum on Saturday night reminding one of Sunday liturgy. Nature is the reality for them—when there is no rain, crops die, when grasshoppers come, it's another kind of food, when the wind blows, it provides a welcomed breeze.

This is the Africa I am coming to know: The beauty of the people, the precious gift of their children, the blessing of the land, the gift of the soil and crops, and the heart of a God who is present everywhere. (Sr. Mary Annete to Sr. Mary Margaret, March 5, 1998)

I am most grateful to all who supported the writing of this book: Sr. Mary Shauna, who when I questioned if I should continue the writing, gave me a resounding "Yes!" and to Sr. Mary Ethel Parrott, who encouraged me to find a publisher. I also appreciate the assistance of Sr. Mary Kathleen Glavich who edited the book and Jodee McElfresh who prepared numerous photographs and assisted in the editing. I am especially grateful to my sisters of the Covington province who read chapters, gave suggestions, and pushed and prodded me to continue writing. Finally, I owe thanks to the many generous benefactors, whose physical and financial gifts –and especially their prayers – helped to make our St. Julie mission possible on the holy ground of Uganda, East Africa.

Webale Kwija! Welcome to the holy ground of Uganda!

Sr. Mary Margaret Droege, SND
June 22, 2019
50th Anniversary of the Canonization of St. Julie Billiart

The Sisters of Notre Dame

The St. Julie Mission in Uganda, East Africa, was begun by the Sisters of Notre Dame, an international congregation of women religious founded in Coesfeld, Germany, in 1850. In Coesfeld, many challenges faced the young community. Even before the rise of Otto von Bismarck as German Chancellor of the Reich in 1871, the forerunners of the Kulturkampf had already made themselves quite visible. The Kulturkampf was a conflict between the civil government and religious authorities especially over control of education and church appointments. The state exerted its influence on the schools, forced the closing of all convents, and finally drove the sisters out of the country. In 1874, the first Sisters of Notre Dame departed Germany and arrived in New York City.

At the invitation of Bishop Richard Gilmour of Cleveland, Ohio, and Bishop Augustus Toebbe of Covington, Kentucky, the sisters initially settled in these two dioceses. Two hundred Sisters of Notre Dame came to the United States as missionaries, often serving German immigrants especially in education. The central government was re-established in Germany in 1888.

As the membership in the congregation grew and other bishops requested sisters to serve in their dioceses, some were sent as missionaries to other countries. This account of the mission in Uganda, East Africa, is yet another chapter in the Sisters of Notre Dame story of proclaiming the goodness and provident care of our good God to people of many lands and nations.

The Sisters of Notre Dame were founded in Europe as were the Sisters of Notre Dame de Namur. In addition to a similar name, the two congregations of sisters share a common charism. The charism or spirit that St. Julie Billiart gave to her Sisters of Notre Dame de Namur in Belgium, in 1804, is the same spirit that was later shared with the Sisters of Notre Dame in Coesfeld, Germany, in 1850.

ST. JULIE MISSION TIME LINE

1990 At the General Conference in India, the sisters are appraised of African bishops' request for Sisters of Notre Dame.

1992 A mission is established in Mozambique by Sisters of Notre Dame in Brazil.

1993 A mission is established in Tanzania by Sisters of Notre Dame in India. Sr. Mary Joell, Sr. Mary Margaret, and Sr. Mary Amy visit the Hoima Diocese in Uganda to pursue the possibility of establishing a mission in Uganda.

1994 Sr. Mary Margaret and Sr. Mary Amy visit the Hoima Diocese and pursue the particulars of establishing a convent and a primary boarding school in the Buseesa area of the diocese.

1995 Sr. Mary Delrita, Sr. Mary Janet, Sr. Jane Marie, and Sr. Margaret Mary from the United States arrive in Buseesa, Uganda.

1998 St. Julie Primary Boarding School (for boys and girls) is established.

2001 First African Conference with sisters from Mozambique, Tanzania, Uganda, and Kenya is held in Tanzania.

2002 First women accepted into the Sisters of Notre Dame formation program

2003 Notre Dame Academy Secondary School (for girls) is established. Three Ugandan women are accepted as candidates for the Sisters of Notre Dame.

2006 First two Ugandan sisters pronounce vows as Sisters of Notre Dame.

2008 Notre Dame Nursery is established in Buseesa. St. Julie Old Students Association (JOSA) is established.

2009 Sisters take up residence in Mpala.

2011 Notre Dame Nursery is established in Mpala.

2013 First Ugandan sister pronounces perpetual vows as a Sister of Notre Dame. Preparations are initiated for establishing the East Africa Delegation.

2015 East Africa delegation is established.

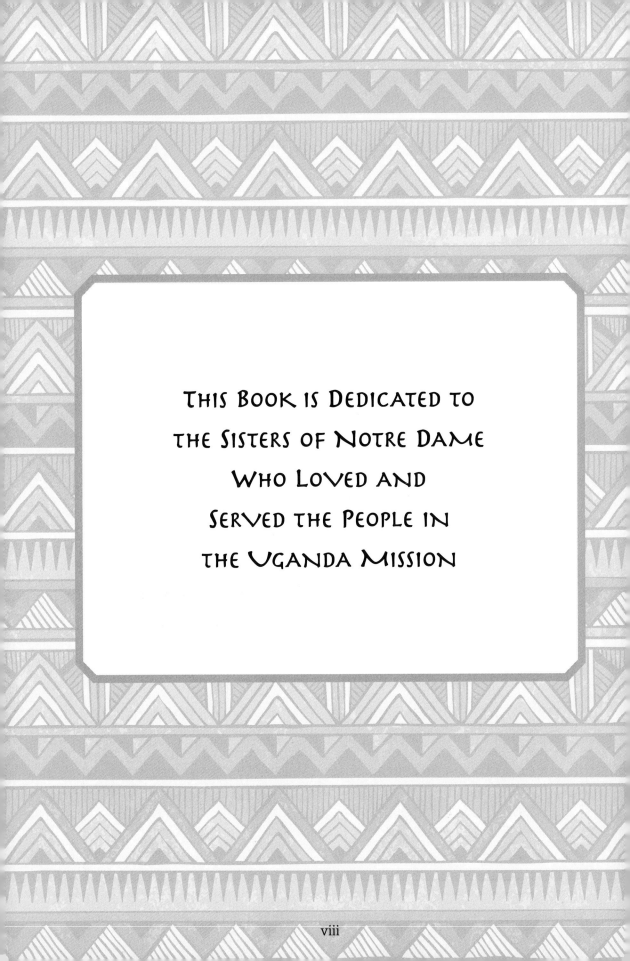

THIS BOOK IS DEDICATED TO
THE SISTERS OF NOTRE DAME
WHO LOVED AND
SERVED THE PEOPLE IN
THE UGANDA MISSION

TABLE OF CONTENTS

The inside of a large bowl woven from plant fibers (traditional art)

1

INVITATION TO AFRICA

The General Chapter of 1992 was well under way. The theme, "Evangelical Poverty in the Light of our Mission in the Church," influenced many of the general sessions as well as formal and informal discussions. At one of the break times, the United States provincials were enjoying a cup of coffee when Sr. Mary Joell Overman, the superior general, approached and joined the group. Sr. Mary Joell announced that she had received requests for sisters from bishops in Nigeria, Uganda, and Kenya. Her question for the provincials was: Would any province be willing to consider assuming responsibility for a mission in one of these countries?

Sr. Rita Mary Harwood from Chardon, Ohio, Sr. Joan Marie Recker from Toledo, Ohio, Sr. Mary Joann Schlarbaum from Thousand Oaks, California, Sr. Mary Amy Hauck (who, in December would be assuming the leadership position in California), and Sr. Mary Margaret Droege from Covington, Kentucky, considered the proposal. Then, slowly, it was recounted that the Chardon province had sponsored the mission in India and still maintained some responsibility there. The Toledo province sponsored the mission in Papua, New Guinea. Only the Covington and Thousand Oaks provinces had no foreign mission.

EARLY INVITATIONS

The congregational interest in Africa sparked in 1989 when some African bishops met Sisters of Notre Dame at conferences or became acquainted with them through other bishops. In a short time, bishops from Kenya, Tanzania, and Mozambique sent letters to the Generalate (the Sisters of Notre Dame motherhouse in Rome) requesting sisters to serve in ministry in their dioceses. In a letter to the sisters on July 31, 1990, Sr. Mary Joell remarked that "every twenty or thirty years, we, as a congregation, have responded to a call from a bishop of a local church in a country where we had no sisters."

In the letter, Sr. Mary Joell announced that she and Sr. Mary Odete would be going for a two-week visit to Africa. They were responding to invitations from bishops in three dioceses: Diocese of Mombasa, Kenya, Diocese of Arusha, Tanzania, Diocese of Beira, Mozambique. The information gathered by the two sisters would be shared with the provincial superiors at the General Conference in India in October 1990. The question set before the congregation was: Is God calling the Sisters of Notre Dame to Africa?

At the 1990 General Conference, the gathering of the provincial superiors worldwide and the members of the General Council, Sr. Mary Joell explained that the Missionaries of Africa, formerly called the White Fathers, arrived in the region around Lakes Victoria and Tanzania in the late 1870s. They introduced the Catholic religion to the people of the area. Although this meant that the Catholic Church had been present in the three African countries under consideration for about 150 years, the faith was not deep-seated. Each provincial superior was asked to reflect on a set of questions pertaining to her province's interest, personnel, finances, and possible commitment.

Many of the provincials found Sr. Mary Joell's information exciting, recognizing that the sisters were being invited to make Christ's presence more visible in these African countries. There was much discussion about the request. Some of the provincials were concerned about making a commitment without the input of the sisters of her province, without exact knowledge of the financial situation of her province, and without sufficient reflection on the deep meaning and implications of the request. At the conclusion of the conference, each provincial responded to the questions, trusting that she had been an attentive listener to the Holy Spirit.

In her 1991 Easter letter to the entire congregation, Sr. Mary Joell addressed the topic of missionary spirit. Sister wrote: "Along with our charism, our internationality and our special devotion to Mary, a MISSIONARY SPIRIT is fundamental in identifying us as Sisters of Notre Dame." But Sr. Mary Joell also pointed out: "Even though a MISSIONARY SPIRIT identifies us as Sisters of Notre Dame, we are not founded as a missionary congregation." Sister wrote that the congregation was considering foundations in two African countries: Tanzania and Mozambique. With these considerations the sisters were being challenged in their willingness to transcend the boundaries of their own countries and provinces.

In May 1991, the provincials were asked to consider the following questions: (1) Is your province willing and able to sponsor a foundation in Tanzania? (2) If you are not able to sponsor, are you able to provide personnel? (3) If you are not able to sponsor, are you able to provide financial support? The sisters were also invited to submit questions about the mission.

In a June letter to the sisters of her province, Sr. Mary Margaret presented Sr. Mary Joell's questions and added one other question: At this point in your life would you see yourself in ministry for a period of time (perhaps five years) in Africa? The sisters were also asked to submit questions, considerations, or ideas concerning establishing a mission in Africa.

During the next weeks, the sisters discussed the possibility of an African mission. They utilized the information they had received from the General Conference, and after reflection they responded to the questions they had received. A report of the sisters' responses was then submitted to Sr. Mary Joell.

Sr. Mary Joell's December 2, 1991, letter announced that the sisters from India would begin a foundation in the Diocese of Arusha, Tanzania, and that the Brazilian province of Passo Fundo would minister in the Diocese of Chimoio, Mozambique.

MISSION TREE

With the prospect that sisters might be missioned to Africa in the near future, the 1992 Covington summer missioning ceremony took a different form. Each local community was requested to bring some soil from its convent yard to the ceremony. During the service, as each local community was called forth, one member brought the soil and poured it into a large bowl by the altar. This soil was to be used for the planting of a mission tree and would represent the sisters' prayers and support that would nourish and sustain the SND mission tree - the Africa mission.

What tree would make an appropriate mission tree? Sr. Mary Virginia Ann Cleves knew someone who managed a garden center and contact was made. The tree had to be special, and the gardener suggested a katsura tree. She indicated that the tree is not very common, is quite resistant to insects, and is slow growing. It is very much like the American Red Bud tree in that it has very tiny reddish-purple buds in the spring, and its rounded leaves are about four inches long. The tree is valued as a shade tree, and its loose foliage allows for a great amount of air circulation. Since the tree is originally from the Orient the sisters thought it might make a perfect mission tree. The gardener suggested that the sisters check out the katsura growing in Spring Grove Cemetery in Cincinnati, Ohio.

Sr. Mary Margaret and Sr. Mary Virginia Ann traveled to Spring Grove Cemetery and found the katsura tree; it was huge! They couldn't begin to estimate the age of the tree. It was decided that the katsura would be the tree representing their African mission.

In November 1992, Sister Mary Joell, who was visiting from Rome, and the sisters of the provincial house gathered in the Sacred Heart circle behind the building. The men had dug a hole, and the katsura was sitting next to the hole waiting to be planted. At one point during the short prayer service, each sister took a scoop of soil from the bowl and placed it in the hole. The tree was then lifted into the hole, and the remainder of the soil was poured in. The people from the garden center completed the planting of the mission tree. The sisters would now wait for God to continue the work that had begun.

LETTERS ABOUND

While communication increased between the two African dioceses and the general administration of the congregation, other African dioceses were making their needs known to Sr. Mary Joell.

A bishop from Nigeria contacted the Generalate, and on April 22, 1992, Bishop Deogratias Muganwa Byabazaire of the Diocese of Hoima, Uganda, wrote to Sr. Mary Joell. The Bishop requested that the Sisters of Notre Dame establish a community in his diocese. Sr. Therese Tinkasimire, a sister from the Hoima Diocese, while studying at Gonzaga University in Washington state, met Sr. Mary Barbara Ostheimer, a Sister of Notre Dame from Toledo, Ohio. Upon her return to Uganda, Sr. Therese told the Bishop about the Sisters of Notre Dame and their ministry of education.

Bishop Deogratias Muganwa Byabazaire wrote to Sr. Mary Joell:

> It has been the ardent desire of our diocese to have the witness, charism, and services of international missionary congregations within the diocese. At the moment, our diocese has little of this important aspect of church life….In the name of the diocese I take this opportunity to present our request to the General Council to establish a community in the Diocese of Hoima in 1994 or earlier if possible. (Bishop Deogratias to Sr. Mary Joell, April 22, 1992)

Thus, the topic of another African foundation was raised during a coffee break at the 1992 General Chapter. The provincials from the Covington and Thousand Oaks provinces agreed to consider the possibility of a mission in Africa through joint sponsorship. The conversation was brief, and Sr. Mary Joell promised to send the provincials information about the African dioceses.

In February 1993, Sr. Mary Margaret reminded the sisters in Covington that when Sr. Mary Joell visited the United States in the fall of 1992, she announced that the Notre Dame community had again been invited to Africa by two Bishops, one in Uganda, and the other in Nigeria. Sr. Mary Joell had remarked that she was looking to the United States provinces to consider a joint venture in one of these dioceses.

In that same month, the sisters in California and Covington received the ad limina report of the Diocese of Hoima, Uganda, and the Diocese of Ijebu-Ode, Nigeria. (The ad limina apostolorum visits are meetings the bishops have every five years with the pope to give him an account of the state of their diocese.) The sisters were asked to acquaint themselves with the information. In each local community, the sisters discussed the information provided and the possibility of joining with another province to address the need in Africa. Any sister who was interested and able to be considered for being missioned to Africa, was asked to make this known. The responses were to be sent to the respective provincial superior. Both the California and Covington provinces followed a similar process in considering a mission in Africa and identifying the future missionaries.

Sr. Mary Margaret wrote to the sisters:

> The task before us is to open our hearts and our minds to see what God might be saying to us; to consider if we have resources we are willing to share (or to sacrifice for others). (Sr. Mary Margaret to Sisters, February 28, 1993)

Enclosed with the letter were questions for consideration by the local communities:

- Do you think our province should consider a mission in Africa? Explain briefly.
- Are you in agreement that we should join with another province in sending sisters to a diocese in Africa?
- Considering the two possibilities, the diocese in Uganda or the diocese in Nigeria, which do you think we should consider if we decide to send sisters to Africa?
- Additional comments, observations, or questions we need to ask ourselves or ask the diocese.

Sisters who wished to be considered for ministry in Africa were asked to respond to these questions/statements:

- The personal gifts I bring are …
- The professional talents I have are …
- I could contribute to the ministry by …
- Can you see yourself in ministry in Africa for a period of at least 3-5 years? (Add comments)
- Other comments

During the next three weeks individuals and local communities reflected and prayed for the Spirit's guidance in this important matter. Sisters reviewed the materials, sought more information, and discussed what they found.

Sr. Mary Philip Trauth, history professor at Thomas More College, contacted the United States State Department about the safety of sending sisters to Uganda. Sister discovered that the country was experiencing a time of relative peace.

By March 20, Sr. Mary Amy and Sr. Mary Margaret had sent their province responses to Sr. Mary Joell. Both provinces indicated a preference for the diocese in Uganda. One of the primary reasons for choosing Uganda was the greater need for woman religious in various ministries.

Covington's response read:

> From the papers returned from the sisters ... it seems we have support for a mission in Africa. There is fairly strong but not overwhelming support as there are MANY questions which surfaced. ... What is our next step?
> (Sr. Mary Margaret to Sr. Mary Joell, March 20, 1993)

Sr. Mary Joell was quick to respond:

> Today is Good News day! I'm excited to think that both of your provinces have given indication of supporting the establishment of a mission in Africa. The next step! I have written a letter to the Bishop in Uganda (Bishop Deogratias Byabazaire) saying we are still interested and would suggest that two sisters come from the United States to visit. (Sr. Mary Joell to Sr. Mary Margaret and Sr. Mary Amy, March 20, 1993)

In a few weeks, Sr. Mary Joell received a letter from the Bishop in Uganda:

> The greatest news of the year! We are most delighted to learn that the California and Kentucky provinces have shown their interest in establishing a community in our diocese.
>
> The contribution of religious congregations in education is ever becoming indispensable and especially on the side of girls' education, the need is great.
> We shall therefore be happy to receive the Sisters to visit us and have first-hand information. (Bishop Deogratias to Sr. Mary Joell, April 13, 1993)

The Bishop suggested the sisters fly with Sabena Airlines because this airline continued flights in and out of Uganda during Idi Amin's time as president. (In 1971 General Idi Amin overthrew the elected government and declared himself president of Uganda, launching a ruthless eight-year regime in which an estimated 300,000 civilians were massacred.) The Bishop promised he would meet the sisters at Entebbe International Airport and work out an itinerary to enable the sisters to visit various parts of the diocese.

On June 3, Sr. Mary Joell was able to fax Sr. Mary Amy and Sr. Mary Margaret:

> Good News! I have received a FAX from Bishop Deogratias that the suggested dates of October 30 to November 7 or whatever dates can be arranged are fine with him. So this means a GREEN LIGHT TO PROCEED AHEAD FOR UGANDA. (Sr. Mary Joell to Sr. Mary Margaret and Sr. Mary Amy, June 3, 1993)

In her October 1, 1993, letter to the sisters, Sr. Mary Joell began with this quote:

Our first task in approaching
Another people
Another culture
Another religion

Is to take off our shoes
For the place we are approaching is holy.

Else we may find ourselves
Treading on another's dream.

More serious still, we may forget …
That God was there before our arrival.

– unknown

Sr. Mary Joell then announced that the Immaculate Heart of Mary Province, Covington, Kentucky, and Rosa Mystica Province, Thousand Oaks, California, were considering an African mission through a joint effort. Sr. Mary Joell wrote that she, Sr. Mary Amy, and Sr. Mary Margaret would be traveling to Uganda to spend one week seeing the various apostolic needs of the diocese. Sr. Mary Amy, as a new provincial, and her council were scheduled to go to Rome in late October for a week-long orientation with the General Council, the chief governing body of the Sisters of Notre Dame. The trip to Uganda was planned to follow these meetings. Sr. Mary Joell and Sr. Mary Amy were to depart from Rome, meeting Sr. Mary Margaret in Brussels, Belgium.

Sr. Mary Joell indicated that although Bishop Deogratias' (as the sisters would come to call him) initial invitation was for an all-girl Catholic high school, he also desired that the sisters have the opportunity to see the other needs of the local church. Thus, the sisters would spend one week in the Diocese of Hoima visiting the various apostolic ministries.

What began as an informal gathering of the United States provincial superiors during the 1992 General Chapter, concretized the chapter theme of evangelical poverty and mission in the Church. In less than two and a half years, two of the United States provinces would jointly sponsor a foundation in the Diocese of Hoima, Uganda, East Africa.

Detail of a 200 Uganda Shilling (money)

2
FIRST TRIP TO UGANDA, 1993

From the beginning, Sr. Mary Margaret's flight seemed to have been "marked by the cross." The plane was scheduled to leave Cincinnati in the late afternoon of October 29, and because of several delays, Sr. Mary Margaret failed to meet her connecting flight in Atlanta, Georgia.

While waiting for the Atlanta ticket agent to confirm the new flights through Shannon and Dublin, Ireland, Sr. Mary Margaret thought she was having a vision: Walking through the terminal were the sisters from Birmingham, Alabama! What a relief to see some familiar and friendly faces in this stressful time! The sisters had driven in heavy rain for three hours to meet sister on her way to Uganda. After a brief visit, Sr. Mary Margaret boarded the plane, and the sisters began their lengthy night-drive back to Birmingham.

Sr. Mary Margaret arrived in Brussels in the afternoon of the following day and met Sr. Mary Joell and Sr. Mary Amy. As the sisters were waiting that evening for their flight, they noticed that the flight number indicated the flight was to Bujumbura. The sisters were totally unfamiliar with Bujumbura, and they inquired of someone at the counter. Bujumbura is in Burundi, a country adjacent to Rwanda and near Uganda. This was not a fact to inspire courage in the three travelers considering the recent genocide that had occurred in Rwanda. At 10:40 p.m., the sisters boarded the plane for Uganda by way of Bujumbura.

The sisters experienced some anxiety when the plane touched down in Bujumbura. The previous week there had been an attempted coup in the country. The small, modern airport was situated on a plain surrounded by high mountains. Heavy security was obvious as the sisters entered the terminal, where they were surprised to be offered soda and tea. During this respite, Sr. Mary Amy disappeared for some time. What could have happened to her? The other two sisters were relieved to discover that sister had trouble with the lock in the restroom.

After an hour, the passengers boarded the plane for Entebbe, Uganda. Since the Entebbe airport is situated on the shore of Lake Victoria, the approach was quite spectacular with the morning sun gleaming off the blue water and the many small, scattered islands.

WELCOME AT ENTEBBE AIRPORT

Upon deplaning, the sisters were met by a gentleman holding a small blackboard on which was written the names of the sisters. The sisters were then escorted to the VIP lounge, welcomed by Bishop Deogratias, and offered refreshments. Everything had the appearance of the arrival of some important dignitaries; the sisters were overwhelmed with the welcome and hospitality. Shortly, the sisters were introduced to Elizabeth Bagaya, who had served as the Ugandan Ambassador to the Vatican and as Secretary for Education. At the time of the sisters' visit, she worked with UNICEF and AIDS issues.

As they left the airport terminal, three priests from the Hoima Diocese greeted the sisters. The Bishop, the sisters, the priests, and the luggage were squeezed into the vehicle. Fortunately, the trip to Kampala (the capital) was only forty-five minutes.

On the way, they passed the former airport where an international incident with an Israeli airline had occurred under the regime of Idi Amin. Over the next few days, the sisters were to see and hear about the disasters inflicted upon the people and the land during the years under this cruel dictator as well as that of Milton Obote, who preceded and followed Idi Amin.

In Kampala, the Bishop and the sisters stopped for lunch at ARU, headquarters for the Association of Religious in Uganda. ARU sponsors a hostel for religious women. While there, the sisters met some Dominican sisters who had recently arrived from Italy. Little did the three sisters know that in a few days they would be staying at the Dominican sisters' new convent in Kakumiro. The Bishop offered Mass in the small chapel at ARU, and by 3:30 p.m., the sisters were on their way to Hoima, the diocesan see. Hoima is the central city in the diocese and the site of the cathedral and the residence of the Bishop.

EXPERIENCING UGANDA'S ROADS

After about an hour's drive on a tarmac road, Fr. Charles Nkende, the Bishop's secretary, pulled over to the side of the road. Because it was quite warm, the sisters were surprised when the Bishop and Fr. Charles stepped out of the vehicle and began donning coats and hats! The Bishop informed the sisters that the roads ahead were dusty and some type of covering was needed. The sisters resorted to what was at hand. Sr. Mary Joell covered herself with a jacket; Mary Amy, a rag (formerly someone's clothing); and Sr. Mary Margaret a plastic bag. Thus, at least their white veils were protected from the fine red dust that continued to come in through the windows and settle on everyone and everything.

The red earthen road was crisscrossed with ruts and potholes several inches deep. The sisters came to call these holes "hippo holes" as they thought some holes were so large that they could easily accommodate a hippopotamus! The vehicle swerved from one side of the road to the other as Fr. Charles attempted to avoid the holes, but it was impossible to miss all of them. Fortunately, very few vehicles were passed. Their car kept a good speed despite the condition of the road.

Three stops were made during the trip: once to greet the Bishop's brother who was traveling to Kampala; another time for refreshments; and a third time to pick up a man whose truck, filled with bananas and workers, had run out of fuel. The sisters were to learn much about the hospitality of helping those along the road.

HOIMA, THE DIOCESAN SEE

When the travelers arrived in Hoima about 7:30 p.m., it was already dark and impossible to see anything. There were no lights because there was no electricity. At the Bishop's house, the young women who cared for the laundry, cooking, and cleaning welcomed the sisters and helped carry the luggage to the bedrooms. Sr. Mary Joell had a private room while Sr. Mary Amy and Sr. Mary Margaret shared a room. The bedrooms had cement floors, windows with screens, and a shower. When the generator was off or there was no solar energy, kerosene lamps provided light and the showers produced only cold water.

The evening meal included bananas, pineapple, and matooke (a green banana that is cooked), some green vegetable, meat, and several ingredients that the sisters did not recognize. A single light hanging from the ceiling lighted the dining room. Sr. Mary Amy was somewhat unnerved when she observed geckos crawling along the walls. Geckos are nature's bug catchers.

After the somewhat lengthy meal at which German wine was served, the sisters were informed that because of their coming, a holy hour had been prepared. All proceeded to the chapel where they prayed evening prayer, night prayer, and the rosary. One of the sisters was so tired that her "prayer" was primarily a concentration on staying upright on her chair. The prayer being completed, the sisters made their way to their bedrooms and began unpacking. It was after midnight when they finally retired for the night.

The three visitors had been told that they had arrived during the rainy season, so they were not surprised that night when a storm arose. The lightning and thunder were quite severe, and the rain came in torrents.

Before the sun had even thought about making an appearance, a rooster announced that the day was to begin. After a breakfast of hot cereal (sorghum and soybeans), and scrambled eggs, bread, coffee, and tea, the Bishop, Fr. Charles, and the sisters were traveling to St. Simon Peter Vocational Training Center. The Missionaries of Africa conduct the center. The purpose of the center is to train young men to become committed Christian craftsman especially in the fields of carpentry, construction, and motor vehicle mechanics.

ST. SIMON PETER Since it was the feast of All Saints, the sisters joined in the Eucharistic liturgy at the chapel of St. Simon Peter. Drums and other instruments as well as clapping and swaying, accompanied harmonious vocals giving joyful praise to God. Some hymns were in the native Runyoro language and others were in English. Even the popular American songwriter Carey Landry made the song list! A group of young children who sat in front of the sisters kept them supplied with songbooks and indicated what song they were about to sing.

TOUR OF HOIMA At 4:00 p.m., after a brief siesta and afternoon tea, the sisters were given a tour of Hoima. They noted that the town consisted of a few dirt roads with buildings resembling a Western movie set. At the one gas station in Hoima, a picture of Pope John Paul II was taped on a window. Pictures of the Holy Father were also seen on lapel pins. This display reflects the reverence and respect with which the people hold this Pope who had visited eight months previously.

OUR LADY OF LOURDES CATHEDRAL The cathedral is a surprisingly large building. Built by the Hoima Construction Department, it was made of "Butema bricks," so called because they are made in the village of Butema. The arches in the building are a characteristic of Br. Karl Siebertz, the architect and member of the White Fathers. The wall behind the tabernacle has individual woodcarvings of Jesus and the twelve apostles.

EDUCATION OFFICE At the education office for the diocese, Fr. Peter Kibuuka explained the educational system in the country:

- The primary schools comprise grades P-1 through P-7. Students are tested after P-7 to determine if they qualify to begin high school. Nationally only 40% of the students pass this exam. For those who do not pass, this means the end of their formal education.
- Parents do not always support education as they themselves are not educated (because of the civil war) and so are not always willing or able to pay for their children's education.

- In government-sponsored schools, the government pays the teachers' salaries. The pay is about $30 to $40 a month, and the payment is sporadic.
- The teacher-training of two to three years is very questionable.
- Teachers are not likely to teach in outlying districts.
- The school system is really on its own.

OTHER VISITS   The sisters then visited a hospital that was a collection of single-level buildings. Volunteers from Italy staffed the hospital.

At St. John Bosco Minor Seminary, the sisters noted that the classrooms looked old and deserted. The sisters wondered if they were no longer in use. At the time, there were 155 students. The sisters were told that many students did not persevere for three reasons; finances, studies that were too difficult, or lack of academic preparation. As the visitors left the seminary, the watchman, carrying a bow and arrows, came to open the gate.

That evening, the sisters joined the Bishop and two priests for supper followed by evening and night prayer. Back in their shared bedroom, the two provincials prepared for the night. Thinking to keep all the bugs at bay, especially mosquitoes, Sr. Mary Amy lit a citronella candle. She put the candle too close to some scarves, and in a few minutes a small fire was ablaze on the table. Sr. Mary Margaret noticed the fire and quickly extinguished it. Sr. Mary Amy remarked that instead of collecting funds for a school in Uganda, she would have been collecting funds to rebuild the Bishop's house!

TO THE SOUTH

On Tuesday, the group headed toward the southern part of the diocese. This time the sisters were prepared for the dusty roads. Sr. Mary Amy had brought scarves to use as gifts, but the sisters converted them into protective head coverings for their travels. On the way, they stopped to pick up some women, one of whom had three children. The sisters learned that an arm raised to a passing vehicle indicated that the person needed a ride.

About 12:30 p.m., the sisters arrived in Kakumiro and the convent of the Dominican Sisters of St. Catherine of Siena. These sisters from Italy had been in Uganda for only one month and were most welcoming. Their convent was very attractive and rather large. After dinner with the sisters, the Bishop, Fr. Charles, and the Sisters of Notre Dame enjoyed a brief rest and then left for St. Cecilly Secondary School in Bukumi.

In his letter to Sr. Mary Joell, Bishop Deogratias had stressed the need for the education of women—especially through secondary education. He proposed a girls' secondary school in Bukumi. He concluded his letter:

> "This is just a proposal. The sisters will eventually make their own choice after considering the various circumstances."
> (Bishop Deogratias to Sr. Mary Joell, April 13, 1993)

ST. CECILLY SECONDARY FOR GIRLS AND ST. EDWARD SECONDARY FOR BOYS

St. Cecilly Secondary School for girls is situated at the top of a hill. When it could no longer be maintained, it was consolidated with St. Edwards Secondary School for boys that is located at the bottom of the hill.

Between the two schools, were several buildings for other educational programs: two primary schools and a catechumenate, a program to introduce and prepare persons joining the Catholic faith. When the Bishop and sisters visited the catechumens, the children offered joyful songs and dance accompanied by drums and clapping. Some of the children wore a rosary like a necklace. This was a sight the sisters were to see often during their visit.

At St. Edward's, the sisters met Brother Aloysius, a Brother of Christian Instruction and the headmaster of the school for over two years. They also met Florence, who had been on the staff for about two years and served as Deputy (person in charge) for the girls. The sisters were told about the poor education that students, especially girls, received, and the poor showing of the school in the final exams.

During the tour of St. Cecilly's, the sisters visited the girls in the dorms. The furnishings consisted of bunk beds and a small storage space for each girl, which was covered with colorful magazine pictures. Because the storage spaces were so small, many of the girls had things piled by their beds.

In front of the brick dorms was a spacious grassy area. Across from the dorms was a brick building that had formerly been used as classrooms. The building had been abandoned and was in great disrepair, so the girls attended classes at St. Edward's.

The pit latrines for the girls raised health and safety issues in the minds of the sisters. Florence explained that there was no running water in this area because the pump was not working. Consequently, the girls had to carry water from the bottom of the hill.

The sisters met a young woman from New Jersey who was with a Mennonite volunteer program. She stated that for her the most difficult aspect of Uganda was dealing with her American mentality of expecting to get things done and seeing quick results. Her experience was that it didn't happen that way in Uganda.

After the tour, the sisters joined the girls assembled near the lone tree in the grassy area and watched them present a program of song and dance. This was followed by tea with the school staff.

KAKUMIRO

That evening, the sisters returned to the Dominican sisters' convent in Kakumiro. The sisters were most gracious, even demonstrating how to light the kerosene lamps.

In the morning, the sisters joined others for Mass at the parish church, St. Andrea Kaahwa, the national shrine of one of the Ugandan martyrs. After breakfast, the Dominican sisters were proud to show their convent garden of corn, beans, carrots, zucchini, eggplant, pineapple, sweet potatoes, and several kinds of lettuce.

MORE EDUCATIONAL STOPS

The Bishop and the sisters returned to St. Cecilly's and met with Florence in her home. In Uganda, it is customary for schools to provide housing for the teachers. All spoke openly about the conditions they had observed the previous day. Florence described the low morale of the teachers and the great difficulty in getting teachers to come to the area. There was also a problem with retention. Again, the sisters heard about the system of paying the teachers. Florence explained that at this school, a parents' group supplemented the salary, but the amount was very minimal.

Florence related that because of poor primary education, the girls were not really prepared for secondary education. Compounding this was the fact that the boys at St. Edward's did not want the girls in their school or in their dining room. Consequently, the girls carried their food up the hill and ate outside the dorm area. This was the spot where the sisters had seen the cows grazing earlier in the day. It was also noted that there were rats in the girls' dormitories.

The Bishop and the sisters later visited Brother Lawrence, the deputy head teacher, who had been with the school for about twenty years. Also present were a husband and wife who had children in the school. The parents agreed that the girls received an inferior education compared to the boys. As the sisters were preparing to leave, the woman voiced the hope that something could be done for the education of women.

The information gleaned and the visit to the various buildings these two days gave the sisters much to ponder.

RETURN TO HOIMA

On the return trip to Hoima, a very ill woman and her companion joined the Bishop and sisters for the last two hours of the trip. The woman had an open wound on her abdomen that was quite distended. It was obvious she was in great discomfort. Before the vehicle reached Hoima, yet another passenger joined the group.

On reaching Hoima, the travelers proceeded to the hospital where the Bishop carried the woman to the entrance and placed her on the floor. There was no nurse or doctor present at the time. The Bishop gave the woman some money for her stay, and the next day he visited her.

At the Bishop's house, prayer in the chapel followed the 7:30 p.m. supper. When the sisters retired, there was no electricity, so they washed out some clothing and prepared for bed in the dark.

HOIMA CONSTRUCTION   In the morning, the electricity was still off. The sisters followed the usual morning routine: Mass, morning prayer, and breakfast. Later, they set out for the Hoima Construction Department. Fr. Heinz-Josef Schakel, a Missionary of Africa, had been the director for the past several months. The company, which employed about 350 workers, built churches, schools, and other such facilities for the diocese. Fr. Heinz explained that the diocesan construction company's work is a little more expensive than that of other companies, but the company paid good wages and provided quality workmanship.

Fr. Heinz then conducted the visitors to the other industries and their shops: auto mechanics and woodworking. There they saw beautiful chairs, tables, beds, cupboards, and desks made of mahogany, a common tree in Uganda. Fr. Heinz pointed out that much of the large machinery used was made in Germany. The German people were very generous in their financial assistance to the diocese. The monies usually came from specific organizations in Germany such as Caritas and Misserio.

TO THE NORTH

The sisters, Fr. Charles, and a driver set out for Masindi in the northern part of the diocese. The Bishop was not able to accompany them as he had a meeting with a coronation committee. The Banyoro tribe of the southern area desired the restoration of the monarchy, and the Banyoro king would be crowned in December. The Bishop, as a member of this tribe, was to be part of the coronation ceremony. Each tribe had its own king, who had no political power but rather was a cultural leader. It was thought that the monarchy would help strengthen the unity within the tribe.

MASINDI   The parish in Masindi had responsibility for forty outstations. The minister, who was also the Vicar General of the diocese, and his assistant minister were able to visit each mission about once every three months.

In Masindi, the sisters visited a girls' secondary school. The sisters were especially interested in the dorms that had recently been built. Near the entrance to the property were large gardens where students from the primary school were working. The sisters learned that it was a common practice for students to assist in the cultivation of the food. As the sisters walked the grounds, children from the primary school ran to meet the visitors and greet them with smiles and handshakes. The children in their green uniforms were eager to have their pictures taken.

On the same property was a catechumenate program with ninety children enrolled. The children lived at the school for one year as they prepared for Baptism. They were also taught to read and write. For most, this would be their only year of school. The children belonged primarily to three tribes, and thus the classes were taught in the languages of these tribes.

During their visit the sisters also took note of the great number of flowers, especially those they readily recognized: marigolds, roses, cosmos, and New Guinea impatiens that were the size of bushes.

The visitors then traveled to St. Michael, one of the outstations of the Masindi parish. A school was begun here in 1950, discontinued during the war years and begun again in 1979. Classes for the 180 students were held in circular thatched huts. The nearby small brick church was in very poor condition.

At the next school the children were having class in small groups under a large tree. At the arrival of Fr. Charles and the sisters, the teachers and children—many of whom were Catholic refugees from Zaire—came and sang. The guests were then asked to sign the guest book. Early in their visit, the sisters learned the custom and the importance of signing the guest book at each place they visited.

At St. Jude Church, which was to be consecrated in a few weeks, the sisters could see the remains of the soldiers' barracks from the time of Amin. The area had also housed an arsenal in the 1970s. Elsewhere there were constant reminders of the civil war and the devastation that affected every aspect of life and culture in Uganda.

MURRO   In Murro, the travelers stopped for tea with the pastor of Mary, the Mother of God Parish. The pastor or his assistant visited each of the fourteen outstations about every six months. Such a visit was an all-day event: confessions for about two hours, Mass, perhaps sixty Baptisms, and the blessing of weddings. In addition to the parish hall – no church yet – there were several signs of life springing forth: a new convent for the Sisters of the Good Samaritan, an indigenous community that will care for the destitute and abandoned, a catechumenate building for children who came for one year while preparing for Baptism, and the beginning of a new primary school.

After tea the visitors were driven to the top of a tall, steep hill situated in a large valley surrounded by low mountains. The small, white chapel was dedicated to Our Lady of Guadalupe. The inside of the chapel was bare except for a picture of Our Lady of Guadalupe and the large corpus from a crucifix.

This tour of the northern area of the diocese was to include a visit to Murchison Falls, but because of recent rebel activity, the visit was cancelled.

BACK TO HOIMA

On Friday, the sisters toured the Hoima brick factory where the Butema bricks were made. Then they visited a sunflower and soybean oil-producing plant established by the Kolping Society, which also conducted a hostel in the area.

The afternoon included the dedication of a nutrition center, a joint project between the diocese and a group from Belgium. The projects of the Belgium group were directed at assisting the people to move from relief help to self-reliance. Previous projects had addressed husbandry, the promotion of rice growing, the processing of maize and rice, and the repair or building of bridges in rural areas to allow people to transport their products to markets.

When the Bishop and sisters arrived at the center, it was raining, but no one used an umbrella. The sisters quietly tried to make their umbrellas as inconspicuous as possible. Fortunately, the actual ribbon-cutting ceremony was brief, and all the guests retreated to a covered area. The program continued with the blessing of the building, speeches, singing by the youth choir from St. Andrea in Kakumiro, and entertainment by the Kinyega dancers. The dancers had *ebinyeges* (leg rattles worn in dances) and wore grass skirts. They sang, danced, and acted out stories in song. Before the meal was served, all the guests were offered water and a towel to wash and dry their hands. The meal was the usual Ugandan fare: matooke, peanut sauce, and cassava (a root vegetable). Since this was a special occasion, meat was served.

When the Bishop and sisters returned to the Bishop's house, there was no electricity. It was the sisters' last night in Hoima. Since the Bishop had a meeting, Fr. Charles and two of the girls, in the name of the Bishop, presented the sisters with carved wooden plaques depicting Our Lady of Lourdes Cathedral in Hoima.

KAMPALA

The rain continued into the night so that the next morning the roads were muddy and quite slippery; frequent fog also slowed the travel to Kampala. After some distance, the Bishop's vehicle met a large truck mired in the mud in the center of the narrow road. The Bishop's driver tried to go around the truck on the right side. In his attempt, the driver drove into a steep ditch that caused the vehicle to get trapped in the mud and to lean heavily to the right. After surveying the situation, the driver put the four-wheel drive into action. All the occupants leaned heavily to the left and offered numerous prayers. Through the combination of skill, pushing by bystanders, and divine intervention, the vehicle moved forward, around the truck, and up the side of the ditch.

When they arrived in Kampala, the Bishop and sisters drove to the Vatican embassy to meet the Pronuncio, Christophe Pierre. After conversing for an hour, the Pronuncio invited his guests to the rooms where John Paul II had stayed during his February visit to Uganda. The Pronuncio pointed out the bedspread that was made of pounded bark and displayed a map of Uganda and various scenes in the country. It was a beautiful work of art! (Barkcloth is a traditional material that was used for clothing before the coming of foreigners and the introduction of cotton and other fabrics.)

While they were in Kampala, the Bishop took the sisters to Makerere University— the only major university in Uganda. The buildings showed the scars of the war. The Bishop wanted the sisters to meet Sr. Teresa Tinkasiimire, through whom he had come to know about the Sisters of Notre Dame.

NATIONAL SHRINE OF THE UGANDA MARTYRS   In the late afternoon, Bishop Deogratias invited the sisters to travel to Namugongo to the National Shrine of the Uganda Martyrs. Twenty-two young Catholic men were martyred at this spot or along the route. (Some Episcopal youths were also martyred nearby, and another shrine honors their memory.) The national shrine is situated in a beautiful park with a small lake. The sisters thought the shape of the church to be much like that of a gleaming space capsule, but in fact it was designed to depict the shape of the traditional Ugandan hut. Scenes from the lives of the martyrs were beautifully carved into the mahogany doors. Each window in the shrine depicted one of the martyrs whose relics were contained in the main altar. On the day of the national feast of the Uganda Martyrs, June 3, thousands of pilgrims walked the seventeen miles from Kampala to celebrate the Mass at the shrine. Other pilgrims came from farther places, such as Kenya.

After some prayer time in the shrine, all returned to Kampala and ARU. A time was set to meet with Bishop Deogratias to discuss the possibility of the Sisters of Notre Dame coming to the Hoima Diocese and in particular assuming responsibility for St. Cecilly School.

WILL THE SISTERS OF NOTRE DAME COME TO UGANDA?

From 5:00 p.m. to 8:00 p.m., the Bishop, Sr. Mary Joell, Sr. Mary Amy, and Sr. Mary Margaret met in a small parlor at ARU. The meeting was positive and direct. The sisters expressed a deep sense of a call to the diocese. They remarked that St. Julie Billiart, the spiritual mother of the Sisters of Notre Dame, would have felt quite at home among the poor and needy of the diocese. It was also noted that St. Julie wore a large medal of Our Lady of Guadalupe, and a chapel that they had visited in Murro was named Our Lady of Guadalupe. Perhaps Julie was telling the sisters something.

The sisters presented to the Bishop their concerns about the situation at St. Cecilly School. The sisters thought that their assuming responsibility for the school was not feasible. The sisters had no experience in the culture, they had no established reputation in the area, and the problems were so numerous that the sisters would not be able to address them. However, there was a definite sense that the Sisters of Notre Dame were being called to participate in the life of the church in the Hoima Diocese.

The sisters asked the Bishop if there were other possible ministries, especially in the area of education. No commitment was made at this time, but it was agreed that Sr. Mary Amy and Sr. Mary Margaret would return to their respective provinces and present to the sisters of the province information about the diocese and its many needs.

GOOD-BYE KAMPALA, HELLO LONDON

Early the next morning, the sisters were on their way to Entebbe airport. Sr. Mary Amy and Sr. Mary Margaret checked in easily. When Sr. Mary Joell gave her name, she was informed that her name was not on the passenger list despite the fact that the sisters had confirmed their flights the previous day. Sister then discovered that her large piece of luggage was missing. In a brief time, both situations were resolved, and Sr. Mary Joell was on her way to Rome. Sr. Mary Amy and Sr. Mary Margaret's flight brought them, but not their luggage, to London. The sisters had stopped in Brussels where there was a problem with a conveyor belt. While they waited in the London airport, they enjoyed a cup of tea with Sr. Mary Patricia Gannon and Sr. Mary Aidan, from the England district house, who had come to meet them. After some time, the luggage finally arrived, and the sisters set out for their two-hour ride to the district house in Kettering.

The next day, one of the sisters of the district house offered to wash the sisters' clothing. She could hardly believe the red dirt that had seeped into every seam and fiber of the clothing.

The sisters of the District of Stella Maris, Kettering, England, were most interested in hearing of the adventures of the two sisters. Sr. Mary Amy and Sr. Mary Margaret related many of their experiences, observations, and impressions of the previous days. The sisters asked questions and promised their prayerful support for the mission in Uganda.

Source of Information: Sr. Mary Margaret Droege, Journal "Daily Account of Visit to Uganda, October 29 – November 7, 1993."

Doll made from corn plant fibers

3
BACK HOME

When Sr. Mary Amy and Sr. Mary Margaret returned to their respective provinces, the sisters were most eager to hear about their adventures. During the days in Uganda, Sr. Mary Margaret had taken numerous pictures and slides and made notes about the places they visited and the experiences they had. Upon returning home, Sr. Mary Margaret typed the notes and distributed them to the sisters. During December, she held area gatherings to show the slides and tell about her experiences and impressions. These gatherings also offered an opportunity for the sisters to ask questions and offer comments.

PROVINCE SAYS "YES" TO UGANDA MISSION

Through a questionnaire, every sister was able to express her thoughts and feelings about undertaking a mission in Uganda. The results of the questionnaire were the following:

California	Covington	
65%	68%	favored beginning a mission in Uganda
25%	12%	were opposed to a mission in Uganda
10%	14%	were uncertain
--	6%	did not respond

Six sisters in California and seven sisters in Covington indicated their willingness to minister in Uganda immediately. Four sisters in California and five sisters in Covington indicated they would like to go to Uganda when their present ministry commitments were completed. (Report to the Covington Province, December 28, 1993)

In her Christmas letter of 1993, Sr. Mary Amy wrote:

> I realize and appreciate the apprehension and fear that may be connected with this new work. Despite my own positive experience in Uganda, I also know well the limitations of our personnel and resources. Yet, "God called into being the Congregation of the Sisters of Notre Dame, and in the unfolding of its history we recognize the sign of his goodness." (Constitutions 1987, p. ix) ... The gifts we offer will entail sacrifice on the part of our entire province, but let us be generous with the God who "so loved the world he gave his only Son."

On December 25, 1993, Sr. Mary Amy and Sr. Mary Margaret sent a joint letter to Sr. Mary Joell:

> We are happy to tell you that in each of our provinces the majority of sisters indicated their support for pursuing the establishment of the model primary school, which we discussed with the bishop of Hoima. At this point, we see ourselves intensifying our investigation of matters relating to the establishment of this mission (e.g., finances, jurisdiction, communication, etc.) as well as discerning which sisters may be called to serve in Uganda.

On January 4, 1994, Sr. Mary Joell wrote to Bishop Deogratias that the sisters were accepting his invitation and making a commitment to participate in the ministry of education in the Diocese of Hoima.

On January 28, 1994, Sr. Mary Margaret and Sr. Mary Amy met with Sr. Mary Joell in Toledo, Ohio, as Sr. Mary Joell was there on visitation. The minutes of the meeting stated that the three sisters discussed jurisdiction, discernment with sisters volunteering for Uganda, contact with the Bishop of Hoima, and other areas that needed to be researched. It was agreed that the Uganda mission would be a foundation under the jurisdiction of the Covington and Thousand Oaks provinces. Both provincials would appoint sisters to the mission, and both provinces would contribute to the financial support of the mission with the Covington province coordinating the finances.

DISCERNMENT FOR THE FIRST MISSIONARIES

The process for the discernment with the sisters who volunteered for Uganda was defined.

1. Each sister was to write a letter addressing specific areas determined by the provincial superiors.
2. Each sister would meet with her provincial to further discern the call to Uganda.
3. The provincial council in each province was to identify two sisters to serve in the Uganda mission.
4. The names of the sisters were then to be forwarded to the superior general in Rome.

On March 16, the Covington provincial council considered the candidates for Uganda. A decision was made, the chosen sisters were contacted, and the necessary information was sent to Sr. Mary Joell. Approval and confirmation of these appointments were received from Rome on March 20.

Finally came the announcement of the sisters to be missioned to Uganda: Sr. Mary Janet Stamm and Sr. Mary Delrita Glaser from Covington, and Sr. Jane Marie McHugh and Sr. Margaret Mary Scott from Thousand Oaks. Sr. Mary Margaret reminded the sisters of the Covington province:

> In sending Sr. Mary Delrita and Sr. Mary Janet, WE are being sent to Uganda. These two sisters go, not as individuals, but as members of our community. … In these two sisters we are each saying our YES once again. (Sr. Mary Margaret to Sisters, March 19, 1994)

Several months later on September 8, a feast of Mary, Bishop Deogratias wrote to each of the four missionaries. The letter to Sr. Mary Janet included the following:

> I am writing on behalf of the Diocese of Hoima to inform you how happy we are that you are coming to found a new community of Sisters of Notre Dame in Hoima and in Uganda. We thank the Lord for this great gift. … As education is a top priority in the pastoral work of the diocese, you as a Teacher and Administrator will contribute greatly to the development of education in this part of our diocese.

PREPARATION OF FUTURE MISSIONARIES

Meanwhile, the immediate preparation of the four missionary sisters was underway. From June 26 through July 12, the two Covington sisters participated in the Institute on Sub-Saharan Africa program held at Notre Dame University in South Bend, Indiana. This program examined many areas including issues for the church in Africa, the rise of African nationalism, the aftermath of independence, traditional African religions, Islam and Christianity, education, and military influence. (Brochure: "Sub-Saharan Africa")

In mid-September, Sr. Jane Marie and Sr. Margaret Mary came from Thousand Oaks to meet the two Covington missionaries-to-be and the sisters of the Covington province. It was also an opportunity for the Thousand Oaks sisters to become more familiar with the Covington province and its ministries and to meet the families of Sr. Mary Janet and Sr. Mary Delrita.

From September 26 through October 26, Sr. Mary Janet, Sr. Mary Delrita, Sr. Margaret Mary, and Sr. Jane Marie participated in the Cross-Cultural Training Services held in Chicago, Illinois, and sponsored by the Maryknoll Society. The Maryknoll program assisted participants in realizing the particular challenges and opportunities of a cross-cultural mission and in determining their readiness to minister in another culture. (Brochure: "Cross-Cultural Training Services")

In letters back home, the four sisters described special liturgies as well as visits to sights in the area. They kept the sisters of the two provinces well-informed about their activities:

> Topics for this week included future trends in mission, justice issues in mission, family-of-origin issues, role and challenges of a missioner in a foreign culture, and a powerful session on leave-taking. ... The family-of-origin discussion took us into styles of interaction, inclusion, intimacy needs and expression, etc. We are, indeed, being stretched and know ourselves to be growing!

> The FIRO-B, one of the tests we took before coming, has been very helpful in understanding ourselves better and especially how we interact in groups. This will be very helpful as we seek to establish our local community and as we enter the new culture. (Sr. Mary Janet, Sr. Mary Delrita, Sr. Jane Marie, Sr. Margaret Mary to Sisters, October 14, 1994)

> One of the presenters led us through a pretend scenario in which all our luggage got lost we as we were enroute to our mission. Just thinking of this possibility caused some panic. She then led us to think about the resources we each have within ourselves and how we really can make it with very little (things) because we have much within ourselves.

> A Comboni missionary from East Africa ... two Comboni Sisters. ... We had a chance to ask them some of the practical questions such as, what kind of shoes should we bring to Africa, etc. In meeting all these missionaries, it has been truly inspiring to sense their love for the people they serve and their desire to be one with Jesus in working for the Reign of God. (Sr. Mary Janet, Sr. Mary Delrita, Sr. Jane Marie, Sr. Margaret Mary to Sisters, October 8, 1994)

When the sisters returned from Chicago, they traveled to the Chardon and Toledo provinces for a visit with missionaries from India and Papua New Guinea. From these experienced missionaries, the sisters learned much about beginnings and the challenges of mission life. The four sisters wrote a joint letter to the sisters in California and Covington telling about their experiences.

> What, you may be asking yourselves, have those four wandering Sisters of Notre Dame been up to these past two weeks? After a few days of rest back in Covington, your missionaries in training completed a week of DRINKING IN THE WISDOM of the returned missionaries of both the Chardon and Toledo Provinces. We feel privileged to have been allowed to touch the flame of their enthusiasm and love of mission life. They shared many practical points and made themselves available to answer our NOTRE DAME MISSIONARY questions. (Sr. Mary Janet, Sr. Mary Delrita, Sr. Jane Marie, Sr. Margaret Mary to Sisters, November 6, 1994)

BISHOP DEOGRATIAS

Meanwhile, communication between Uganda and the United States continued. On May 6, 1994, Bishop Deogratias wrote to the two provincial superiors about plans for their visit.

I have already informed the Parish Priest and the people of Bujuni about your kind acceptance to serve in that Parish. The people are extremely happy to hear the news. They are waiting for you to make a final choice of the place when you come. In the meantime, they are suggesting two places, one in the Sub-Parish called Buseesa, that is between Kakumiro (where the Dominican Sisters are) and the Parish Centre of Bujuni. The other place is about 3 miles from the Centre.

In a visit to Rome in June, Bishop Deogratias had met with Sr. Mary Mechtilde and Sr. Margaret Mary, members of the General Council. The Bishop was quite up front in saying that he was in no position to pay the sisters a salary. He indicated that their salaries would have to come through tuition fees or in-kind gifts. The people are extremely poor, but would offer things, such as fruits, vegetables, and chickens. Nevertheless, the Bishop indicated his desire to support and help the sisters in whatever way possible.

The draft of the Agreement of Understanding between the Diocese of Hoima and the Sisters of Notre Dame was drawn up. The two provincial superiors were to discuss the Agreement with the Bishop at the time of their visit. Sr. Mary Joell asked the provincials to review the proposed Agreement with their respective councils, note any modifications, and concur on the document's stipulations. A copy was then to be sent to Sr. Mary Joell who would take it to the General Council for approval. The two provincials were to have copies of the final Agreement when they left for Uganda.

TWO PROVINCIAL SUPERIORS TO VISIT UGANDA

By September, the travel plans for Sr. Mary Amy and Sr. Mary Margaret were in place. The two were scheduled to leave on October 12 and were to meet in Frankfurt, Germany. They would stay two days with the sisters in Mülhausen, Germany, and leave for Uganda on the 15th and arrive on the 16th.

Shortly before the two sisters left for Germany, Sr. Mary Joell sent a letter with some final instructions about the proposed Agreement, the purchase of property, and the convent.

Concerning the erecting of a convent, I hope that you are able to obtain sufficient definitive information regarding property and building materials, et al [sic] during your visit. Then you hopefully will be in a position to send us a joint petition asking to build a convent after final drawings are completed. (Sr. Mary Joell to Sr. Mary Margaret and Sr. Mary Amy, October 7, 1994)

Sr. Mary Joell added the following;

The small Coesfeld crucifixes were made for the first time last May. One of the local shops in Coesfeld has begun to produce them. If, and how long the man will continue to do this is not certain. We bought twenty. I thought you would perhaps like to use them as missioning crosses for the four sisters being missioned to Uganda. (Sr. Mary Joell to Sr. Mary Margaret and Sr. Mary Amy, October 7, 1994)

With their many questions prepared, Sr. Mary Amy and Sr. Mary Margaret made their final preparations for their second trip to Uganda.

CONGREGAZIONE SUORE DI NOSTRA SIGNORA

VIA DELLA CAMILLUCCIA, 687   00135 ROMA, ITALIA   (39-6) 327-9144   *Telefax: (39-6) 327-7003*

CASA GENERALIZIA

10 January, 1994

REGISTERED MAIL

Rt. Rev. Deogratias Byabazaire
Diocese of Hoima
Bishop's House
P.O. Box 34, Hoima
UGANDA - East Africa

Dear Bishop Byabazaire:

I am happy now, Bishop, to make a commitment in the name
of the Congregation of the Sisters of Notre Dame to accept
your invitation to have our Sisters participate in the
ministry of education in the Diocese of Hoima. The two
provincial superiors, Sisters Mary Amy and Mary Margaret have
agreed to initially make available four sisters as an opening
foundation in your Diocese.

Dear Bishop Byabazaire, we look forward to working with
you and others in the Diocese of Hoima. May Our Lady of
Uganda intercede for God's blessings for all of us. The kind
hospitality shown by all of you at the Bishop's House to the
three of us during our stay with you is a constant reminder to
us of God's Goodness.

With every good wish and our prayerful remembrance,

Sincerely in Our Lady,

Sister Mary Joell Overman SND

Superior General

Excerpt of a letter of Sr. Mary Joell to Bishop Deogratias

The Colobus monkey is found in the Buseesa area

4
SECOND VISIT TO UGANDA, 1994

With the announcement of the names of the four sisters, intense communication and planning began. Much was learned from the first visit to Uganda. The second visit was to be more focused. In a letter to the Bishop, the sisters stated their primary goals for the visit:

- Purchase land for the convent
- Meet with the diocesan construction company to arrange for the construction of a convent and the digging of a well
- Investigate purchase of a vehicle, including license and insurance, etc.
- Discuss the particulars of a Model Primary School
- Consider ways the sisters could become familiar with the language, customs, traditions, and educational system of the Hoima Diocese.

(Sr. Mary Amy and Sr. Mary Margaret to Bishop Deogratias, May 26, 1994)

Recognizing that each of these goals would require a substantial financial outlay, the two provincial superiors wrote to Bishop Deogratias:

In order to assist in financing this project, we are asking for funds from various foundations and boards. These organizations require a letter from you indicating that you have invited us to minister in the Diocese of Hoima, that we will indeed be arriving in the spring of 1995, and that we have your permission and blessing to solicit funds for the following:

- establishment of a Model Vocational and Primary School, including residence facilities
- construction of a convent, including digging of a well
- purchase of a vehicle
- transportation of Sisters from USA to Uganda

(Sr. Mary Amy and Sr. Mary Margaret to Bishop Deogratias, May 26, 1994)

All was in readiness for the second visit to Uganda. Sr. Mary Amy and Sr. Mary Margaret met in Brussels on the evening of Saturday, October 15, 1994, and by 11:00 p.m. they were on their way to Uganda via Sabina Airlines.

Arriving at Entebbe International Airport on October 16, the sisters were met by Bishop Deogratias, Fr. Charles, and two other priests. After Mass and lunch at ARU, the Bishop, Fr. Charles, and the two sisters began their trip to Kakumiro, taking a more southern route than they had taken the previous year. Enroute, they visited the Bishop of Mityana. On the same property as the Bishop's house was a convent of indigenous sisters as well as a Carmelite monastery that also served as a retreat center.

KAKUMIRO: THE DOMINICAN SISTERS

Because of the stop in Mityana, the sisters arrived at the Dominican sisters' convent in Kakumiro about an hour and a half late. The Dominican sisters quickly prepared a meal, and all sat down to renew their acquaintance from the previous year. During the conversation, the Dominican sisters told about the brutal death in February of their own dear sister, Sr. Monica. While on a trip to Kampala at night, Sister was shot by bandits; she died in the vehicle. Sr. Mary Amy and Sr. Mary Margaret remembered the lively sister who was a native of Argentina. The Dominican sisters related that when Sr. Monica died, the people of the area expressed their sorrow and concern that the sisters would be withdrawn from Uganda. The superior general in Rome renewed the commitment of the sisters to the people of the area. Sr. Monica's body was buried near the Kakumiro convent.

After a lengthy meal, all proceeded to retire for the night. Sr. Mary Amy and Sr. Mary Margaret shared a bedroom and unpacked their suitcases by kerosene lamp. Their greatest challenge that night was taking a shower. They had only one lamp and there were no lights in the shower area. Since there were two shower stalls, the sisters decided to take their showers at the same time. They gathered their towels, soap, and lantern and slowly made their way to the showers, singing (quietly, of course) "We Three Kings." They discovered that they had the best light if they placed the lantern on top of a wooden cabinet and left the doors to their shower compartments open. Since this worked so well, it became their ritual for each of the four nights they were with the Dominican sisters.

VISIT TO BUSEESA

The next morning Bishop Deogratias, Fr. Charles, Sr. Mary Amy, and Sr. Mary Margaret traveled the half-hour to Buseesa. The road was often narrow, and tight curves and a steep and muddy roadway slowed their progress. The road reminded the sisters of a trail in some remote area of a farm.

Suddenly the sisters saw children lined up on both sides of a road to the left. There was no question that they had arrived in Buseesa. The vehicle turned onto the road, and the children welcomed the sisters with rhythmic clapping. As the vehicle passed the children, they followed jogging the 1.5 km up to the church. Since there were so many deep ruts in the road, the progress was slow. The sisters noted that flowers had been attached to banana plants along the road.

Part of the way up the hill, the sisters were met by a group of singers who preceded the vehicle. Periodically the singers paused, turned, and threw flower petals on the vehicle and on the path.

On reaching the top of the hill, the sisters were welcomed by hundreds of adults and children. The sisters were directed to the entrance of the church where chairs had been arranged. The adults, as well as the children, presented a program of song, dance, and drama. Drums accompanied much of the singing and dancing. Speaking in Runyoro, the native language of the people, Bishop Deogratias introduced the sisters and explained the nature of their visit. One of the priests translated for the sisters. A basket was placed on the table in front of the sisters, and people came forth to offer gifts of welcome: a pineapple, a bunch of small onions, jackfruit, and a papaya. The sisters also received some local handicrafts.

After the sisters had said a few words, with a priest translating, the sisters were led down the other side of the hill to look at the proposed sites for a convent. The sisters considered building on a site on a hillside nearby. The Bishop informed the sisters that Br. Karl, the architect, had visited, and he also chose this site. The sisters walked the hillside trying to imagine how it would look with a convent.

The Bishop then explained that the church at Buseesa was still a mission church. The sisters explained the importance of the availability of liturgy and the sacraments for the sisters who would come. The Bishop assured them that the mission church would become a parish in the near future, but an aspect of becoming a parish was the building of a rectory to house the parish priest. At that point, the sisters wondered who was responsible for the building of the rectory.

Walking up the hill, the Bishop and the sisters stopped to visit Buseesa Primary School operated by the government. The school had an enrollment of over 500 students; over half of the students were girls. The rooms had dirt floors, one blackboard, and little furniture. Some had walls of brick that were in great disrepair. One structure had wooden poles supporting a thatched roof. Because the buildings could not accommodate all the children, some classes were held outdoors. Beyond the school was a large grassy area used as a soccer field.

At a sound from the headmaster of the school, all the children assembled in front of the administration building (a one-room building). The national anthem was sung, and the Bishop and headmaster spoke to the children.

After the assembly, refreshments of tea, cola, and Mirinda soda were served at the church. This building, made of brick with a cement floor, was barren of furniture except for an altar and a few benches. As the sisters were preparing to leave, there were additional handshakes and the playing of drums.

Because the Bishop was to be in Masaka for the dedication of a new Catholic university, the sisters spent the remainder of that day at the Dominican sisters' convent. The next day, Sr. Mary Amy and Sr. Mary Margaret met with Sr. Paola O.P. who told the sisters about the Dominicans' first year in Uganda. She patiently answered the many questions the sisters raised. Sr. Paola also gave the sisters a tour of the convent pointing out certain aspects of the building and what the sisters wished they had done differently, how rainwater was collected, stored, and heated by solar energy. The sisters also visited Sr. Monica's grave.

BUJUNI: SCHOOL VISITS AND EDUCATION MEETING

On Wednesday, Bishop Deogratias and the sisters traveled to Bujuni, about fifteen minutes beyond Buseesa. The church and rectory, built by the Missionaries of Africa about seventy-five years ago, were quite large and in need of repair.

PRIMARY SCHOOLS   The visitors were directed to the front porch of the rectory where the children from the two primary schools were assembled in straight lines. One school was referred to as the "boys' school" with some girls; and the other was the "girls' school" with some boys! Sr. Mary Amy and Sr. Mary Margaret later referred to these schools as the "blue school" and the "pink school" because of the color of the uniforms of the students of the respective schools.

The Bishop, the sisters, and the teachers, were introduced. The Uganda national anthem and another song were sung, followed by brief talks by the Bishop and the sisters. During this period of about thirty minutes, the children remained quiet and attentive. Since the teachers were on the porch with the visitors, the older students served as monitors for the younger students.

Some of the youngest students stood at the bottom of the porch stairs. As the program continued, one foot from each of several children in the front row appeared on the bottom step. In a short time, the second foot advanced to the step. As the front row moved up, the children behind also moved forward. After some time, the older girls noticed the movement and moved the little ones to their original positions. In a short time, the little feet once more began inching forward.

DISTRICT EDUCATION OFFICE   While in Bujuni, the sisters visited the District Education Officer, whom they would later call the DEO. The sisters passed through the secretary's office that was equipped with a table, chair, and a manual typewriter. The DEO's office was located in a small room with a desk and a few chairs. A bench was brought in, and all the visitors crowded around with their knees touching the desk. The walls of the office were covered with maps and enrollment charts of the Kibaale District. Again, the sisters heard about the plight of education, about the Kibaale District in particular.

- 70% of the teachers were not certified.
- There was a large drop-out rate from P-1 to P-7 (from 1,100 students to 200 students).
- A teacher's salary was about $50 a month.
- Many teachers do not live at the school, so there is a high absentee rate among teachers.
- Although there is a government program that helps to build schools, there are numerous stipulations attached to these funds.

The DEO recognized that the sisters would want good teachers for their school. He explained that he assigns the teachers to the schools, and he assured the sisters that the teachers assigned to their school would receive special training.

The sisters listened carefully and wondered how this would work in their model primary school. They were sure they would want a strong voice in deciding which teachers were sent to their school. They wanted teachers who shared their philosophy and with whom they could work. The sisters suspected that they would be expected to assume the cost of the special training of the teachers.

As the meeting was nearing its conclusion, the sounds of a rooster could be heard. With each passing minute, the sounds seemed to be coming closer. As the visitors left the DEO's office, they encountered a rooster strutting around the secretary's office! The DEO did not seem the least surprised at the sight of this winged creature in the office.

SECONDARY SCHOOL   From the DEO's office, the sisters traveled to a secondary school situated on a hilltop. The view from the school was magnificent, but everything else about the school spoke of poverty. The science room was equipped with some glass beakers and a few other pieces of equipment that easily fit on four shelves. The sisters met with the headmaster in his office that was partitioned from the other part of the room by means of reeds and sticks lashed together to form the walls.

MEETING WITH SCHOOL COMMITTEE   After lunch and a rest in the rectory at Bujuni, the Bishop and the sisters walked down the hill to the assembly hall. Here they met with members of the school committee that had worked on a proposal for a model primary school. The Bishop, the sisters, and a few others were invited to sit on the chairs on the stage (a raised platform about three feet high).

In the meeting of about two hours, the following topics were discussed:

- The location of the model primary school
- The grade or grades to start with (grade three or higher)
- Population: just girls, or girls and boys
- The possible effect on the present school in Buseesa—if the school were located in Buseesa
- A boarding school versus a day school
- The head teacher (principal)
- The inclusion of lay teachers

It was agreed that the sisters would make the final decision on the location of the school.

The sisters sensed a great support for the potential model primary school. They also had a sense that the people of the area had high expectations of the sisters even though the people did not specifically identify these.

ON TO HOIMA

On Thursday, the sisters left Kakumiro for Hoima. In some places, the road was quite muddy because of the rain, but the driver maintained a good speed most of the way. At one point, a monkey quickly jumped into a tree—the first and only wild animal the sisters saw on this trip. As usual, extra passengers were added along the way: three men who squeezed in among the luggage and a small child who sat on the Bishop's lap.

At the Bishop's house, the sisters met with Bishop Deogratias and reiterated the importance of the convent being near a parish. Thus, the most logical place for the new convent and school was Buseesa. Later in the afternoon the sisters met with the Bishop and three of the consultors for the diocese. They discussed an agreement between the Diocese of Hoima and the Sisters of Notre Dame. Some points of the agreement included the availability of Mass, ownership of land, and various financial responsibilities. They also considered the need to begin construction of the convent and a time frame for the missionary sisters to arrive.

In the evening, the sisters celebrated the Bishop's Silver Jubilee of ordination. Then, as in the previous year, all gathered for evening and night prayer in the Bishop's chapel.

On Friday, an early morning liturgy and morning prayer were celebrated so the group could get started for Kampala. Again, the sisters were prepared with their protective head covering.

KAMPALA, MANY STOPS

The first stop in Kampala was the Catholic Secretariat. Fr. Charles remained to begin copying the book on the Runyoro language he had written. The sisters were to take the copies back with them to the United States so the sisters preparing to come to Uganda would have some idea of the local language in the Buseesa area.

In Kampala, Bishop Deogratias took the sisters to the Toyota dealership. They examined the Land Cruiser that the sisters would need when they came to Uganda. Since the sisters knew little about the purchase of such a vehicle, they requested printed information they could show to a Toyota dealer in the United States. The sisters learned that in addition to the base cost, there was a 30% import tax. On that total, there was an additional 30% tax! The Bishop assured the sisters that he would check into the possibility of some of the taxes being reduced.

The Bishop and the sisters then drove to Interservice, an organization initiated by the Missionaries of Africa. (Interservice later became an arm of the Ugandan Bishops' Conference.) Fr. Callist Rubaramira explained the nature of the organization and the services offered, e.g., transferring money into the country, assisting in receiving mailed parcels. In discussing the vehicle, the sisters also learned that a ten-passenger vehicle would be less expensive than a nine-passenger vehicle.

After lunch at ARU, Sr. Tarcisia, the Secretary for ARU, drove the sisters to Schimoni Teacher Training College. The sisters explained to the assistant director of the college that sisters who would be coming to Uganda were trained and experienced teachers but were not familiar with the methods used in Uganda. The assistant director suggested that the sisters observe some methods classes or demonstration lessons. Since much depended on the arrival date of the sisters, nothing definite could be decided.

From the visits to schools like the one in Buseesa and from information the assistant provided, the sisters came to understand that the basic materials available in the schools were blackboards and individual copybooks (notebooks). They were also told that the children were very auditory, and rote learning was standard. (Rote learning is the memorization of concepts based on repetition.) Earlier the Bishop had commented to the sisters that he wanted the children to be challenged to think. He asked that leadership be developed in the children.

On Saturday, the Bishop traveled to Tororo in the eastern section of the country. The next day, Mission Sunday, there was to be a special ceremony for those preparing to become catechists, teachers of religion. (The role of catechist is one of great importance in Uganda.) Each year this ceremony is held in one of the dioceses, and all the bishops come and celebrate together.

Sr. Tarcisia provided a driver who took the sisters to the bank to exchange US dollars for Ugandan shillings. The sisters arrived forty-five minutes before the bank was scheduled to close. They were surprised that the exchange rate was different for bills of different denominations: the larger denominations had the better exchange rate.

With their Ugandan shillings, the sisters visited a bookstore operated by the Daughters of St. Paul. Here the sisters found what they needed: maps, print material of the history of Uganda, batiks, and a book (mimeographed) on the Runyoro language. When the sisters went to pay for the items, they discovered that they did not have sufficient Ugandan shillings. Because the bank was now closed, the clerk agreed to accept US dollars.

Fr. Charles returned to ARU late afternoon and explained the difficulty he had in copying the language book. Sometimes the electricity was off or not strong enough—this was common—so the copy machine would not function. With the materials he was able to copy, Fr. Charles punched holes in the pages and assembled them.

Remaining for a day and a half at ARU and four days with the Dominican sisters in Kakumiro, gave the two provincials the experiences of being confined to one place, of being totally dependent on others, and of not having transportation readily available—all situations the sisters coming to Uganda would experience.

On Sunday, Fr. Charles and Fr. John Mary from the mission office drove the sisters to the Entebbe airport. The sisters quickly checked in, said their farewell, and proceeded to the waiting area. Here the sisters began making a list of the questions their visit had generated and the many things they would need to do upon returning home to Covington, Kentucky, and Thousand Oaks, California.

At each step of this visit to Uganda, the sisters recognized God's goodness and provident care and strong guiding hand. This sense of God's special care was present from the very beginning and continued through every step of growth of the mission in Uganda.

Source of Information: Sr. Mary Margaret Droege, SND, "Narration of Visit to Uganda, 1994."

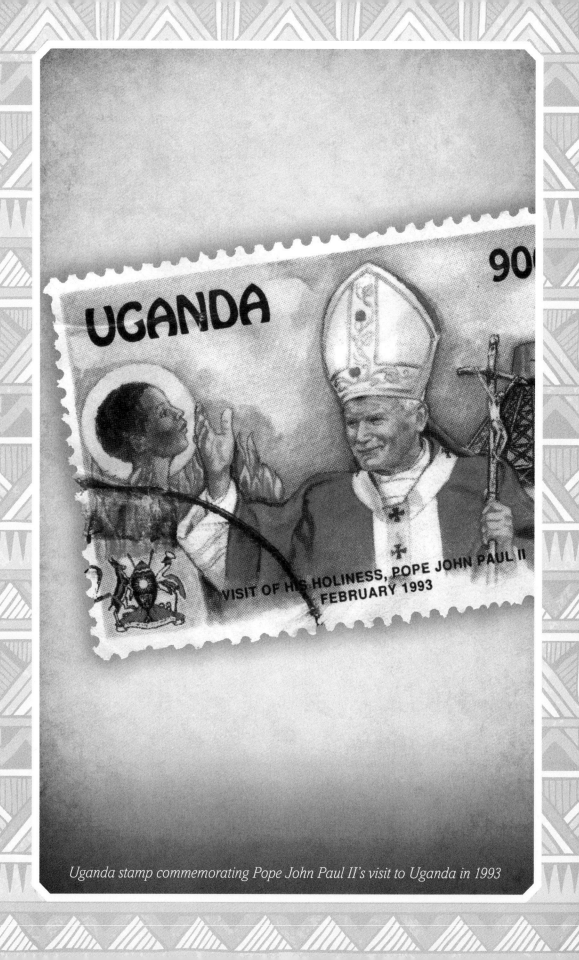

Uganda stamp commemorating Pope John Paul II's visit to Uganda in 1993

5
FINAL PREPARATIONS, DEPARTURE, AND ARRIVAL

On their return trip from Uganda in 1994, Sr. Mary Amy and Sr. Mary Margaret stopped in Mülhausen, Germany, to visit with the Sisters of Notre Dame there. The two sisters shared what they learned in Uganda. They also had the opportunity to meet with Sr. Mary Alexandra who had been a missionary in Brazil and one of the first missionaries to Korea. At the time of the sisters' visit, sister was working at the mission office in Aachen. She was able to offer many insights, challenges, and cautions relevant to beginning a mission in a foreign country.

On one of the days in Germany, Sr. Mary Amy and Sr. Mary Margaret visited the community cemetery, a short distance from the provincial house. They began a search for the grave of Sr. Mary Bernarda. Sister was an early pioneer in the Sisters of Notre Dame community and was considered the Teacher of Teachers. Her dedication provided a firm basis on which the educational system in the community flourished. After wandering up and down the rows of graves, the two sisters finally discovered Sister's grave. They bent down and began digging a small hole in the soil. Carefully, they placed in the hole, a rock they had brought from Uganda and gently covered the treasure. The sisters then prayed to Sr. Mary Bernarda. They requested her to intercede for the foundation in Uganda, that the educational endeavor be strong and faithful to the Gospel and to Sisters of Notre Dame principles of education.

At a later date, the two provincials contacted the Sisters of Notre Dame de Namur in Belgium and asked if a plaque could be placed in the small chapel where St. Julie Billiart is buried. The plaque, which was placed near the statue of St. Julie, reads

St. Julie, bless
our Uganda Foundation 1995
The Sisters of Notre Dame
of Coesfeld
California Province
Kentucky Province

While in Mülhausen, Sr. Mary Amy and Sr. Mary Margaret called Sr. Mary Joell to give her an update on their visit. The sisters reported that the Agreement of Understanding (with some minor changes) had been signed. They also discussed the building of the convent.

Upon their return to the United States, the two sisters became immersed in the activities of their respective provinces. They remained in close communication as they began addressing the building of the convent, the purchasing of a vehicle, the preparing of the future missionaries, as well as other situations and questions that arose. This required numerous phone calls, letters, and faxes to each other, Bishop Deogratias, Sr. Mary Joell, and the Hoima Construction Company.

The Uganda mission was a multifaceted undertaking. Preparation required identifying and utilizing resources and opportunities in the United States as well as in Uganda. The projects were often challenging and at times frustrating. Negotiations were with persons at a great distance, and the means of communication were very limited. Understandings in the American culture were quite different from those in the Ugandan culture. One great advantage was the fact that the two American provincials, on visits to Uganda, had been introduced to many of the persons with whom they would be communicating.

BUILDING FROM AFAR

One of the major undertakings in the preparation for the sisters' going to Uganda was the building of a convent. One challenge was to build a convent that met the immediate needs of the sisters and would be functional in future years. A second challenge was to build a convent that fit into the culture, was secure and provided enough communal and private space. Three concerns were how to build the convent, to make important decisions relative to the building, and to check on the progress without being physically present at the site or even in the country.

On their first visit, Sr. Mary Amy and Sr. Mary Margaret had met Fr. Heinz-Josef Schackel, a Missionary of Africa and the administrator of Hoima Construction Company. In May 1994, Sr. Mary Amy wrote to Fr. Heinz with questions about building a convent in the Hoima Diocese. (A specific location had not yet been determined.) Some of the questions posed were:

- How do we arrange for the transfer of funds?
- How do we arrange for purchase of property for the convent? Approximately how much would it cost to purchase about two acres of land?

- How can we arrange for construction of the convent and digging of the well?
- How much would a convent somewhat like the Dominican sisters' at Kakumiro cost?
- Do you see yourself in a position to direct us in any of the above matters?

In a faxed letter, Fr. Heinz explained that money could be transferred to Uganda via the Missionaries of Africa in Washington, D.C. He also wrote that the Bishop informed him that the diocese had land and would give it to the sisters. Fr. Heinz projected the cost of building to be about $192,000 but explained influencing factors included the United States-Uganda exchange rate and the type of brick used. If Butema bricks, which endured the climate better than other bricks, were used, the cost would be higher. And finally, the Hoima Diocesan Construction could construct the building. Things were moving along. Surely a convent could be completed by the time the sisters arrived in Uganda the next spring.

In September, Br. Karl responded to some questions the sisters had sent. Because of the size of the proposed building and the fact that it was made of brick, the sisters were concerned about the appearance of luxury. Br. Karl assured them this would not be a problem as other convents had similar structures. He also indicated that the convent floor would have to have several levels to maintain the slope of the hill. The water supply would have to be investigated on site. Boreholes (wells with small diameters) were common and wells were seldom used. Large storage tanks that collect rainwater and require a pump were also common. Further discussion about the convent could be continued when the sisters visited in October. In another fax, Br. Karl indicated that the kitchen would have a gas or electric cooker near the dining area and an outside kitchen using firewood, would also be used.

Prior to their 1994 visit, Sr. Mary Amy and Sr. Mary Margaret had faxed Br. Karl some preliminary plans prepared by a California architect whose plans included some ideas of what the sisters wanted in terms of rooms and clustering of rooms. When the sisters came in October, Br. Karl identified some aspects that were not practical or feasible for the climate in Uganda. He pointed out that verandas are popular in Uganda, and the California plan showed an enclosed passage only. Corridors need plenty of light and ventilation, which the presented design seemed to be missing. The three also discussed possible sources of water (rain, borehole) and energy (solar). Br. Karl agreed to rework the convent plans and fax them to the sisters.

With the plans underway, the two provincials made a formal request to the Superior General in Rome for permission to build a convent in the Diocese of Hoima, Uganda. The building would be constructed in Buseesa at the site the sisters had identified in October 1994. Diocesan land was available, building plans had been discussed with the architect, and a Uganda Mission Fund had been established in Covington. The exact cost was unknown but, including furnishings, would probably be approximately $200,000.

A few days later Sr. Mary Joell wrote that she had presented the request in the council meeting and additional information was needed:

- How soon will the construction begin? What is the anticipated completion date?
- Will a school also be built as the convent is being built? If something should happen that a school would not be built, what alternative plan can be considered for the sisters' ministry?
- When will a parish priest actually take up residence?
- Please provide your most recent sketch of proposed convent along with some narrative, e.g., how many rooms, approximate square footage of building, nature of construction materials to be used.

(Sr. Mary Joell to Sr. Mary Margaret and Sr. Mary Amy, November 1, 1994)

The next day another letter was received. Sr. Mary Joell wrote that in a special council meeting further discussion was held and approval was given to build the convent. Sister requested that the following information be forwarded to her when the sisters received it from the Hoima Diocese Construction:

- A revised set of plans with a breakdown of costs. For example, the cost of boring a well, electrical, plumbing, etc.
- A description of the convent: number of bedrooms, bathrooms, etc., and size.
- Is the estimated cost of $200,000 for construction only? What about furnishings?

Sr. Mary Joell added, "We would like to have the opportunity to comment on the plans before construction is underway." (Sr. Mary Joell to Sr. Mary Margaret and Sr. Mary Amy, November 2, 1994)

Later experience would educate the sisters to the fact that the estimated cost would contain no specific costs, e.g., for plumbing, site work, labor. In addition, if this information were known, there was no way to judge or compare it to other construction companies. The building required a trust that this was to be God's work and God's hand was guiding the project.

Before discussion on the building continued, there was the need to obtain property in Buseesa. Sr. Mary Joell had written:

> Regarding the purchase of property in the name of the Congregation, Bishop Byabazaire explained clearly that the only way to get property in Uganda at this time for a religious community is through the Diocese. (Sr. Mary Joell to Sr. Mary Margaret and Sr. Mary Amy, October 7, 1994)

The two sisters requested from the Bishop a letter stating that two acres of land would be given to the Sisters of Notre Dame as a permanent gift so the congregation could build a convent.

The Diocese of Hoima offered five acres of land in Buseesa as a permanent gift to the sisters. The Bishop stated that a hundred acres for the future parish of Buseesa and for the educational activities of the sisters had been surveyed but not yet mapped. When the mapping was accomplished, the exact spot of the plot of land offered to the sisters would be identified.

The next month the Bishop expressed his pleasure that the sisters had agreed with Br. Karl's plan to construct the first part of the convent so that the sisters could arrive as planned.

In early December, a fax to Sr. Mary Amy from Fr. Heinz contained a startling sentence: "Working time: Starting in May 1995 and finishing within a year, provided there is no delay of either funds or building materials." Quickly a letter was sent to Bishop Deogratias stating that Fr. Heinz had indicated that the convent would not be completed until May 1996 at the earliest. Sr. Mary Amy added, "I must admit my heart sank. We were hoping to send our sisters in May or June." (Sr. Mary Amy to Bishop Deogratias, December 9, 1994)

Because of the slope of the land, the sisters received two proposals for plans for the convent. One proposal would require considerable leveling and expense. Thus, the second proposal with revisions to fit the contour of the land was accepted. But the best news came from Fr. Heinz. If he received a quick answer, then the company could start with the building in January, 1995. $75,000 was transferred to the Missionaries of Africa for the account of Hoima Construction Company. Now it was up to Fr. Heinz and his crew of workers.

Initiating the construction in January and completing it by May or June was a daunting task. To work with the slope of the land, the plan was to divide the building into four separate blocks connected by stairs; the buildings would surround an inner courtyard. It was decided to build the convent in stages so that each block would be completed before the next one was begun. At least some block, called

Stage I, could be completed by the time the sisters arrived. Fr. Heinz suggested that a provisional fence would separate the sisters from the work area during Stage II of the construction.

The first month of the new year brought more good great news.

Bishop Deogratias wrote:

> We are happy to inform you that today a group of workers have left for Buseesa to begin the construction of the St. Julie Convent. We are sure that that part of the Convent will be finished on time. We have put there our best people to do that work. (Bishop Deogratias to Sr. Mary Margaret, January 24, 1995)

The Bishop also mentioned that he had recently visited Sr. Mary Joell and had given to her some photographs showing the progress on St. Julie's convent. These photos were quickly sent to the USA.

Within a short time more good news began arriving. By March 25, the patronal feast day of the Sisters of Notre Dame, two of the buildings of the convent were partially completed, and work was being done on a third. In May, Bishop Deogratias wrote, "The workers are working around the clock in order to beat the dead-line (sic). We are eagerly looking forward to the arrival of the Sisters and it will be a happy and great event." (Bishop Deogratias to Sr. Mary Amy, May 9, 1995)

Overseeing the construction of a building while being thousands of miles away and utilizing a company whose director the sisters had only met twice was a daring venture. Telephone contact was virtually impossible, and thus the fax machine was employed. During these months, questions and answers flew back and forth between the United States and Uganda. Some of the questions related to the placement and cost of solar light installation and heating water, the location of the borehole, screens in the windows, a stove for the kitchen, the size of a generator, curtains, and cutlery. By the end of March, Br. Karl sent drawings of how various rooms could be furnished. Fr. Heinz offered that the furniture could be made in the diocesan carpentry/joinery, "HIOCA." The furniture for Stage I could be ready by the time the construction was completed.

THE UNEXPECTED – WELL, MAYBE NOT SO UNEXPECTED

As the planning continued in the last months, more and more issues began to surface. Some were expected, but others were somewhat of a surprise.

One of the major issues was that of a resident priest in Buseesa. The provincials had discussed this with the Bishop especially during the 1994 visit. In March 1995,

Sr. Mary Margaret wrote to Bishop Deogratias asking when he anticipated having a resident priest at Buseesa. The Bishop responded that a priest had been appointed and was ready to move to Buseesa, but there was one problem: There was no priest's house. The Bishop further indicated that the diocese had no money for such an undertaking and requested that the building of a rectory be part of the convent project so that both houses could be ready about the same time. With the letter, the Bishop included Br. Karl's two plans for the priest's house.

The sisters had not anticipated this extra expense, but they were not especially surprised at the request. Since the availability of the liturgy and the sacraments was so important, what were the sisters willing to do to assure the presence of a resident priest?

Sr. Mary Amy and Sr. Mary Margaret discussed the situation and met with their respective councils. With some rearranging of finances, the sisters concluded that they could provide funds for the construction of the rectory. The sisters chose the simpler of the two plans presented. This plan included a building with a dining/ sitting area, office, bedroom, guest room, bath and WC, two storage rooms, and the cook's room. A separate building housed the kitchen, and another building, a pit latrine and bath. The construction cost of the rectory amounted to $33,556. Funds were sent to the Missionaries of Africa. With all this information, the Bishop gave the assurance that the construction of the rectory would begin immediately.

These two construction ventures were only the beginning of a partnership between the Sisters of Notre Dame and the Hoima Construction Department, which continued for many years.

A TROUBLESOME VEHICLE

Little did the sisters know that the vehicle would be one of the most complicated and frustrating issues they would be required to address. When Sr. Mary Amy and Sr. Mary Margaret visited Uganda in the fall of 1994, Bishop Deogratias accompanied them to Walusimbi's Garage, a Toyota dealership in Kampala. They discussed the purchase of a Land Cruiser, but no final decision was made.

Upon returning to the United States, Sr. Mary Margaret visited a local Toyota dealership. The salesperson could offer little assistance as to the specifications of the vehicle since vehicles are made to address the conditions of a country. In December, Sr. Mary Margaret wrote to Fr. Callist Rubaramira at Interservice in Uganda, inquiring about some specifics of the vehicle and received a timely reply.

- Do all Land Cruisers come with manual transmission? (Generally, yes. There is also trouble with maintenance with automatic transmission.)

- Is the 3.0 or 2.8 diesel engine large enough? (The 2.8 engine should be sufficient. A petrol engine is also available but is expensive to run.)

- Are the seating cushions covered with fabric or vinyl? (You can choose. However, fabric seats take in quite a bit of dust).

During that same week, Bishop Deogratias faxed that the process of ordering the car through the dealership in Kampala could begin. It would take about four months for the vehicle to arrive and for the taxation and registration to be processed. When Sr. Mary Margaret received the fax, she wrote to Sr. Mary Amy saying she thought that if it took four months to deliver the vehicle, and it arrived in April, what would happen to the vehicle until the sisters arrived? And then the sisters would have to learn something about driving in Uganda and get the driving permits.

In a communication, the Bishop summarized his conversations with Fr. Callist at Interservice and Walusimbi Garage. He explained that the sisters should order the vehicle through Interservice and transfer the money to the account of Interservice. Then came the disappointing news: The only disadvantage was that the car would not arrive in Kampala by May. It took about six months. He then expressed his hope that the minister of education would grant a tax exemption for the vehicle.

As events unfolded, the vehicle was not delivered early, and obtaining a driving permit was also to be a major challenge.

During the next six weeks, several faxes were sent to Interservice inquiring about the exact cost of the Land Cruiser. An April 5 fax contained the following information:

Here below is a breakdown of the costs associated with the purchase of the vehicle, Toyota Landcruiser II, as per your request:

Price CIF Kampala	$31,000
Import duty	30%
Sales Tax	30%
Excise Duty	50%
Registration	2%
Uganda Clearing	2%

As for paying or not paying the import duty and sales tax, all that would depend on the answer received after submitting the application for tax exemption. (Fr. Vincent Bimanywarugaba [from Interservice] to Sr. Mary Margaret, April 5, 1995)

Finally, on April 24, Fr. Vincent, the diocesan treasurer, faxed that he had been having difficulty in obtaining a confirmation of the exact cost of the vehicle, but he estimated that the total cost would be about $80,000.

Sr. Mary Margaret immediately faxed Sr. Mary Amy, "I can't imagine a vehicle costing this much but what choice do we have?" The following day, $80,000 was wired to the Missionaries of Africa for the vehicle payment, and the Land Cruiser was ordered.

Sr. Mary Amy had been pursuing the possibility of obtaining funds from some outside sources. Donations from individuals and a foundation were received, and Sr. Jane Marie applied to the Sisters of Notre Dame Solidarity Fund in Rome, Italy. The Solidarity Fund provided funds for various ministry projects in the congregation.

PAPERWORK

Another important item was that of paperwork. Sr. Mary Amy sent to Bishop Deogratias, the teaching credentials, degrees, copies of passports, and other items, for the sisters destined for Uganda. She also included letters stating that the two provinces would support the four sisters during their stay in Uganda. These documents were needed in order to secure residency permits.

COVINGTON SISTERS VISIT CALIFORNIA

While all these letters were being exchanged, another component of the preparation was underway. Sr. Jane Marie and Sr. Margaret Mary had spent time in Covington in September 1994. Now Sr. Mary Janet and Sr. Mary Delrita traveled to the Thousand Oaks province in February 1995. The sisters visited the Sisters of Notre Dame ministries as well as local historical and tourist sights.

Sr. Mary Margaret went to California for a few days to meet with Sr. Mary Amy and the four missionaries. A gathering was planned with the McHugh family (Sr. Jane Marie), and the Scott family (Sr. Margaret Mary). This was similar to the one in Covington the previous fall with the Stamm family (Sr. Mary Janet) and the Glaser family (Sr. Mary Delrita). Sr. Mary Amy and Sr. Mary Margaret gave presentations for the families, responding to their questions and helping them to feel better about letting their beloved daughter/sister go to Africa.

In a letter dated March 18, 1995, to the sisters in Covington, Sr. Mary Janet and Sr. Mary Delrita wrote about their meetings with the two provincials.

Both Sister Mary Margaret and Mary Amy spoke inspiringly of the openness we must continue to have, the readiness to live peacefully with the questions we want so much to be answered, the willingness to be sent wherever the Lord wills. It was at this time that we received the announcement that Sister Mary Janet will be our Local Superior. We received the news with gratitude and promised each other full support.

In the same letter Sr. Mary Janet and Sr. Mary Delrita wrote that the last supper in California

was an experience of love tinged with sorrow. Partings are sometimes difficult. This one was plain hard. As we have visited the four American provinces we have realized more and more how much we are all united in this endeavor, but Rosa Mystica and the Immaculate Heart of Mary provinces are joined in Buseesa with special bonds. Sister Mary Amy and the Sisters of Rosa Mystica have given us such a warm and generous reception into their midst. Sr. Mary Amy said it well, "We are inextricably bound together."

DEPARTURE NEARS

For the future missionaries, the months passed quickly. They visited with family and friends saying their good-byes. A small room at the provincial house was set aside for storing the many items that were destined for Buseesa: dishes, soap, bedding, food, and personal belongings. July 9 was designated as Missioning Day with departure on July 11. As these days drew closer, large boxes were packed, sealed, addressed, and numbered.

MISSIONING CEREMONY

On Sunday, July 9, the sisters of the Covington province gathered at St. Joseph Heights to participate in the missioning for Sr. Mary Janet and Sr. Mary Delrita. First on the agenda was a brunch in the dining room that was decorated with an African theme. During this time, each sister of the province gave a blessing to each of the two sisters. It was a very moving event. A much lighter element of the celebration was the singing of the song "Please Don't Send Me to Africa."

At 2:00 p.m. sisters, family, and friends of the two missionaries gathered at St. Agnes Church, Ft. Wright, Kentucky, for the formal missioning liturgy. After the Scripture readings, Sr. Mary Margaret called forth Sr. Mary Janet and Sr. Mary Delrita. Through a series of questions, the sisters proclaimed their commitment to walk with the people of Uganda, to assist the people to recognize their human dignity, and to give hope and courage to those who struggle.

The mission crucifixes were then blessed and presented to the two sisters. These crucifixes are replicas of the Coesfeld crucifix. This crucifix is associated with the beginnings of the Sisters of Notre Dame in Coesfeld, Germany. The two sisters were challenged to preach Christ crucified and expect the crucifix to be a source of strength and hope in times of difficulties. Each sister responded:

> With a heart full of gratitude, yet very much aware of my own weakness, I accept this mission crucifix. Called and strengthened by God's goodness, I desire to walk with my sisters and brothers in Uganda, deepening with them, my call to live the life of Jesus. Moved by the spirit of St. Julie, Aldegonda and Lisette, and the many sisters before me, I desire especially to witness to God's goodness and provident care. (Missioning Booklet, July 9, 1995, pp. 6 and 7)

In response, the community prayed:

> Guide their steps with your mighty arm, and with the power of your grace strengthen them in spirit, so that they will not falter through weariness.
> Make their words the echo of Christ's voice, so that those who hear them may be drawn to obey the Gospel. (*Missioning Booklet*, July 9, 1995, p. 8)

All then extended their right hand and petitioned blessings for Sr. Mary Janet and Sr. Mary Delrita.

The liturgy was followed by a reception at St. Joseph Heights where all could wish the sisters farewell and offer best wishes and promise of prayer. Those present could also view maps and photos of the area where the sisters would be ministering.

DEPARTURE DAY

On Tuesday morning, July 11, the provincial house community gathered in chapel for a final blessing. All proceeded to the front steps for a good-bye and *auf wiedersehen*. Even the Ugandan flag was in evidence.

After the sisters and their belongings were safely tucked into the car, the vehicle slowly made its way down the front drive to Dixie Highway. Earlier, some of the lay staff had loaded the many boxes and suitcases onto the truck.

In about twenty minutes, the car and truck arrived at the Greater Cincinnati Northern Kentucky International Airport. Fortunately, the sisters were traveling American Airlines that has a small terminal and was not crowded. When the sisters arrived with all their boxes and suitcases, they were the only ones at the check-in counter. The sisters carried a letter about the numerous boxes. Weeks earlier, the sisters had contacted the airline with the result that the sisters from California were given 210 pounds of free freight, and the sisters from Covington were given 320 pounds.

With their thirteen boxes checked in, the sisters were ready for boarding the plane. Several family members and friends had come to the airport to wish them well. There were long hugs and large tears, and the sisters boarded the plane. While friends and relatives waited for the plane to take off, a noise from the other end of the terminal was heard. There were sisters running to see the sisters before they left. How disappointed they were to see the sisters gone. One sister approached the attendant at the check-in area to ask about having the sisters return for a moment to see the new arrivals. The attendant was definite in explaining this was only done if the police needed to see someone. After much pleading, the attendant agreed, and the two missionaries were called. The two sister missionaries thought something had gone terribly wrong and they would not be going to Uganda. How relieved they were to see the late arrivals. (Remembrance of Sr. Mary Martha Beiting) After a few minutes, they again boarded the plane for Pittsburgh where they would have a three-hour layover and then travel to London, England. By 6:00 the next morning, the two sisters were at Gatwick Airport in London.

The sisters then traveled to Heathrow where they were to meet Sr. Mary Patricia Gannon and three Korean sisters. Uncertain of the exact meeting place, the missionaries utilized the airport paging system. The two groups finally met, and after a "spot of tea," they began a tour of London. Sr. Mary Patricia treated them royally, but since the two missionaries had not slept on the flight to London, they had a difficult time staying awake during the bus tour. They returned to the airport where Sr. Jane Marie and Sr. Margaret Mary had arrived from California. At 11:00 p.m. the plane lifted off, and the four sisters were bound for Entebbe, Uganda.

In her journal, Sr. Mary Delrita wrote the following, describing her thoughts at this time:

> Yes to you, Jesus, whatever lies ahead. What we are walking into is unpredictable, but whatever it is, it is OK. Our sense of confidence, joy, and gratitude can only be the gift of God's grace in our hearts. We both feel a firm assurance about God's call and his accompaniment. This is his work, and he will be with us. I feel an eager anticipation. Finally our dream will have flesh and blood. It's like being in the birthing room in the final stages of labor. Watching waiting, encouraging. In a moment the baby is born, and everything changes. (Sr. Mary Delrita's Journal, July 12, 1995)

ARRIVAL IN UGANDA

There was a brief stop in Nairobi. On the final leg of the flight, passengers included the Ugandan Special Olympics Team. The plane landed in Entebbe on Thursday, July 13,1995, about noon.

The sisters descended from the plane and were met by Isoke Bugama, a MP from the Kibaale District, his wife, Margaret, and several of their children who presented the sisters with roses. Bishop Deogratias, Bishop Edward Baharagate, the retired bishop of Hoima, government officials, parish leaders, priests, and sisters also greeted the four missionaries. All were escorted to the VIP lounge while all the paperwork for the sisters was taken care of and the luggage checked through customs. All went well except one box was missing. The sisters were to discover which box at a later date.

As they exited the terminal, the sisters were directed to the parking area where they each received a bouquet of flowers. Fifty representatives from Buseesa, Bujuni, and Kakumiro parishes formed a reception line and shook the hand of each sister. The sisters were interviewed by the press and radio reporters. Sr. Jane's interview was heard throughout the country as she shared the Runyoro phrases she had studied back in the States.

The sisters boarded two vehicles that took them to the Kampala Diocesan Leadership Center for the official welcome reception. One vehicle went directly to the center, but the other took a side trip to the Hoima Construction Company's Kampala house so the sisters could send a fax home telling of their safe arrival. At the welcome gathering, everyone waited and waited and waited for the two delayed sisters. Finally, they decided to start the program introducing the two sisters present and the other sisters "in absentia."

The welcome included songs and traditional dances by several children from Buseesa. The songs and dances were accompanied by drums and by dancers with *ebinyeges* strapped around their legs. There were welcome speeches by religious and government leaders, and the sisters then experienced their first Ugandan meal. After the festivities, the sisters proceeded to ARU where they spent the night.

While in Kampala, the sisters registered at the American Embassy and visited the Pronuncio, Cardinal Emmanuel Wamala. They then traveled to the cathedral, and St. Teresa Primary, a highly respected primary school where they spoke with the headmistress and visited classrooms. Fr. Heinz introduced the sisters to the "supermarket" ($9.00 for a box of cornflakes) and the fabric shop where he had purchased the material for the curtains for the convent bedrooms.

TO KAKUMIRO AND BUSEESA

On Saturday, July 15, the sisters set out for Kakumiro. The Dominican sisters who had provided hospitality for the two United States provincial superiors the two previous years, warmly welcomed the newly-arrived missionaries. Since the missionaries were excited about seeing their new convent home, they drove to Buseesa. When they arrived, Bishop Deogratias had a brief prayer in the church where they sang "The Battle Hymn of the Republic" and prayed through the intercession of the Uganda Martyrs and St. Julie. The sisters were led in procession from the church to the convent. Girls from Buseesa Primary led the way dancing, and children lined the road on both sides. Peter, the construction foreman, showed the sisters through the completed area of the convent. In a fax the sisters wrote, "Our house at Buseesa is beyond expectations – Hoima brick and beautiful woodwork!" (Sr. Jane Marie, Sr. Margaret Mary, Sr. Mary Janet, Sr. Mary Derita to All, July 19, 1995) In typical Ugandan fashion, there was a welcome program of song, dance, and speeches. The four SND missionaries remained with the Dominicans until their partly- completed convent was ready for occupancy.

WELCOME! WELCOME! WELCOME!

The sisters were not prepared for the many welcomes they would receive. The first weeks were filled with ceremonial welcomes.

Sunday, July 16, the celebration at Buseesa began with Bishop Deogratias processing around and through the convent, blessing each room. The congregation then proceeded to the parish church where the four sisters had places on the left side of the sanctuary. The singing throughout the pontifical high Mass was mainly in Runyoro. When the Bishop spoke in the local language, he translated for the sisters. After the liturgical celebration, all gathered outside under a gloriously blooming yellow acacia tree. Here the sisters were again treated to many songs, dances, and speeches. An elder of the parish bestowed upon the sisters their *empaakos* (pet names) to show that they were one with the people: Amooti (Sr. Mary Janet), Atwooki (Sr. Mary Delrita), Ateenyi (Sr. Margaret Mary), and Akiiki (Jane Marie). A meal was then served at the church.

The welcome on Sunday, July 23, at the parish in Bujuni was much like the one at Buseesa with the liturgy followed by speeches, songs, and dances. However, here the sisters shared the spotlight with Bishop John Baptist Kagwa who was from the Bujuni parish. The Mass and programs lasted from 10:00 a.m. until 5:00 p.m. Gifts included avocados, pineapple, sugar cane, passion fruit, and a musical wall clock.

The following week was spent at the Bishop's house in Hoima. The orientation to the Diocese of Hoima included visits to six of the parishes in the Kibaale District. These are the parishes whose children would be coming to the primary boarding school that the sisters planned to establish. The Bishop also acquainted the sisters with the various diocesan institutions and projects such as the brick-making factory and Hoima Construction. During their visits, the sisters were introduced to many of the diocesan clergy and religious.

On Sunday, July 30, the pontifical Mass at Our Lady of Lourdes Cathedral in Hoima began at 9:30 a.m. with a procession. The liturgy included the ordination of one young man to minor orders and six men to deaconate, the reception of about 100 youths of St. Simon Peter Association (lay apostolate), and the diocesan welcome of the Sisters of Notre Dame. The religious celebration concluded about 1:30 p.m., and the welcome program began. There were the usual speeches and songs with one group of students singing some verses of "She'll Be Comin' 'Round the Mountain." The program concluded at 4:30 p.m., and the sisters were taken to the Bishop's mother's home for supper. "Mama Veronica" wanted to give the sisters a cock and a hen, but the animals squawked so badly that the sisters had to decline.

BUSEESA AT LAST

It wasn't until Friday, July 21, that the Sisters of Notre Dame bade farewell to the Dominican sisters and thanked them for their gracious hospitality. The four missionaries were eager to take up residence in their home in Buseesa.

Fr. Aloysius Mugisa, (name means "blessing"), who was stationed temporarily at Buseesa, and one of the sisters traveled in the pickup truck loaded with baggage and the supplies purchased in Kampala. The Bishop and his driver Charles brought the other sisters and the remaining baggage.

What a joy when the sisters arrived at their home! The rooms of the convent are built around a rectangular courtyard. At the time of the sisters' arrival, three sides of the convent were nearly complete. The section yet to be built contained the chapel, the bedrooms, and the lavatory/shower room. Even though the convent was not completed, there was ample space including a large community room/dining room. Some substitutions for the missing rooms were made: a small storage room became the chapel, the guest rooms and storerooms became temporary bedrooms for the sisters, and the guest room lavatory/showers were shared.

The sisters were delighted to find in the kitchen, a gas stove with two cylinders of gas (propane). There was also a refrigerator run by paraffin (which was to cause problems later), and water coming from the taps! The water lasted only one day, and the "well went dry." The gas stove was a life-saver – literally – since it was used almost constantly to boil water. Preparing water suitable for drinking became an all-day, exhausting task.

On Monday, the sisters began unpacking the many boxes they had brought from the United States. The boxes had arrived in good condition except for box thirteen. This box was the last one packed, and contained some last-minute things including books and rosaries. When the box arrived late in Uganda, the top of it was intact, but the bottom had fallen out.

With the damage to the box, Sr. Mary Janet experienced a major loss. She wrote to Sr. Mary Margaret explaining that when she went to claim the lost box, the contents had been placed in a plastic bag, and some of the things were missing. In box thirteen, Sr. Mary Janet had placed important papers she wanted to keep, some medical books, and her Bible.

> It really broke my heart that I lost my Bible! I had pictures, cards, treasured things I wanted to keep ... just feel I lost something important to me. ... We thought for a while that our mission crucifixes were in this box. We were overjoyed when we found them, plus the Mother Julie statue. ... There were tears of joy when we made this discovery. (Sr. Mary Janet to Sr. Mary Margaret, August 5, 1995)

When the sisters arrived at the convent that was still under construction, it was difficult to get up to the veranda from the lower level. Knowing that the Bishop was planning a visit, the sisters asked the men to add some steps for easier entry into the convent. They arranged some bricks. It was better, but still not very safe. Sr. Mary Delrita went to check on something and when she stepped on the bricks, one brick went out from under her foot. She landed on her back in the mud. It was a hard fall and a near disaster. Sister said that the way she fell she should have hit the concrete but it was as if a mysterious hand pushed her, and she landed in the mud. Sister was very muddy, her dress was torn about twelve inches, and she was badly shaken.

During the first days the people of the area brought fresh vegetables, fruits, eggs, and even a live chicken; but later they brought very little because they were very poor and had little themselves. In a short time, the sisters needed food. They had heard of a market day in Matale village, so two of the sisters and the two house girls, who had recently been hired, set out on a forty-five-minute walk to the market with each pair taking a different route. The pairs agreed that they would pretend not to know one another, and the two girls would make the purchases because foreigners would be charged more than the usual price. When they arrived, people were gathered at the market place, but the event seemed to be more social and centered around the local brew and roast pork with little else available.

PASTORS

The newly assigned pastor, Fr. Peter Isingoma, was just completing an assignment as rector at the national seminary in Fort Portal. In his place, Fr. Aloysius Mugisa came to assist the sisters. Because the rectory was not yet complete, Fr. Aloysius stayed at the convent occupying the rooms allotted for the house girls. Father assisted the sisters by prompting them to respond in culturally appropriate ways, translating for them, putting the water filter together, showing them how to prepare local foods, helping with chores, cleaning the fated chicken, and fixing kerosene lamp wicks. The sisters wrote that Father was a real godsend.

On August 4, Fr. Peter took up residence in the priest house, and celebrated the first Mass in the temporary chapel at the convent.

To assist the sisters in learning Runyoro, Fr. Peter met with them frequently almost the entire first year. The lessons usually focused on parts of speech or words or phrases used in specific situations, e.g., conversation at a meal. When the provincials visited in October, they noted:

> They have worked hard at their language lessons, and this is most apparent in their meeting with the people at church, along the road, and those who stop by the convent. The people are delighted to hear greetings in their own language, and a brief "conversation" often ensues. (Sr. Mary Margaret to Families of Sr. Mary Janet and Sr. Mary Delrita, October 30, 1995)

MINUS ONE

When the sisters first arrived in Uganda, Bishop Deogratias told them about the Conference of South East African Religious that was being held in Kampala in the next weeks. Sr. Margaret Mary expressed an interest, and thus on Tuesday, August 1, sister traveled to Gaba Seminary for the conference. Sister remained there until August 15, enjoying excellent talks, running water, electricity, and prepared meals. The other three sisters in Buseesa had to face some serious and potentially life-threatening situations. The preparing of food, collecting and purifying water, taking care of laundry, unpacking boxes, and deciding on a location for all the materials they had brought placed considerable strain on them.

In Buseesa, Sr. Mary Janet, Sr. Mary Delrita, and Sr. Jane Marie met Businge Ednah and Mbabazi Angela, two young women from Hoima, who came as house girls to assist with the housework in the convent. Sr. Jane Marie was placed in charge of training Ednah and Angela in cleaning and doing laundry. (Angela became ill and had to return home. In November Natabi Mary came to take her place.) Even with the additional help, there was much to do in setting up the house, and trying to keep it clean in the midst of construction. In her journal, Sr. Mary Delrita wrote that she swept and swept and mopped the dining/sitting room, and then swept again. It was impossible to keep ahead of the red dirt!

When Sr. Margaret Mary returned from the conference, she was excited about all she learned. The sisters began having sessions in which Sr. Margaret Mary shared what she learned from the conference experience. Gradually, the sisters eased into the routine and challenges in Buseesa.

CELEBRATIONS

The sisters used every opportunity to celebrate: birthdays, feast days, and the monthly anniversary of their arrival in Uganda. Mary and Ednah had never celebrated their birthdays because it is not a custom in Uganda. The sisters wanted to make their day special, so decorations were put up, and favorite baked items were prepared. The girls were thrilled to have their own special day.

UGANDA INDEPENDENCE DAY (October 9)   This day was celebrated by serving popcorn and a fruit drink to the construction workers and listening as they explained their new Constitutions and sang the national anthem. The sisters celebrated July 4th with hamburgers and a game of Yahtzee, a dice game.

PROVINCE CELEBRATIONS   The first province celebration of the interprovince foundation was that of the Thousand Oaks province celebrated on October 7, the feast of the Holy Rosary. The dining room and chapel were decorated with placemats and napkins of green and rose fabric. The liturgy included special readings and the singing of "You Are All Beautiful" in three-part harmony. In the evening, the celebration continued with special treats sent in a "care package." The Covington province was celebrated in June, the feast of the Immaculate Heart of Mary. Decorations this time were pink, blue, and lavender hearts, pink crepe paper, and confetti. Special prayers and Mass added to the day.

THANKSGIVING proved to be a very special day.

> Recalling the story that the pilgrims invited their Indian neighbors to join them in giving thanks to God, we invited our construction workers and parish staff to a Thanksgiving feast. Invitations in Runyoro were sent. The site for our feast was the still incomplete main convent. We used bricks and boards for a table and chairs and benches from church. Decorations included flowers suspended by banana fibers from window frames and bouquets of flowers picked from the bush. We served matooke (cooked bananas), beans, rice, salad, and drink. The celebration began with a speech delivered in Runyoro about the history and tradition of the day. After the speech everyone shared one thing he/she was grateful for and we joined hands and recited the "Our Father" in Runyoro. Then

> Fr. Peter led the meal prayer. At one point during the speech, a sister mentioned that football games are a tradition on Thanksgiving Day, so as a thank you for the meal, the workers played a soccer game – California vs. Kentucky.
>
> That evening we ate our traditional Thanksgiving dinner, substituting chicken for turkey. The cock we decided to dine on somehow escaped from the hen house. (The Buseesa SNDs to Sisters and Friends, November 26, 1995)

ADVENT AND CHRISTMAS   At the beginning of Advent, the sisters erected a Jesse Tree in church and in the convent. In a letter Sr. Mary Janet remarked, that there was no sign, not even a hint of the commercialism that is such a part of the pre-Christmas scene back home. When Sister asked one of the house girls how she decorated for Christmas at her home (a mud hut), Mary had a hard time thinking of what they did. She finally said that people might find a picture in a newspaper (something rare in Buseesa) and hang it up. Fr. Peter related that in his home in Masindi, his family had a Christmas tree decorated with Christmas cards and sweets. When visitors came, they would receive sweets from the tree. There was also singing, dancing, and food.

Sr. Jane Marie sent Christmas greetings.

> Mwebale Noeli! A very Merry Christmas to you all! Believe it or not, if we didn't have calendars, we'd have no idea that Christmas was so near. We're living in a land where none of the children have ever heard of Santa Claus, where there are no Christmas decorations, parades, or tree lots, and where gift exchange is not a common practice! We are preparing ourselves to celebrate a COMMERCIAL-FREE Christmas. (Sr. Jane Marie to All, Christmas 1995)

Signs of Christmas began appearing in Buseesa on December 23.

> Some local man came forward with hand-carved mahogany crib figures his father had made years ago. They made a grass hut in the front of Church and set the figures there. The kneeling Mary is about two feet tall. Beautiful! We had midnight Mass by lantern light and Runyoro Christmas carols to the beat of the drum. In the morning our pastor went on safari to three outstations for Mass so we had a communion service in the church. Our tree is something else – bare cassava branches we had used for our Jesse Tree during advent but now covered with rice fern taped to each branch. A little tinsel and a few ornaments and presto! I love it! (Sr. Mary Delrita to her brother, December 28, 1995)

After celebrating with a cock for dinner, they opened a few packages they had wrapped for one another.

After lunch on December 26, Sr. Jane Marie and Sr. Margaret Mary traveled to Mubende to call their families. They had pre-arranged that they would call between 10:00 p.m. and midnight California time. What joy it was to hear the voices of their family members during this special season! On their return trip, the sisters stopped to pick up seven Dominican sisters in Kakumiro and brought them to St. Julie Convent for a relaxing afternoon in appreciation for all the sisters had done for them.

HOLY WEEK AND EASTER   Holy Week presented a very different experience for the sisters. Earlier, Fr. Peter had been injured in an accident when a goat ran in front of his motorcycle. He was thrown and hit his head so hard that his helmet was cracked. Father sustained a broken jaw, cut tongue, and other cuts and bruises. Father recuperated at the Bishop's house in Hoima for about three weeks.

In the absence of the priest, the catechist conducted the Palm Sunday service. The people came to church carrying palm branches they had cut from the forest. Some tied fresh flowers around the palms, while others had their palms braided. The people gathered on Buseesa Road for the blessing of the palms. Then all joined the procession to the church singing and waving palm branches. The sisters couldn't help but feel that this must have been what it was like that first Palm Sunday morning.

Since there was still no parish priest on Holy Thursday, services were held at the convent. The sisters and a few local people gathered in the temporary convent chapel (now the kitchen) that had been decorated with flowers and greens gathered from the bush. At the end of the communion service, the Blessed Sacrament was carried to the altar of repose in the convent sitting room. A large pink drape, earthen water jar, and long grasses provided the setting for quiet prayer. On Good Friday, the sisters again conducted their own prayer service.

Fr. Vincent Kirabo, diocesan treasurer, accompanied Fr. Peter back to Buseesa. The Easter Vigil Mass, with Fr. Vincent as celebrant, began at midnight. Christians gathered around the fire outside the church for the beginning of the celebration. The first Mass after such a long time took place by lantern light. Fr. Peter and Fr. Vincent concelebrated the Easter Mass. The Christians rejoiced in the resurrection of Jesus and the return of their parish priest.

UGANDA MARTYRS   The Diocesan celebration of the Uganda Martyrs was held on May 19 at Kakumiro. Mass was outside and a large covered area sheltered the many participants. On the actual feast, the local celebration in Buseesa began with morning liturgy at Denis Kamuka's grave. Catechists and Christians from various outstations attended. There were three choirs. At the end of Mass, speeches were made by the parish council chairman, an older man who knew Denis personally, and Sr. Jane Marie.

BUSY DAYS

Almost no day was without its visitors: clergy stopping by to check on the sisters, curious children peering in the windows, villagers coming to welcome and meet the sisters. Hours were consumed each day with boiling water and preparing food under very new conditions. But with all this, one of the sisters wrote to her family:

> I'm convinced we've come to the right place to do God's work; the poorest part of a poor country. I'm happy that the SNDs said yes to this mission and happier that I was chosen to be part of the beginnings. I love being here. I love doing what I'm doing. We're still not really involved in anything specific (only been here three mo.) but are quite busy learning language, customs, basic skills, cultural history, and present reality. We are warmly accepted by the people – they bask in the fact that we chose to come to Kibaale District. Nobody chooses to come here; this area is called the Lost Counties because of shuffling back and forth between kingdoms and powers. Even the rest of an underdeveloped county is better off than this district. Well, I could go on. (Sr. Mary Delrita to Bob and Kay, n.d.)

Dear Sisters,   2:50 pm

We were about to call California on the telephone when we realized your time was 4:00 am. We are now at Horma House with Father Heinz. The ride to Kampala was beautiful. Leaves are coated with red dust and the air has the odor of smoke from small fires. It is now raining heavily as our belongings are unloaded. Father Heinz said it we good that we brought so much since duty isn't usually exacted upon entering the country. Kampala seems spread out. There are a lot of people around. We experienced our first Ugandan traffic jam — cars, bicycles <u>and</u> pedestrians! To the Californians it does seem humid. We should feel tired after two nights on an airplane, but the excitement is winning out over fatigue! Thanks to all the sisters who made our missioning and last few days so memorable!   Much love !!

Fax that the first missionaries sent when arriving in Uganda in 1995

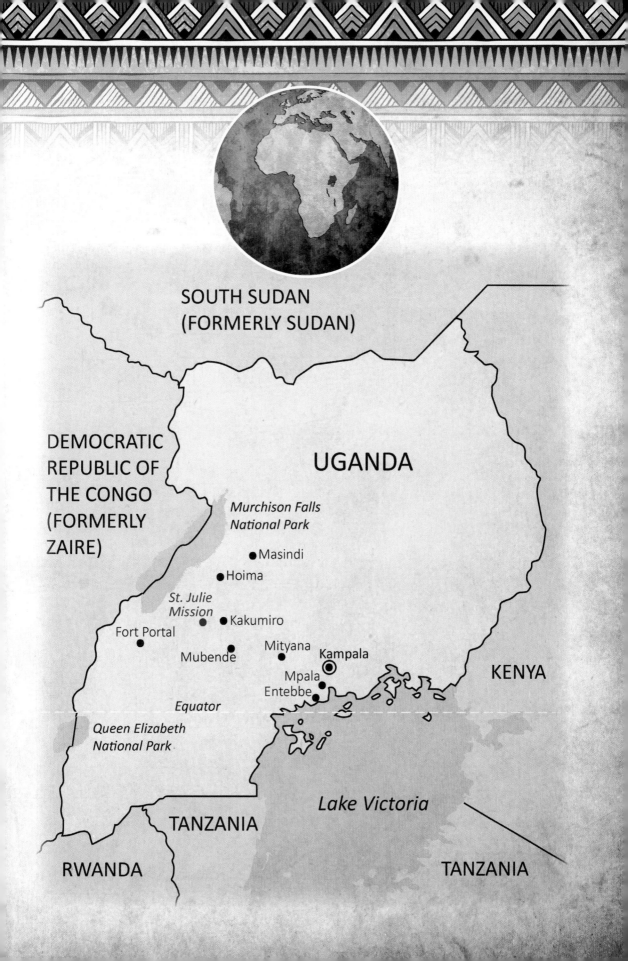

The PLACE WE APPROACH IS HOLY GROUND

TOP Prayer card published by the province in Thousand Oaks, California
MIDDLE Sr. Mary Margaret presents mission crosses to Sr. Mary Delrita and Sr. Mary Janet
BOTTOM The sisters plant a "Mission Tree" at Provincial Center in Covington, Kentucky

TOP School at St. Michael Mission in Masindi MIDDLE Sr. Mary Amy, Sr. Mary Joell, Sr. Theresa Tinkasiimire, Bishop Deogratias BOTTOM Common sight: overloaded truck on the highway

TOP Boda-boda, (motorcycle) MIDDLE Road near Kampala lined with small shops
BOTTOM Kampala, capital city

KITCHEN ↑

↑ STORAGE →

← FOOD PREPARATION

← DINING ROOM

GUESTS ROOMS →

GARAGE   "SUN' PORCH"

↑ CHAPEL   ↑ SISTERS' BEDROOMS

TOP Diagram of the convent MIDDLE Beginning of the convent construction, January 1995
BOTTOM Property for future convent

TOP Laying the rock foundation for a section of the convent MIDDLE Construction of the convent
BOTTOM Bishop Baharagate visits the women preparing the meal for ground-breaking for St. Julie Primary School

TOP Tabernacle is in the shape of an African grain barn MIDDLE Sisters at prayer in the convent chapel:
(left) Sr. Mary Rozaria, Sr. Anita Marie; (right) Sr. Mary Janet, Sr. Mary Delrita, Sr. Mary Rita
BOTTOM High grasses; Sr. Mary Margaret, Sr. Margaret Mary, Sr. Mary Delrita, Sr. Mary Janet, Sr. Jane Marie

TOP Blocked muddy road, October 1995 MIDDLE Road between Buseesa and Hoima
BOTTOM Our Lady of Lourdes Cathedral, Hoima Diocese

6

THE FIRST YEARS IN BUSEESA

The first years in Buseesa were times of first adventures, first experiences, the formation of a new community, and the planning of how this mission would live and share the Gospel of Jesus. The most ordinary task frequently took longer than anticipated. There were times when perseverance, ingenuity, determination, and the helping hand of God resulted in amazing accomplishments.

Daily life was never lived in isolation. There were always visitors and villagers slipping in and out of each event. There were new discoveries, new challenges, and new friends. Water, medical care, construction, vehicles, and farm animals presented a continuous supply of challenges. But a reliance on prayer, on each other, and on the hands of many good people provided the means for the sisters to address each situation.

The sisters lived in the midst of the continuing construction of the convent, the ever-present search for water, and the continuing concern about food. In essence, Sr. Mary Janet, Sr. Mary Delrita, Sr. Jane Marie, and Sr. Margaret Mary were encountering, as never before, some of the basic elements of survival. They were blessed with a generous and caring Bishop and pastors, and with the Ugandan people who shared even the little they had. The first years were characterized by hardships and challenges, but also by friendships, achievements, growth, and celebration.

In November 1997, the sisters developed a policies and procedures handbook. An important part of this document is the Mission Statement.

> As Sisters of Notre Dame, we are sent by the Church and by the congregation to be a witness of God's goodness and provident care. We dedicate ourselves to the following of Jesus through our vows, our life of prayers and community and apostolic service.
>
> In Uganda we strive to help people experience God's goodness, realize their own dignity and enjoy a standard of living that befits the children of God. Our primary mission is to empower people, especially women and children, through education and catechesis. Sensitive to the culture, we work with people to help them recognize and utilize their own resources.

Our Goals:

1. *To collaborate with the local church and educational authorities in raising the educational standards of the Kibaale region.*

2. *To respond to the invitation of Pope John Paul II to participate in the evangelization and catechesis of Africa.*

3. *To actualize the statement of the 1992 General Chapter calling us to action for the poor.*

Our Objectives:

1. *To witness by our presence and care for people.*

2. *To establish a model primary school.*

3. *To provide opportunities for teacher training and in-service, literacy programs, catechetical instruction and other educational services.*

FOOD

In letters home, the sisters made frequent reference to running out of supplies. This often meant their food supplies were getting low. This was a potentially serious situation since there was no close place to purchase food. Then the sisters made a trip to Kampala. Because they had no vehicle, the sisters relied upon the parish priest to drive them to the city. Such trips included visits to the money exchange, post office, Star Market for groceries, the open market for fruits and vegetables, and another store for meat.

Initially, the sisters' meals were primarily American style. They had brought a number of spices and other ingredients needed for such meals. In addition, the sisters received many packages from the United States. They also relied on donations from the local people and purchases at markets in Kampala. Bishop Deogratias often stopped by the convent to visit, and began bringing a variety of foods: pineapples, potatoes, sugar, dried peas, rice, sugar, butter, eggs, and oranges. The sisters wondered what they had said that caused the Bishop to bring all the food and supplies, but they were deeply grateful.

Gradually the sisters moved into more Ugandan foods including bananas. These were served at almost every meal; there was always matooke with the main meal. Sr. Mary Janet described matooke as being "like squash, sort of pasty." Cassava and millet were also standard fare.

Some of the sisters proved adventurous in eating fried grasshoppers and white ants that are considered a delicacy in Uganda. Two sisters enjoyed them somewhat. One night after having both dried and fried ants, Sr. Mary Delrita had just gotten into bed when she became aware that she was scratching her arms quite a bit. Then her legs and ankles began to itch. Sister got up and checked her arms and legs: hives! She realized that an allergic reaction was developing. Sister quickly swallowed two Benadryl caplets. No more white ants for her!

THE GARDEN   Soon the sisters recognized the need to provide for many of their own nutritional needs. They had been told that the Christians would plant a garden for the sisters, but at their arrival, no garden was seen.

The sisters began planning a garden within the compound. One day Sr. Mary Delrita spent five hours in the courtyard preparing the soil for a garden. She planted cucumbers, cantaloupe, and carrots. Shortly, Theresa Katunzi, a young woman whom Sr. Mary Janet had met a few days earlier, appeared at the convent to help the sisters with the garden. With her assistance, the sisters prepared the soil and planted beans and peas. But the plants did not grow very well. It seemed that with all the construction, the soil had been disturbed. Topsoil, always very fragile and limited, had been turned over, and construction materials became mixed in. Quickly the sisters decided they needed to cultivate land outside the compound.

Beyond the convent, the ground had to be cleared of bush before any planting could be done. Workmen, using large hoes, began chopping at the tall grass that attains a height of twelve to fifteen feet. Sometimes the grass was slashed and sometimes burned. Then the men had to dig out the long, tangled roots of the stubborn couch grass and prepare the soil for planting. Since the area was the size of two football fields, the project took almost two months to complete. Sr. Margaret Mary considered what had to be done and designed the school garden and a poultry project.

The first to be planted were 140 banana seedlings. Each plant required a hole two meters deep and two meters wide. Coffee hulls were mixed with soil and put into the hole with the plants.

The newly cultivated matooke field was so large that the pastor assisted the sisters by recruiting local Christians to plant. Over forty Christians responded to the appeal for help. Men, women, and children scattered throughout the field filling every corner with seed. Papaya, sweet potatoes, and groundnuts (peanuts) were also cultivated.

Coffee trees were the next to be planted. Fifty coffee trees were placed between matooke seedlings. This planting forces the trees to grow tall because both compete for sunlight. Also planted was a field of cassava, a plant with a starchy root that can be prepared in a variety of ways and is a staple food.

In the following months, Fr. Peter, the pastor, negotiated with the cultivators to clear a plot above the convent for $350. In January, an area at the side of the house was also cultivated.

As each small plot close to the convent was cleared and prepared, a variety of plants was planted in rows: lettuce, carrots, beans, pineapples, spinach, cabbage, and tomatoes. Orange trees were planted in January; avocado, mango, and jackfruit in March; and banana trees in April. This was the beginning of the farm. Sr. Margaret Mary coordinated much of the farm work and often assisted in the tedious labor.

Occasionally, some Christians and children from the area helped in the task. Even with all this attention, the farm was ultimately dependent on the weather. The alternating wet and dry seasons determined not only the time for planting but also the very survival of the crops.

Within three months of their arrival, the sisters had acquired three hens and two roosters, mostly received as gifts. The animals ran freely in the courtyard garden and helped themselves to the emerging plants. In time, a chicken house of sticks and mud with a metal roof was constructed behind the convent.

One evening upon checking the chickens, Sr. Margaret Mary discovered part of the chicken wire pulled back. She repaired the enclosure with nails but was more concerned that the chickens not escape than with the possibility of theft. The next morning, she discovered another area of chicken wire and reeds torn away and eight layer hens missing. A report was filed with the police with no result. Although the hens were never recovered, the sisters did learn to take better security measures with the property.

Sr. Margaret Mary learned about the types of food the chickens needed to increase egg production. A veterinarian from the area came and assisted sister in assessing the health and readiness of the hens to lay eggs. He also instructed sister how to build boxes for the hens to enter when they lay. Periodically, sister ordered more chicks from a source in Kampala, and the population quickly increased. The chickens provided the sisters with eggs and an occasional chicken dinner.

PREPARING AND STORING FOOD   Sr. Mary Janet described her first experience of preparing a chicken.

> I promised her [Jane] I would help clean the chicken. This was my 1st attempt at such a task – Yuk!!! Sr. Margaret did the 1st one some months ago and couldn't do it again. I didn't think I should enjoy the chicken dinner without being willing to help with the preparation. Well, it was pretty gross, but I did get through it. Tonight, we had the chicken for dinner. I wasn't sure I could eat it without thinking about the pre-dinner scene. The dinner was delicious. (Sr. Mary Janet to Family, November 19, 1995)

In another letter, sister described some of the meals.

> Sunday dinner was chicken soup and beans. Monday – end of chicken soup and beans. This morning, because it was a feast day, we splurged and had something very rare here – an orange. We bought four at the market last time we went. They were green then, now they are orange. We used two today and each had a ½. Wow! An orange never tasted so good! We portioned out the bread so we could stretch it. Tomorrow we will have cooked rice for breakfast. We have come to realize how precious basic things like food and water are. (Sr. Mary Janet to Family, August 22, 1995)

Trips to Kampala for necessities, such as flour, sugar, and rice, became routine. Eventually, the sisters began purchasing some items in bulk through the construction company: fifty-pound bags of flour, oats, rice, and sugar. These supplies created another challenge: how to store the items and keep out ants, rats, and other creatures. One day the girls found ants in the sugar and spent a good part of the afternoon sifting the fifty-pound bag of sugar. On the next trip to Kampala, the sisters purchased six large plastic buckets in which to store food.

Preparation and storage of food required considerable time; there were no short cuts. Sr. Jane Marie was the primary cook, and she worked with the girls, teaching them to prepare foods with which the sisters were familiar.

The gas stove was the first real stove. At the beginning, the sisters only had a charcoal burner. Sr. Jane Marie cooked the first foods on the charcoal burner. The wood-burning stove was ordered but had not yet arrived.

The sisters were delighted with the propane stove, but occasional problems arose when the propane ran low. On one occasion, Angela announced that the stove had run out of gas. What a disaster! Sr. Jane Marie had three loaves of bread ready to bake and a chicken killed and prepared for cooking. Fortunately, the sisters were able to borrow Fr. Peter's gas cylinder for an hour. In the beginning, the stove was also used to boil the water used for drinking and cooking, but soon this task moved to an outside fire.

Another surprise for the sisters was a refrigerator. This was run by kerosene (locally called paraffin) and did a good job—when it worked. The flame had to be just right or it smoked or went out.

One evening Sr. Jane Marie and Sr. Mary Delrita worked on the refrigerator until about 11:30 p.m. with no luck. The next day, because of Sr. Mary Delrita's persistence and endurance, it was discovered that the kerosene tank was too full, and the flue needed to be cleaned. By the end of the project, sister had black soot all over, but the refrigerator worked. The refrigerator continued to need careful tending.

Occasionally, the sisters were able to purchase meat. Shortly before Easter, Sr. Mary Janet walked to Matale, a neighboring village.

> Cows are brought to a grassy area, slaughtered, skinned and cut up for sale. As I stood by the meat waiting for the butcher to wait on us, I noticed piles of fresh manure and was careful not to step in it. A dog kept trying to get at the part of the cow that lay on the grass covered with banana leaves. Of course, there were lots of flies. People crowded around looking over the meat. When the butcher went to cut us a good piece from what was under the banana leaf, I noticed the tail and legs of the cow were still there. When people make a purchase, it is wrapped in banana leaves. ... When we got home I told Sr. Jane, "You better cook this meat good and long."

> Christmas and Easter are meat sale times. These are special days when people have meat to eat; otherwise it is rare. (Sr. Mary Janet to Lisa, Curt, Erica, and Kevin, April 10,1996)

WATER! WATER!

Water was a problem from the beginning. When the sisters arrived in Buseesa, the water tank was dry because it was the dry season. Within the first days in Buseesa, Sr. Mary Delrita and Fr. Aloysius collected five jerry cans (twenty-liter plastic containers) and traveled to Kakumiro to get water from the Dominican sisters. These trips continued for a number of days.

Rain from the roof flows into the gutters, then into pipes, and finally into the storage tanks. When water is needed, it is pumped to the upper tank where it can flow by gravity through a pipe into the house.

From the very beginning, survival activities, such as getting, purifying, and storing good water took almost all day. Water from the water tank that was used for drinking and cooking, was boiled for twenty minutes, filtered drop by drop, and finally poured into liter bottles.

Another source of water was the local water hole. This was a natural spring that flowed into a depressed area. The water attracted insects of all kinds, and there was little question about the impurity of the water. The sisters were appalled when they realized this water was a main source of water for many people living in the area. However, when the water in the tank was low, the sisters also made trips to the water hole to procure water for various uses.

People told the sisters, "The rain will come!" Finally, in early August there was a heavy evening rain that lasted about forty-five minutes. The next afternoon it rained again. Whenever it looked like rain, the sisters put out whatever pots and buckets were available to catch the precious drops. The water was then stored in plastic jerry cans. When these were filled, they were very heavy, and the sisters were surprised to see young children easily balancing these cans on their heads as they carried precious water to their homes.

With water being so undependable, the sisters began looking into the possibility of a borehole. Contact was made with the district water officer in the Kibaale District.

After research on the area, someone in the department responded that the current sources of water used by residents were protected and unprotected springs, and a borehole might have to be very deep, and the yield might be low. A complicating factor was that there was only one drill in the country. The response also included a cost estimate of the project based on an analysis of typical costs throughout Uganda. The quoted costs did not include any costs for storage tanks or piping systems.

When the borehole workers arrived on March 24, 1996, they inquired of the sisters where they wanted the borehole. The sisters were of no help as they had never even seen a borehole. The men walked around the area and pointed to a spot not too far from the convent. The crew of nine workers labored for a day and a half drilling to a depth of 200 feet, before successfully tapping into water. (The average depth of boreholes in the Kibaale District is about eighty-two feet.) The huge drilling machine provided on-site instruction for the students and staff at Buseesa Primary who gathered in awe at the imposing sight. The sisters had to provide two nights' lodging and food for the men. Fortunately, there was sufficient room in the unfinished convent wing.

With the installation of the hand pump, cement platform, and drain, the borehole was completed in September. The borehole quickly became a source of water for the village inhabitants and the students at Buseesa Primary. The bad news was that, although the quality of the water was a thousand times better than the local swamp, it was not fit for internal consumption.

A few months later, a crew arrived to test the borehole. They discovered less water than had been expected, and it was determined that although it could produce water, it was not enough to meet the needs of boarding school children.

On June 20, 1997, the borehole pump broke. This was not totally unexpected because the children from the local school gave it quite a workout. The borehole was not repaired until sometime later.

LAUNDRY   Laundry was an all-day task. It required building an outdoor fire, boiling the water, and washing and rinsing the clothes by hand. The soft water made it difficult to get out the soap. The sisters hadn't expected to iron their clothes, but with the method of laundry, ironing was necessary. They purchased a charcoal iron, but it wasn't possible to purchase charcoal locally. One of the construction men advised using a hot piece of wood from the fire. Sr. Mary Janet decided to try it. The iron worked amazingly well, but smoke spilled from the iron. Sister immediately thought of an old song from home, "Smoke Gets in Your Eyes."

After the experience of doing laundry, the sisters were surprised at the appearance of the people when they came for the Sunday liturgy: Their clothing was always clean and orderly. Many came to church carrying their shoes, protecting them from the muddy or dusty roads.

COMMUNICATION

The sisters made great efforts to communicate with those back in the United States. Initially, they sent faxes through the Hoima Construction Company's office in Kampala. Each trip to Kampala was an opportunity to send a fax or make phone contact with the United States. When the sisters were in Kampala on July 31, they discovered that their fax of July 24 had not yet been sent!

The sisters wrote letters and made videos of the people and surroundings. On one occasion, the sisters needed authorization for a fairly large expense. They set off for the Kakumiro post office to make the call. They arrived at 7:00 a.m., but since the post office did not open until 8:00 a.m., they stood outside and waited. When they finally got inside and tried the phone, it would not work; it was an overcast day and the phone relied on solar energy. With no results yet by 11:00 a.m., the woman at the post office suggested the sisters go to Mubende. At the Mubende post office, about an hour from Buseesa, the sisters succeeded in completing a call to California – 1:00 a.m. California time. What a joy it was to speak with someone back home!

One sister explained to her family that the "means of communication are nil here. There is no mail service, not even a post office anywhere close." Initially letters were sent and received through the Bishop's house, several hours away. With construction supply trucks traveling back and forth between Hoima and Buseesa, the sisters were able to send and receive mail more readily. Packages from the United States were sent to Kampala because someone from the construction company went regularly to the airport or post office to pick up deliveries. The security of packages sent from the United States to Hoima could not be assured.

There was always excitement when the construction company lorry came rumbling down the road, for it often carried boxes and mail from the sisters, relatives, and friends back home.

Within two years, the sisters obtained a PO box in Mubende, about an hour away, that enabled them to get their mail more quickly. Packages still had to be sent to Kampala where the construction crew would bring them to Buseesa if there was room in the lorry.

The sisters felt very isolated and cut off from the world outside. In the beginning there was no newspaper, no radio, no telephone, so they had little idea what was happening in the other parts of the globe. With the ordinary means of communication extremely limited, the sisters yearned for news from home and were always most grateful for every letter and box. On one occasion, the sisters said it was like Christmas because they received a large pack of mail from the sisters in Covington and Thousand Oaks.

The sisters were interested in knowing what was happening in the outside world, so eventually they were able to use a twelve-band radio that Sr. Margaret Mary had brought. They had difficulty getting Voice of America, but did succeed with the BBC. The sisters discussed the possibility of a radio call system that would permit them to contact Hoima and some of the parishes.

Because the sisters were without a source of daily news, they later arranged to have the daily paper, *New Vision*, delivered to the bottom of the hill. Thus, they were able to read national and international news – from an African perspective. They continued this for some time.

In December 1996, two men arrived and brought the equipment for the installation of the radio call. This included surveying the site for the best location for the set, positioning the antennae, threading the cable through the roof, connecting to the solar batteries, and joining the radio with others on the air. After the sisters were instructed in the use of the set, they called Hoima to share the good news. Later, the sisters hoped to upgrade the unit to be able to send e-mails.

HEALTH CONCERNS

LOCAL HELP   On one of their tours of the diocese, the sisters were taken to Hoima Hospital. Being a nurse by profession, Sr. Mary Delrita was very attentive to what she saw. She described the conditions as "Pitiable!" Patients brought their own bedding, and families were responsible for meals and other things. The medical care provided was very poor because the facility was so poor. The need for medical care was a major issue in the area. A forty-five-minute walk brought the sisters to a clinic that was run by a male nurse. The nurse kept the clinic clean and organized, but Sr. Mary Delrita quickly recognized that his knowledge base was very small and not completely accurate. Fairly good health care could be found in Kampala, but that was hours away. Thus, the sisters made great efforts to remain healthy.

Many people sought Fr. Peter out for advice. Father was well known for his skill in healing. He used herbs and other kinds of native medicine and treatment. The local medicine was mostly herbal and surprisingly helpful in many ways.

NEIGHBORS COME FOR HELP   The sisters had come to Uganda bringing only those medicines and medical supplies that they thought they would need. As soon as the people learned that Sr. Mary Delrita was a nurse, more and more of them arrived at the convent seeking medical attention. Sometimes mothers came with their infants or young children suffering from malnutrition or disease, and there was nothing Sister could do. Adults and children arrived with open sores on their legs and feet because they wore no shoes. The complaints were mainly in three areas: "worms" (anything they felt inside like congestion, gas, or heartburn), "malaria" (any fever), or "pain" (the most elusive because a good description could not be obtained).

Sister was hesitant about getting too involved for several reasons. First, the language was such a problem that sister could not get good information about the problem. Second, sister hadn't come prepared to deal with the types of concerns she met. In addition, the medical supplies the sisters had brought were limited. Sr. Mary Delrita had to limit her treatments to wounds, coughs, sore throats, and stomach aches. She dispensed antacids and Tylenol with lots of TLC and a prayer for each person.

One little boy deeply touched the hearts of the sisters. Deogratias came to the house often to get cough medicine for his grandmother.

> He looked so pitiful. He shuffles rather than walks and he never smiles. He looks like an old man in a baby's body. ... We thought at first that he was about three years old. We have found out that he is going on six years. We weighed him and he weighs twenty-five pounds! I wish you could see his poor little feet. They were so sore from jiggers and wounds he was limping. African jiggers are not like the kind you get at home. African jiggers are gross! They get under the skin and

lay eggs in a LITTLE sack. … You get them from the dry dirt floors. (February 11, 1997, Sr. Mary Janet)

One day Deogratias came to see Sr. Mary Delrita because he was sick. The sisters tried to convince him that sister couldn't come because she was sick. He wouldn't leave and began acting strangely. One of the sisters went to get sister, and by the time they returned, the child was convulsing and had a very high fever. The sisters laid him on the table and started to sponge him down. With the help of a dropper, Sr. Mary Delrita managed to get some medication into him. Because Deogratias had a low tolerance for pain, he ordinarily would not have allowed sister to remove the jiggers from his feet. So, while he was still "out of it," sister started to work as much as she could on one little foot. The jiggers can cause fever, and when removed, they leave a small hole that takes a while to heal.

The sisters were amazed that no one came looking for the small boy. He remained with the sisters from morning until mid-afternoon. Sr. Mary Delrita carried him home with the bandaged foot to his grandmother's mud hut. The grandmother was not there, but those who were there, seemed not too concerned about him. The sisters continued to check on him for several days.

Sometime before this, the sisters had given Deogratias a pair of shoes which he wore for only a short time. They had also given him shirts and pants because his clothes were literally filthy rags. He would get dressed up when he came to visit the sisters, then change back to his usual outfit later.

On another occasion, when the sisters answered the doorbell, the pastor's house girl was there with another girl. A mother had sent her daughter to "get Father to come and baptize the baby before he dies!" Father had sent the girls to get Sr. Mary Delrita to see what she could do to help. After collecting some supplies, Sr. Mary Delrita and Sr. Mary Janet went with the girls to a home a short distance down the road.

When they arrived at the mud house, they found the mother, Tereza, sitting sadly with the infant, Christopher, lying quietly on her lap. The infant was non- responsive. God's help was definitely needed here.

Sister asked for some boiled water and pulled out the sugar, cooking oil, and a small dropper she had brought. By the time she had filled the dropper, the baby was beginning to convulse. Quickly, Sister began to give Christopher some of the "formula" drop by drop under his tongue. Slowly Sister worked to get more into the baby. Gradually his convulsions subsided and he began to awaken.

Tereza had nursed all of her other children with no problem, but for some reason this little one and his mother just had not connected, and Christopher was starving.

Eventually the baby began to nurse. With a grateful heart, Sister left them with great hope for continued progress.

Six years later, Christopher was a happy and healthy student at St. Julie School who especially loved and participated in the traditional dances. One day, when he was in the library, Sr. Mary Delrita heard him call to her. Sister responded, asking how she could help him. Christopher looked at Sister and said, "My Momma told me how you saved my life." Sister was awe-struck.

SISTERS' HEALTH   Health issues were a major concern from the beginning. The sisters had taken medical supplies with them to treat a variety of medical conditions. Even with this, they recognized the need to take special care of themselves, for example, when they experienced the flu, a heavy cold, a scraped leg, or even blisters on their feet from so much walking while shopping in Kampala. But two major illnesses are vivid reminders of just how vulnerable the sisters were especially in view of the limited and extremely poor medical resources in the area.

In April 1996, Sr. Mary Janet developed a throat infection and cough. Despite some days of bed rest and Sr. Mary Delrita's treating her with antibiotics, Sr. Mary Janet could not overcome the illness. On May 4, the Bishop sent a driver to Buseesa to bring the sisters to Hoima to the celebration of the fifth anniversary of his consecration as bishop. Sr. Mary Janet was not able to go, and the Bishop became concerned when he heard about Sister's illness. About a week and a half later, the Bishop made the two-and-a-half-hour trip from Hoima to Buseesa to check on Sister. When he saw Sister's condition, he wanted her to go to Hoima to see a doctor there. But Sr. Mary Janet did not want to go. Because she was feeling very bad, she dreaded the trip over long and very rough roads. Besides, she remembered visiting the hospital in Hoima, and that was the last place she wanted to go. Finally, Sr. Mary Janet agreed to go, anticipating that she would be gone for about three days. How grateful Sister was when Sr. Mary Delrita volunteered to accompany her.

Arriving in Hoima, the Bishop drove directly to the home of an Italian doctor. When the doctor took Sr. Mary Janet's blood pressure, it was 180/140. Sister was sure this was due to the great stress and difficulty of the trip. The doctor wrote an order for tests at the hospital the next day.

The visit to the hospital went well. Sister had a chest x-ray and a blood test and returned to the Bishop's house with some medication. Sister seemed to be feeling a little better, but two days later she was worse and sick to her stomach. The Bishop sent his driver to fetch another doctor for a second opinion. Dr. Stella, a Ugandan, had recently left her position as assistant administrator and supervisor of the medical staff at Mulago Hospital in Kampala. She desired to set up a private practice in her home village. The doctor confirmed the diagnosis of pneumonia, prescribed penicillin, and ordered other treatments. After eight days, Sister was feeling much better and returned to Buseesa.

On June 18-19, Sr. Mary Delrita felt rundown and then began to experience night chills and a fever. During the next days, since she did not respond to medications, Sister began to suspect malaria, despite taking the regular steps to prevent it. On Sunday, June 23, Fr. Peter drove Sister the two hours to Kahunde, the closest place where a slide could be made to check. The test came back negative, but this did not answer the question of what was causing the fever

Sr. Mary Delrita then decided it was time to go to Hoima to see the doctor who had cared for Sr. Mary Janet. After examining Sister, Dr. Stella accompanied the sisters to the Bishop's house so she could start Sr. Mary Delrita on an IV. Sisters from the diocesan dispensary provided round-the-clock nursing care, sleeping on a mat next to Sister's bed at night. The IV was continued until Friday because the slide made in Hoima proved positive for malaria, but the species could not be identified.

On Wednesday, another doctor was called for a second opinion, and through the use of a stethoscope and finger tapping – no x-ray – the doctor diagnosed pneumonia. There was no great improvement by 8:00 Monday morning, so Fr. Phillip Ballrkudembe drove Sr. Mary Delrita, Sr. Mary Janet, and Sr. Regina, a Ugandan nurse, to the Franciscan hospital, Nsambya, in Kampala. They had packed everything they would need: sheets, blanket, silverware, dishes, basin, jerry can for water, and food.

By 1:00 p.m. the sisters reached the hospital, but all the physicians were out to lunch until 2:00 p.m. Finally, a physician arrived, read the letter from the Hoima doctor, and sent Sister for a chest x-ray. After the x-ray was read, Sister was sent to admissions, a table at the end of the waiting area. There was some consternation because the room booked for Sister was given to another woman. At that point, Sister just wanted a bed. They gave her an admission packet (a roll of toilet tissue) and walked her to a ward on the other side of the campus.

The ward contained forty plus beds, no privacy curtains, and about three feet of space between beds. After some discussion and a phone call at the nurses' desk, Sister was directed to the next ward. This ward was more spacious and had curtains around each bed. There was a white metal hospital bed, a bedside stand, and a chair. Sr. Mary Janet and Sr. Regina made the trip back across the campus to the vehicle to retrieve their supplies. It was 5:00 p.m. when Sr. Mary Delrita finally slipped into bed.

Shortly, someone came and said that if they paid, Sister could go to a private room. Sr. Regina objected to the arrangement, but in a few minutes, approval was given for the move, and personnel transported Sister in a wheelchair.

Sr. Mary Delrita's private room had a wooden bed with an innerspring mattress, a throw rug, an electric ceiling light, and a small lamp by the bed that the nurses borrowed twice: once because there was no light in the treatment room, and once to begin an IV. There was also a full bath between Sister's room and the next patient's room.

During Sister's stay, blood was drawn, and she had an ultrasound and a repeat chest x-ray. At one point, a CT was suggested, but the one CT in Uganda was at another hospital, and scheduling was a problem. Later it was decided that a CT was unnecessary.

The sisters in Covington had been notified. Sr. Mary Delrita's lengthening stay was raising grave concern. On June 28, while the sisters were still in Hoima, Sr. Mary Janet sent a fax explaining that Sister Mary Delrita was very sick, but that she seemed to be improving a little. This was a complicated time in the Covington province because Sr. Mary Margaret was completing her term as provincial superior, and Sr. Mary Shauna was assuming the responsibility on July 1. Covington received other faxes on July 1 and July 3. On July 4, both Sr. Mary Shauna and Sr. Mary Margaret spoke with Sr. Mary Janet. The situation seemed to be critical as Sister was experiencing headaches, nausea, and vomiting. A sonogram was taken to look for an abscess, and the test was negative. The cause of the fever was still unknown.

During the course of the day, Sr. Mary Margaret contacted Sr. Mary Patricia Gannon, SND, in Kettering, England. Sr. Mary Margaret explained the situation in Uganda to Sr. Mary Patricia and asked if she could explore the possibility of Sr. Mary Delrita's being accepted at a hospital in London provided they could get her on a plane. Sr. Mary Patricia accepted the challenge and worked late into the night contacting medical facilities in London. Finally, Sr. Mary Patricia called with the news that depending on the diagnosis, there was a hospital that would accept Sr. Mary Delrita. In fact, they were willing to send a nurse to Uganda to accompany Sister to England. Fortunately, Sr. Mary Delrita did not have to make the trip to England.

Contact between Covington and Sr. Mary Janet continued to be made through the Catholic Secretariat that was near the hospital and through ARU where Sr. Mary Janet was staying. During this time, Sr. Mary Shauna also kept in close contact with Sr. Mary Delrita's family. Within a day or two Sr. Mary Delrita's stomach settled, her headache was gone, and her temperature gradually returned to normal. By July 10,

Sister was assured that this was not a recurring illness, and Sr. Mary Delrita and Sr. Mary Janet started back to Buseesa. For more than a week, Sr. Mary Delrita spent 90% of the time in bed and gradually began to feel much stronger.

A detailed description of Sr. Mary Janet's and Sr. Mary Delrita's health situation is given so that the reader might recognize the very limited and strained medical supplies and equipment in Uganda. (Sr. Mary Delrita and Sr. Mary Janet to Sr. Mary Shauna and sisters, July 13, 1996; Sr. Mary Delrita to Dearest Friends, July 23, 1996)

The two sisters wrote home:

> We have walked the path of each other's illness together, have been overwhelmed by the many signs of our loving Father's goodness and provident care, and now feel the urge to sing with you, our companions on the journey, "How good God is!" (Sr. Mary Janet and Sr. Mary Delrita to Sr. Mary Shauna and sisters, July 13, 1996)

After experiencing the illnesses, the sisters more actively pursued the radio call. They had procured some donations toward the project, but not enough to cover the expense. They then made a request to the Sisters of Notre Dame Solidarity Fund in Rome and also requested grant monies from the Diocesan Department of Social Services.

TRAVEL

The sisters were on the road quite a bit, especially during the first weeks. Sr. Mary Janet wrote:

> One of the most difficult and worst things here is travel. I have seen and experienced no good roads. Almost all are dirt roads even in the capital city. There are many potholes and in one situation we positively had to use the 4-wheel drive to get through a long stretch of loose mud. There are no road signs, traffic lights, and there seems to be no rules about driving except to drive on the left side (usually) and in such a way that you don't get killed or knock someone down. (Sr. Mary Janet to Bill, Mary, Al, Tom, Hazel, Blanche, Leo, Ann, and Family, July 20, 1995)

Sister remarked that she almost had to close her eyes when they drove through Kampala. "At the intersection all the cars pile up in a huge jam and dare to squeeze through."

But sometimes it wasn't just the roads themselves that presented a problem: Distances were also a major challenge. A trip on dry roads to Kampala ordinarily took about four hours. The trip to Hoima generally took about three and a half hours. However, one trip to Hoima took the entire day because the Bishop wanted the sisters to visit the parishes in the Kibaale District. At each stop the sisters were given a greeting, a brief tour, and soda or tea. At each place they also signed the guest book.

On an early trip to Kampala, Fr. Aloysius and two sisters stopped at the post office and then walked quite a distance from one market and then to another. At a stop along the way home, the sisters purchased some eggs with no protective carton. On her lap, Sr. Mary Delrita made a nest out of a jacket and placed the precious eggs in it. It had rained and the road was muddy and slippery, so Sister had to tend to the eggs carefully. Despite the fact that the vehicle slid into a ditch, the eggs arrived home safely.

When the sisters went to Kampala for shopping, they employed someone familiar with the area to bargain for what they needed. Because of the color of their skin, when the sisters tried to bargain for items, the cost sometimes became more than double the worth. In time, a shopping area called Metro offered many items at a fixed price.

Heavy rains often made the roads impassable, and lorries bringing the building supplies from Hoima often got stuck in the mud. Sometimes the drivers had to unload some of the gravel or bricks to lighten the load before they could extract the lorry from the mud. Several times the lorries remained stuck overnight. This meant that the workers in Buseesa were left without materials, and construction came to a halt.

The missionary sisters arrived in Uganda on July 13 and seven days later Sr. Mary Janet wrote to her family that the sisters had no car, but it was expected to arrive in September.

After a short time, the Bishop arranged with a nearby medical facility to use their Toyota until the sisters' vehicle was ready. The large Toyota had been used as an ambulance and it had no power brakes or power steering. Seats in the back could accommodate five or six people facing one another on each side. There was very little shock absorption, and the vehicle was very expensive to operate, about $80.00 to fill the tank with gas. The sisters sometimes used the local taxi that cost about $3.50. The taxi was a large van licensed to carry fourteen people, but on one trip there were twenty-two people in the van. The cost and destination of the taxi often varied according to the notions of the driver.

In the spring, the ambulance had to be returned. Sr. Mary Janet wrote to her family that it was a great problem for the sisters to be so stuck in "the bush" and dependent on others for transportation. Their friends John and Susan McDermott from the Irish Aid Society came to their assistance. When the couple was making a trip to

Kampala, they went out of their way to take the sisters along and even made trips to the airport. The sisters were always conscious that the good God's gracious providence was ever with them.

A letter from the sisters in June contained the news that they had a car! No, not the long-awaited vehicle, but the Bishop's car. He had a new one and sent his old one for the sisters' use until they had theirs.

VEHICLE   In October, while Sr. Mary Amy and Sr. Mary Margaret were visiting, the sisters received word that their vehicle had arrived. On the way to the airport to fly home, the provincials "visited" the Land Cruiser. The sisters could not get the vehicle because the tax exemption application was still pending. There was concern that if the sisters took possession of the vehicle, it might be impossible to receive a refund for the taxes.

In December, the Ugandan President, Yoweri Museveni, visited Bujuni, the nearby parish. When the sisters were introduced to the President, they asked his influence to obtain tax exemption on their car. Progress on obtaining the vehicle was so very slow.

A shock came when Fr. Peter returned from an ordination ceremony and announced the news: If taxes were not paid within fifteen days, the vehicle was to be auctioned by the government. Early the next morning some of the sisters left for Hoima to check out the situation with the Bishop. The sisters had understood that the he was taking care of the taxation situation. The Bishop could not explain what had happened. The sisters decided it was time to take the matter in hand, so Sr. Mary Janet, Sr. Jane Marie, and Fr. Peter drove to Kampala. They traveled from one government minister to another and back again. They visited government offices every day from Tuesday through Friday. One person would raise their hopes and then send them to someone else, only to have their hopes dashed. They also discovered that as of July a new tax law had been in effect.

Finally, good news: On December 19, 1996, almost two years after being ordered, the 1995 Toyota Land Cruiser was driven by Sr. Jane Marie down the Buseesa road and into the convent yard! The sisters had been granted a waiver of the numerous taxes. Now they needed to get their drivers' licenses.

DRIVER'S LICENSE   Filling out forms and standing in line was just part of the process. The sisters traveled two hours to the test site. At 1:00 p.m., the examiner sent word that he would not arrive until the following day. The sisters then set out for the licensing center in Kampala. By 4:00 p.m. they arrived at the center only to be informed that the examiner did not show up that day. The sisters returned to

Buseesa. The following day, the sisters traveled to the first center and arrived at 10:00 a.m.; the examiner arrived at 2:00 p.m.

Sr. Jane Marie was the first to obtain her license, an experience she later described:

> Fill out form in triplicate using carbon paper.
> Wait in line to have application approved.
> Take application to another building to make payment.
> Fill out payment form in triplicate using carbon paper.
> Wait in line to make payment. ($5.50)
> Wait in line for receipt.
> Return two days later with receipt to pick up Learner's Permit.
> Go through same process to receive a form to take the driving test. ($20.00)
> After passing test, go through process again for the Ugandan Driver's Permit. ($25.00) (The Buseesa Four to Sisters, Family, and Friends, February 8, 1997)

A driver's license allowed one to drive on dirt/muddy roads that are often one lane with numerous potholes.

On a typical trip to Kampala, the first stop was the Mubende post office. Receipts for postage were painstakingly written by hand in duplicate, and no one was in a hurry for anything. All patiently waited their turn. The favorite line of the sisters was "Nothing is simple in Uganda!"

PLUNGING INTO MINISTRY

TEACHING ENGLISH   Some women of the village approached the sisters about teaching them English. In January 1996, one-hour weekly classes were begun. The first time fifteen women attended; the next week, twenty-two women came. The sisters considered these lessons a means to assist in raising the level of women, even if it was just a bit. Sr. Jane Marie coordinated the sessions, and after a few sessions the group was divided. Sr. Mary Delrita and Sr. Mary Janet each had a small group of women who knew some English. At the conclusion of each lesson, Sr. Mary Delrita instructed the women in nutrition and distributed some vegetables from the garden. Sr. Jane Marie began teaching those who knew little or no English. (Some could not read or write; some had only one or two years of education.) The women were so eager to learn.

SPECIAL CLASSES FOR P-7   On January 15, Sr. Mary Janet, Sr. Mary Delrita, and Sr. Jane Marie offered special classes to selected P-7 students at Buseesa Primary who would be candidates for the Primary Leaving Exam in November. They needed to pass the leaving exam if they wanted to go to secondary school. Kibaale District is known for having the poorest scores, and few, if any, students from Buseesa Primary pass this important test. Twenty-eight students from the school participated in the three-week session that included instruction in English, math, and religion.

TEACHING AT BUSEESA PRIMARY   The sisters volunteered to teach during the first term at Buseesa Primary. (There are three terms: February to April, June to August, and October to December.) The sisters began in February with the following assignments: Sr. Jane Marie teaching P-7 English and math, Sr. Margaret Mary teaching P-5 science, Sr. Mary Janet teaching P-4 English and religion, Sr. Mary Delrita teaching P-6 English. This new work gave the sisters an opportunity to learn about education in Uganda.

About the time of the sisters' arrival, the government had initiated free primary education for up to four children from each family. Buseesa Primary's enrollment skyrocketed from about 550 to 800. There were 112 students registered for P-4. After two weeks into the academic year, about ninety students showed up—all in one room! There were not enough seats so some students sat on piles of bricks. Actually, P-4 was not the worst. P-1 had 300 children and two teachers. Buseesa Primary had only seven classrooms. Sr. Jane Marie reported that there were 79 students in her P-6 English class. The students had to squeeze even closer in order to share one of the nine copies of the text. Sister commented that this was making her prayer to establish their own school even more urgent. There was word that the district was to going to supply some iron sheets for roofing and put up some shelters for some classes at Buseesa Primary.

In June, the second term began at Buseesa Primary. Once again, each sister assumed the responsibility for teaching classes. One day as Sr. Mary Janet was teaching her ninety-five P-4 students, she heard a commotion outside; it sounded like children crying. Suddenly the children in the class began to panic: some ran out of the room, some jumped out through the holes in the walls, one girl threw herself on the floor sobbing. All the children had frightened looks on their faces. Sister could hardly get the remaining students under control. After class, she went to the office to inquire what had happened and learned that the twenty-year-old brother of several students had died. Death is something very fearful for these people.

RELIGIOUS EDUCATION   During these months, the sisters also prepared a young boy for First Communion and assisted one of the house girls with her secondary education by teaching her math, biology, and geography.

The sisters realized that the P-7 students would complete their elementary education in December. For some it would mark the end of their formal education. Because the students received such poor religious education, the sisters initiated weekly classes to explain the faith, help students deepen their faith, and nurture a relationship with God. The voluntary class met each Sunday after Mass at the convent. About a dozen students participated in an hour's instruction followed by an hour of games and a snack.

WOMEN'S GROUP   Yet another endeavor evolved during these first months. A woman from the parish requested help in purchasing chicks to begin a business of selling eggs. The woman was a second wife, had eight children, and needed to provide for her family. It was not uncommon for a man to have more than one wife and family, and the responsibility of providing for the family generally fell to the women.

Although the sisters had learned that it was not good to lend or give money to people, they were eager to help the woman. After many inquiries, the sisters discovered the possibility of forming a women's group. A group of about ten women worked together for about six weeks to save and lend money to one another and thus get experience in saving and borrowing. The sisters used a self-help education program sponsored by the Belgian government intended to educate and train women to save, borrow, repay, and develop a business project.

The first meetings were held at the sisters' house, where they tried to model how to host a meeting. Soon, each of the women was expected to host a meeting at her home. This rotation encouraged the women to improve their homes by having a reason to do so. Meetings were held every other Saturday, and the women called themselves the Mukisa (blessing) Women's Group.

A constitution was written that included name, purpose, time, place, and frequency of the meetings, rules, and so forth. The sisters were surprised when the women made a rule that a fine would be charged to a member who came late or missed a meeting. At the second meeting, Sr. Mary Janet had said a few encouraging words about being on time. The women easily identified a chairperson, vice-chairperson, secretary, and treasurer. The lack of education made note taking and bookkeeping very difficult. Sr. Mary Delrita prepared a notebook in which financial accounts were kept and worked with the treasurer. She also created passbooks for each woman to record transactions. Sr. Mary Delrita used the opportunity to teach the women about healthy practices. Sr. Mary Janet worked with the secretary in maintaining minutes. Sister developed a form that the secretary could copy and fill in the particular information for each meeting. The differences in language and culture created great challenges for the project. (At the request of some women, Sr. Jane Marie began teaching English. This endeavor was short-lived as some of the men did not like the idea of the women learning English.)

In the first month, the group had managed to save about $50-$60. Marita, the first woman to borrow money, requested $25 to purchase a mixing bowl, spoon, ingredients, and other needs to begin a baking project. Cissy, one of the girls working at the convent, taught Marita to make bread. (Cissy had learned from Sr. Jane Marie and became quite proficient.) Marita created an oven using pans, one inside the other, with cooking stones above and below. She developed a market for her bread and quickly made her repayment with interest to the group. After her first baking success, Marita exclaimed, "They won't believe that Marita who didn't go to school can do this!"

Sr. Mary Janet and Sr. Mary Delrita continued to work with the group until the women were willing and able to carry on among themselves. The women welcomed each Sister of Notre Dame superior general and provincial superior when she visited, and were on hand to welcome home each sister as she returned from her visit to her home country.

In between these major teaching opportunities, the sisters were involved in smaller ministries. A fourteen-year-old girl had never attended school. Sr. Mary Delrita had her come Tuesdays and Thursdays to learn some English and basic reading. James was applying for advanced technical school. Sr. Margaret Mary assisted him to write letters of inquiry, fill out applications, and gather letters of recommendation. Sr. Mary Janet helped people find and correspond with their pen friends. In the first draft of a letter, a man opened with, "Dear Sweetheart." Sister tactfully directed him to find another salutation. Sr. Jane Marie's students knew they were welcome to come for extra help in English and math. One student came faithfully after school to borrow Weekly Readers and storybooks to help improve her reading skills.

CELEBRATIONS

FIRST CHRISTMAS   When one of the sisters asked a child how her family celebrated Christmas, the child replied, "We eat meat!" Early in the morning of December 24, the sisters could hear the mooing of the seventeen cattle being slaughtered for the Christmas feast. The people of the area would be going to the market to buy their meat.

In the convent, the sisters took the bare cassava branches of their Jesse Tree and covered it with asparagus fern and tinsel to become a Christmas tree. Gifts included small gifts from the United States, gifts for the house girls, and a trio of gifts the sisters had made for each other. It was quite a challenge to be creative with basically nothing. Some gifts were coupons for taking a sister's turn at pumping water or to clean shoes. The two house girls got into the spirit and wrapped up a bag of radishes for one sister and carrots for another. All the gifts were placed at the foot of the tree along with white porcelain nativity figures.

That night the sisters attended midnight Mass by lantern light. The sisters were struck to hear familiar Christmas carols sung in Runyoro. Because the pastor went to three outstations for Mass on Christmas, the parish had a communion service at 10:00 a.m.—in Runyoro. They sang many songs and many verses. One song had twelve verses, and they sang the entire song twice! For dinner, the sisters had a special treat: real meat, not just a tiny hint of meat in pasta or beans, and later enjoyed opening packages.

SPIRITUAL NOURISHMENT

From the very first day, the sisters were privileged to celebrate Mass on weekdays and have the Blessed Sacrament take up residence in a poor wooden tabernacle in the storeroom chapel. As the construction progressed, the chapel was moved from room to room.

To support one another in the spiritual realm, the sisters began each day with morning prayer together. After breakfast, they devoted some time to faith sharing on some passage from Scripture. They then discussed concerns they might have. On weekdays, whenever their pastor was home, they celebrated Mass in their chapel and joined the parish community on Sunday.

The sisters considered how they would make their annual spiritual retreat. The Camboni center in Kampala didn't fit their schedule. September seemed to be a good time because it was between two terms at school. The sisters decided upon the Carmelite monastery in Mityana. The Carmelites were a cloistered contemplative community with German origins. They had a guesthouse, and the grounds hosted numerous flowers, plants, and trees. Sr. Mary Janet, one of the first to make her retreat here, wrote home: "I hope they have decent bathroom facilities. I dread the thought of having to use a pit latrine all week. (Sr. Mary Janet to Blanche and family, September 1, 1996)

During her retreat, Sr. Mary Janet wrote that she felt like she was in paradise. "Wow, it is better than anything we could wish for!" The community was so welcoming and supportive with their prayers. The grounds were beautiful, and Sister had never seen so many exotic flowers. She thought it was a perfect place for retreat.

The sisters made an exciting discovery while on retreat. The artist who designed and executed the décor in the Carmelite chapel was Egino Gunther Weinert, the German artist who also designed the crucifixes worn by Sisters of Notre Dame throughout the world.

FINANCES

Early in the beginning of the new year the sisters scheduled a trip to Kampala to open an account at Stabic Bank and accomplish other errands. They planned to meet with a priest whom the Bishop was sending to assist with the bank business. Because of miscommunication, they failed to connect, but the sisters did succeed in opening an account with the bank. They actually had two accounts, one with Ugandan shillings and the other with USA dollars. Soon they would be able to write checks.

Later, two sisters received checks from a mission group in a parish. They were able to deposit these into their United States dollars account. But checks from individuals were virtually impossible to deposit and had to be sent to the home province for deposit.

SOLAR ENERGY

When the sisters departed for Africa, solar energy was still somewhat of a novelty in the United States. Knowing that there was no electrical power in the Buseesa area, it was decided to include solar panels and electrical outlets in the convent.

During the first months, there was one solar panel. This panel provided energy for the fluorescent overhead light in the community/dining room and a fluorescent light attached to a movable pole in the bedrooms. If it had been sunny most of the day, the sisters had light throughout the evening. On cloudy days, less energy was able to be stored, so lanterns and flashlights were used. Later, more solar panels were installed, and some of the energy was used to heat water for the kitchen and for showers.

COMPUTERS AND FLUSH FACILITIES

The sisters wrote to Sr. Mary Amy and Sr. Mary Margaret with a request regarding the possibility of computers and flush facilities being installed in the school over a five-year period.

Apparently, the provincial superiors were less than enthusiastic about the requests. In response, one of the sisters wrote a letter of explanation in support of their request. The superiors' letter must have suggested speaking to local people about these ideas. (A copy of this letter cannot be found.) In a few days, the sisters provided a follow-up letter with rationale for the proposals.

COMPUTERS   The sisters suggested that the school would open without student computers, but by the time the first students were in P-6 and P-7, computers would be installed. Therefore, the students would have two years of computer experience before leaving primary level. Two pages of rationale followed. A few days later, some of the sisters met Fr. Mugisa Aloysius, the priest who took such good care of them during their first weeks in Buseeesa. The sisters highly valued Father's opinion on matters relating to Uganda and her people.

They asked Father if he thought including computers as an educational aid in the school would be a good idea, or would it be too much for an area like Buseesa because computers are so foreign to the culture. Father's response was:

> Computers? Yes, I would be for it! We need it. … No one here knows anything about computers. We have to bring in people from the outside. … If you could prepare the children here it would be a gift to the area. We need it. … We are anxious to learn.

Sister explained that the sisters had been advised to be careful about imposing the American culture on the people. Father's reply: "Imposing? Not at all! … you would not be imposing—you would be helping us to progress. Education is the key to change and progress."

FLUSH TOILETS   The sisters requested being permitted to add flush toilets and showers on a small scale (one or two of them in the beginning) to give students an opportunity to use them. Then they could assess whether flush toilets and showers would be practical or advisable. It was acknowledged that adequate water might be an issue.

Fr. Aloysius' response to flush toilets was: "Yes, but begin on a small scale. But plan and make provisions for future expansion."

The sisters also spoke with Fr. Peter, and he repeated many of the same points as Fr. Aloysius. At lunch, he spoke about the great changes and growth in Uganda since the destructive times of Milton Obote and Idi Amin. He commented that many people, even former missionaries, who say, "Don't impose your culture," have no idea of the Uganda of today, the Uganda which is ready to accept change for progress.

(The quotes above are from letters: Unsigned to Sr. Mary Margaret and Sr. Mary Amy, February 24,1996; Sr. Jane Marie to Sr. Mary Margaret, Sr. Mary Amy, and members of the respective councils, Feb 22, 1996).

VISITORS

It surely must have seemed to the four sisters that visitors appeared at their door each day and sometimes more than once a day

On September 10, 1995, the first visitor from the USA arrived. Nancie Kress Beg was a friend of Ron Seibert, brother of Sr. Mary Kevan Seibert (from the Covington province). Nancie's main purpose in coming to Africa was to visit the gorilla reserve in southern Uganda near the Rwanda border. While in Kampala, Nancie hired a driver and a car to take her to and from Buseesa.

Nancie related the events of her trip and brought a "care package" from home. The sisters gave her a tour of the convent and visited Buseesa Primary, the waterhole, and other sites of interest in the immediate area, including several families.

> Nancie was struck by the poverty, yet the cleanliness of the children. She commented that the people are curious and shy but very friendly. The sisters speak a little of the native language, and the people have a few words of English. Somehow they are able to communicate. (Sr. Mary Margaret to Sisters, September 16, 1995)

In a phone conversation with Sr. Mary Margaret, Nancie spoke about the sisters' enthusiasm and their positive contact with the people. Nancie's final comment was, "How happy they are!"

In mid-October, Sr. Mary Amy and Sr. Mary Margaret arrived for an eight-day visit. Fr. Heinz and some of the missionaries met the visitors at the airport. After taking care of errands, they began the long ride to Buseesa. When they were within twenty minutes of Buseesa, they were halted because three vehicles were mired in the mud creating a total blockade of the road. After a two-hour wait and no progress in the removal of the vehicles, Fr. Peter appeared up the road beyond the mired vehicles. Since it appeared that the road would be blocked for yet some time, the sisters decided to walk to meet Fr. Peter. The sisters cautiously made their way up the road passing the blockade and walking carefully in the deep slippery tire tracks.

When the sisters reached Buseesa and drove down the road to the convent, the provincials were stunned: Never had they thought that the convent compound would be so large! They had received the needed permissions for the building from the superior general and the General Council, but now they thought, "Wait until Sr. Mary Joell sees this!" But after spending just the few days with the sisters, Sr. Mary Amy and Sr. Mary Margaret realized the need for such space. This was the only place the sisters had. There were spaces for communal activities, but there would also be times when each one needed some private space. There was also the trust that the mission would grow and all this space would be needed.

The next day, the provincials shared community news, and in the afternoon, the truck from Kampala arrived with the sisters' luggage as well as boxes that had come in the mail. With the sisters opening boxes and exclaiming over the contents, it was like Christmas in October. During the provincials' stay, the sisters repeatedly pointed out items that had been sent, and they expressed their gratitude for each one and especially for the love and prayers that accompanied these gifts.

While the visitors were there, construction continued on the convent. Morning prayer was a real challenge. The prayer was accompanied by a crowing rooster, two men hammering, one shoveling stones, one singing, and one whistling. Evening prayer and liturgy were usually more quiet.

The provincials toured the convent and explored the section under construction. The missionary sisters relayed their many discoveries and understandings. They told about their attempts at adjusting to the Ugandan culture. They also discussed their plans and hopes for the future.

After Mass on Sundays and holidays, parishioners often came to greet the sisters to visit, or to express some need or request. The sisters were becoming more adapted to visitors coming throughout the day – almost always unannounced. The sisters would stop their work and come to welcome and talk; hospitality is not taken lightly in Uganda. These visits usually lasted at least an hour and included refreshments.

On March 17, two Sisters of Notre Dame arrived: Sr. Elizabeth Mary Biebelhausen from Chardon, Ohio, who had served in India for forty years and was visiting Tanzania, and Sr. Mary Aruna of Patina, India, missioned in Tanzania. The two visitors told about the beginnings of the mission in Arusha and shared many practical things: garden tips; how to make curried cassava (a great improvement since cassava is basically tasteless) ; and how to make cough medicine from garlic, ginger, and pepper.

A SPECIAL VISITOR

One day, an older woman rang the convent bell. What a surprise to discover that she was the daughter of Denis Kamuka, the almost Ugandan martyr. (The local people consider Denis to be a martyr because he was ready to give up his life for Christ.) Denis and his wife are buried on church property which Denis once owned. Many of the bricks in the church are from the house where Denis lived.

The sisters learned that the daughter lived in Kampala and had come to see friends and visit her parents' graves. She had a picture of her parents, and the sisters noticed how much she looked like her father. She related that Denis and two other boys were wrapped in reeds and told they would be burned later. Denis' older sister pleaded for his life and succeeded in getting him free. Denis spent a year in prison after he was spared the cruel death his companions had suffered.

CONVENT CONSTRUCTION
CONTINUES

During the entire first year, the sisters constantly heard the voices and the hammering of the construction workers. While the sisters settled into the completed rooms of the convent, the workmen continued with the construction of the fourth side that contained the chapel, bedrooms, and lavatory area.

The sisters were both fascinated and amazed to see what the men did with hardly any tools or machinery. Working on the foundation of the remaining section of the house was slow. The crew had been held up because of the rain; the lorry couldn't get the needed rock from the rocky hillsides in Bujuni because of the muddy roads.

For the foundation, a wall of brick was constructed around a designated area. Dirt was then shoveled into the area, and a machine was used to press down the dirt. This machine was the only piece of such equipment the sisters observed in use. Sheer muscle power was used to move the boulders from the lorry onto the pressed dirt. The boulders were then pounded into smaller pieces. The space between the rocks was filled with even smaller rocks, and the foundation was ready for the cement.

After a year of dirt, construction sounds, and interruptions, the convent was finally completed at the end of August 1996. The next step was the varnishing of the concrete floors and the brick walls. The varnish made cleaning easier and added to the brightness of the room by reflecting light. (Each bedroom had one brick wall and three plastered and painted walls.)

One coat of varnish had been put on the floor of the sitting room, but it was walked off in one week. The sisters then requested that the floors have two coats of varnish. At this point, the sisters examined the label on the can and read, "at least three coats." It was decided to complete the varnishing after the furniture arrived and had been moved to the designated areas.

The chapel windows were finally installed. The windowpanes were composed of tinted rectangular shapes, some textured. The chapel was nearing completion when the furniture arrived. The beautiful woodwork tabernacle was fashioned after an African grain storage bin to symbolize the Bread of Life. On September 16, 1996, Bishop Deogratias blessed the chapel, the altar, and the tabernacle. What a blessing to have a permanent and dignified dwelling for Our Lord!

September 26, 1996, was the official moving day. Fortunately, the school construction workers assisted with the carrying and placement of the furniture. With things well under way, Sr. Mary Janet and one of the house girls began cleaning all the windows so the curtains could be hung. Now the sisters could transfer their personal items from their temporary bedrooms to their new rooms.

The convent was now complete and free of construction workers, dust, and noise!

Alleluia!

Our house is beyond our expectations. It is beautiful! The brick is uniquely African. Today we went to see the brick-making factory. What an operation!! We actually went into the huge kiln where the bricks are baked at about 900° temp. (We were in the "cooled" off section of the kiln.)

What are my impressions of Africa? It is beautiful, very beautiful, but also very, very poor — beyond what I imagined. What you see on T.V. about the poverty is real and it is all over. Even in the capital, Kampala it is very poor. One of the most difficult and worst things here is travel. I have seen and experienced no good roads. Almost all are dirt roads, even in the capital cities. There are many pot holes and

Sr. Mary Janet's letter to family, July 20, 1995

The Crested Crane is the national bird of Uganda and appears on the flag

7

ST. JULIE PRIMARY BOARDING SCHOOL

MISSION STATEMENT FOR ST. JULIE SCHOOL (October 1996)

Saint Julie School is a Catholic, private, co-educational, primary boarding school located in the Kibaale District. The mission of Saint Julie School is to proclaim God's goodness in an educational ministry aimed at:

— forming a firm foundation for committed Catholic living;
— promoting the development of leadership qualities in the children;
— providing quality education in the basic Ugandan course of studies.

Pupils who successfully complete their primary education at Saint Julie School will be prepared to enter secondary school and encouraged to return to the Kibaale District after they have achieved their educational goals.

In her 1996 Christmas letter to the sisters and her family and friends, Sr. Jane Marie explained that the schools of the Kibaale District were the lowest-ranked in all of Uganda. Qualified educators refused to teach in this area commonly referred to as "the bush," an area of high grasses and great poverty. Sister thought that if left to its own resources, the district could never pull itself up. Therefore, the planned St. Julie Primary Boarding School would aim to provide a solid Catholic education developing the leadership skills of the young people of the Kibaale District. After having taught at the Buseesa Primary School, Sister was more convinced that what the Sisters of Notre Dame community was striving to do in Uganda was truly God-directed.

EDUCATIONAL PLANNING

On November 19, 1994, an educational meeting was held in Bujuni. Sr. Mary Amy and Sr. Mary Margaret participated with Bishop Deogratias, the diocesan council, the education committee in Bujuni, and lay representatives of parishes and substations in the Kibaale District of the Hoima Diocese. The District Education Officer (DEO) considered it urgent to establish a model primary school in Bukumi and in another deanery. The members agreed with the idea of a model school with the hope that it would produce future leaders. Issues discussed were finances, name for the school, number of classes, construction of buildings, and the appointment of a steering committee.

It was decided to erect a primary boarding school beginning with P-3 (primary, grade 3) and add a grade each year. There was concern about very young children (P-1, P-2) living away from home. The purpose of a boarding school was primarily to address the problem of distance to and from school each day. There was also the concern that since many of the parents had little or no education, they would not be able to assist with home assignments.

At the conclusion of the meeting, the Bishop asked the members to pray for "the realization of our request to the congregation of the Sisters of Notre Dame to found a model school in the Diocese of Hoima." (Minutes of Meeting, November 22, 1994, at Bujuni Parish)

When the sisters arrived in Uganda in July 1995, the focus of resources was on completing construction of the convent. But even before the convent was completed, the sisters began scouting out sites and making plans for the new school. Since the Church owned a great expanse of land, property was not an issue. During their orientation to the Diocese of Hoima, the sisters met with the Bishop and Fr. Heinz to discuss preliminary ideas about the school.

In early September, the Bishop, accompanied by Fr. Heinz and Hoima Construction personnel, visited Buseesa to decide upon a site for St. Julie School. The group identified a site across from the convent. The school would consist of several separate buildings including dormitories, dining hall, and classrooms. In Uganda, each building is referred to as a "block" and is usually one story.

Fr. Heinz had brought some initial sketches and plans and asked for comments from the sisters. During the next days, sisters devoted several hours to studying the plans and sent their comments to Fr. Heinz.

In October, Fr. Heinz submitted plans and a cost estimate for the school for Phase 1 of the school: about $626,540. The provincial councils in the Thousand Oaks and Covington provinces considered the proposal. After discussion, the plans were not accepted. The councils considered the cost to be too great and thought that the plans reflected more the American culture than the Ugandan culture. The provincial councils requested the sisters in Buseesa to work with the plans and the construction company on a revision.

In January 1996, an estimate of $98,558, for the furniture for the classrooms and dorms had been received.

In April, a revised cost estimate for the school (Phase 1) was sent ($244,084). The provincial councils of the two provinces approved, and a formal request was sent to Sr. Mary Joell and the General Council in Rome on April 30. It was stated that the project would be financed through the efforts of the two provinces, and payments would be made over a period of time. On May 2, the General Council approved the request.

In mid-August, a meeting with the headmaster of the local government school in Buseesa regarding the beginning of construction, led to a distressing discovery: Buseesa Primary School also had plans for the site the sisters had identified for the boarding school. The next morning, Fr. Peter and the sisters set out to determine a new site. One was quickly found about a five to seven-minute walk down a footpath. The Bishop approved the site and the clearing of the land began. Within a month, the survey was completed and the workmen began digging the foundation.

Sr. Mary Delrita reported to her family:

> We have a new construction crew for the school … They arrived on 13 Aug. and spent two weeks clearing the bush. Now they are working on the foundation of the first building, a shell of a classroom block that will initially serve as dining hall. Later when we need more classrooms we'll add the interior walls. The other buildings of the first phase are a classroom block for classes, dorm, kitchen, and latrines. I am encouraged at the pace of the progress there. (Sr. Mary Delrita to Bob and Kay, September 28, 1996)

OFFICIAL GROUNDBREAKING: THE "BIG-TO-DO"

The question of an official groundbreaking posed a number of problems. It would be a grand celebration with many invited, and there was the desire for the two provincials from the United States to be present. These sisters were not scheduled to arrive until October. Meanwhile, the construction of the school proceeded along smoothly.

October 17, 1996, was the date chosen for both the blessing of the convent and for the groundbreaking of the school. The Bishop informed the sisters that they would need to send official invitations as soon as possible. After checking with Fr. Peter and the head of the parish council, the invitation list totaled 200 people. The program for the day included the blessing of the school site and the convent, Mass, and a meal for the invited guests. What the sisters thought was going to be a simple blessing with photo opportunity, had suddenly become "the BIG-TO-DO!" (This was the sisters' expression for the event.)

Sr. Mary Amy and Sr. Mary Shauna arrived from the United States. A few days before the event, the Bishop told the sisters that he could not be present because President Museveni was coming to Hoima. Instead, the Bishop arrived for supper on the fifteenth, stayed overnight in the guest wing, and on the next day went to the building site for a mock groundbreaking photo with the two provincials, the other sisters, and some workers.

On the sixteenth, the food the sisters had purchased, including twenty-five live roasting chickens arrived along with twenty women who would prepare the meal. A temporary shelter with four sets of cooking stones was constructed, and the women went to work preparing matooke, beans, rice, ground nut sauce, mashed potatoes, cooked cabbage, salad, fresh pineapple juice, and seventy pounds of beef and chicken.

That evening, Bishop Baharagate, Bishop Emeritus of Hoima Diocese, arrived to assure his attendance at the celebration. Victoria, a great-granddaughter of Denis Kamuka, would also be present.

October 17, 1996, dawned with a bright blue sky, chairs in place, chapel supplies, and nametags all prepared. With Bishop Baharagate presiding, the ceremony began with the blessing of the new wing of the convent. Next, everyone walked to the school site where the area was blessed, and many leaders took a shovel of dirt to break ground. Then all proceeded to the church for Mass in English with Runyoro and Swahili hymns. At the conclusion of the Mass, everyone returned to the convent for dinner that was served by the women of the village. During the meal, children from Buseesa Primary School provided entertainment. Nearly 300 guests, invited or not, ate their fill, congratulated the sisters on the event, and eventually bade farewell.

The women assisted the sisters with the massive cleanup, which lasted three hours. That evening, the sisters sat down to a wonderfully quiet supper. The collective sighs of relief were accompanied by a prayer of gratitude that the BIG-TO-DO would not occur again until the school was completed!

At the end of December 1996, the first school meeting was held while construction continued. Serious planning for the St. Julie Primary Boarding School in all its details would have to be accomplished in only a year, as the first students were scheduled to arrive in February 1998.

> Sister Jane Marie, appointed "headteacher" in October by our provincials, assumed responsibility for mapping out the agenda of January's tasks: writing letters, making official contacts, compiling lists of furniture, equipment, and supplies, and drawing up job descriptions for our hired help. We divided up the responsibilities. (Sisters of Notre Dame Buseesa Annals, January 31, 1997)

SEARCH FOR STUDENTS

In 1997, the sisters received a request from Kahunde parish to visit and meet the parish members. The people of the parish had heard about the arrival of the sisters but had never seen them. Since the people were reluctant to send their children to distant Buseesa to board with strangers, the sisters traveled to Kahunde and met with them. Pictures of the school were shared, and the people had an opportunity to ask questions. The sisters followed this same procedure at other parishes that were distant from Buseesa.

Selecting the first students for St. Julie School was a time-consuming venture. The plan was to identify students throughout the entire area by sending eight application forms to each of the district's eight parishes: Bukumi, Bujuni, Buseesa, Kahunde, Kakindo, Kakumiro, Muhorro, and Mugalike. The parish priests, in conjunction with their respective councils, were to select their own candidates for the final screening process. The sisters were hoping for two boys and two girls from each parish.

Every Wednesday and Saturday throughout the month of June, the four sisters traveled to the individual parishes. Sr. Mary Delrita performed a simple medical check-up on each prospective student and obtained a rudimentary medical history. Sr. Margaret Mary conducted a personal interview with each child and his or her parents. Sr. Mary Janet and Sr. Jane Marie administered individual academic screenings.

CONSTRUCTION

The construction of each school building proceeded well. By January, the temporary dining and classroom blocks were nearly completed, and the administration block was ready for its roof of iron sheets. The administration building had an office for the head teacher, a room for the secretary, a staff room, storage, and lavatory facilities. The dining block was actually a multipurpose building that had no inner walls; the classroom block was divided into three classrooms, each having a generous storage area.

An area for the kitchen block was cleared of vegetation. A large banana plantation behind the dining block was also cleared, and in February the foundation of the first dormitory block was completed and bricklaying commenced. The dormitory contained a sick bay for children who were ill. This room, off the dormitory, offered children privacy and, if needed, isolation because of contagion. Here, students could receive special nursing care.

The sisters noted each day's progress with great interest. A major factor in the progress was the radio call system recently installed at the convent. With the radio, the construction crew could contact Hoima for quick delivery of materials to keep construction moving forward.

PROBLEM WITH WORKMEN   The sisters remarked that the men on the construction crew worked well, and the sisters truly appreciated their skill. However, in August, a problem arose. Many of the workmen were young, and since their homes were at a distance, they camped out in an old building near the church. They slept on old mattresses on the floor and did their own laundry and cooking outside.

Around Buseesa there were no opportunities for entertainment except the bars, mud homes with an outside shelter. One weekend the men went to the local bar and imbibed too much *Waragi* (distilled beverage). Some of the men got into a fight, and a villager was seriously injured. The construction men who were guilty were arrested and held in the local jail. After some time, the foreman managed to get them free probably by paying a good fee, which was illegal.

The sisters realized that the men needed something to occupy their evenings and promised some assistance. They provided the workers with decks of cards, some jigsaw puzzles, and a UNO game. The men were fascinated with the jigsaw puzzle. One puzzle had only 100 pieces and was a picture of a pig in a supermarket pushing a grocery cart. It was a funny picture, and the workmen laughed and were thrilled to see that they could put the pieces together and create a picture. None had ever seen or worked a jigsaw puzzle before.

FACULTY ASSIGNMENTS

At a meeting in September, Sr. Jane Marie reviewed the school year calendar, and the sisters received their faculty assignments for the 1998 school year.

Sr. Jane Marie	Head teacher, math, reading, creative writing, Runyoro
Sr. Mary Janet	Deputy head teacher, religion, reading, handwriting, phonics
Sr. Mary Delrita	School nurse, librarian, reading, grammar, social studies, health
Sr. Margaret Mary	Liturgical choir, reading, science, agriculture, physical education

Music, art, and storytelling were to be taught on a rotational basis

(Sisters of Notre Dame, Buseesa Annals: September 23, 1997)

A few months later, Musiimenta Ruth, who had met the sisters while she was a temporary secretary at ARU in Kampala, accepted the position of the first matron of St. Julie School.

In the midst of all the preparations, the sisters received word that Sr. Mary Annete Adams from the Chardon, Ohio, province would be joining them on January 14. Sister was an experienced teacher and had also been part of a formation team for young sisters in her home province. In an email, Sr. Mary Janet wrote:

> We are so excited about welcoming Sr. Annete. On Sunday, Jan. 18th the parish and local community will have a welcome for her. We are trying to keep the 14th low key. We remember how we felt after the long journey. … Things are looking more hopeful for the school. The construction crew returned and they sent extra help. … There is still so much to do. (Sr. Mary Janet to Sr. Mary Shauna, January 10, 1998)

Because of the heavy rain on the 18th, the parish welcomed Sr. Mary Annete on January 25th, a beautiful sunny day.

Toward the end of January 1997, Sr. Jane Marie led a faculty retreat, reflecting on the image of the seed as a symbol of beginning and new life. Spiritually refreshed and oriented, the sisters were ready to begin the school year. Later, the sisters gathered for a faculty meeting and considered the Sisters of Notre Dame Educational Cornerstones (principles) and how these would guide the educational efforts in Buseesa. In addition to teaching, each sister was assigned other responsibilities.

Kitchen – Sr. Mary Delrita

After-school Coordinator – Sr. Margaret Mary

Faculty Room and School Supplies – Sr. Mary Annete

OTHER SCHOOL NECESSITIES

In June 1997, the first pieces of furniture for the school arrived. Munteme Technical School was commissioned to make individual desks and portable stools for the students. In December, the sisters were still awaiting the arrival of the other furniture. Concerned that the other school furniture would not be ready for the beginning of the school year, Sr. Mary Janet and Sr. Mary Delrita made a trip to the Munteme Technical School to confer with the principal. He assured the sisters that materials and carpenters would be at St. Julie School soon. The sisters advanced the principal some money to pay for the needed materials.

A boarding school requires many types of supplies. Sr. Jane Marie and Sr. Mary Janet made shopping trips to Kampala to purchase supplies for the school kitchen, classrooms, and dormitories. They were successful in purchasing many needed items. In a letter, the sisters asked the sisters to pray so they would find a good cook and also find a way to transport fifty-five mattresses from Kampala.

On one trip, purchases included plaid material for the girls' jumpers, brown for the boys' shorts, and white for blouses and shirts. The Dominican sisters at Kakumiro had begun a domestic science school. The students at this school assisted Sr. Orestina in making the St. Julie School uniforms. The first year, Sister arrived at St. Julie's with several completed uniforms for the new P-3 students. She then took measurements of the children who did not have accurate data in their uniform measurements.

The sisters gave serious consideration to the matter of what texts to use in the school and were aware of the need to use those suited for the Ugandan child. They purchased English, social studies, science, and readers like those used in the Ugandan school system. They felt strongly about the primacy of religion and believed they needed to provide a truly Catholic text for the children. Thus, they made the choice of the Loyola series from the United States and authored by the Sisters of Notre Dame in the Chardon, Ohio, province.

On the Friday before the students arrived, there were still six bunk beds in the process of construction, and half of the completed beds were not yet varnished. Mattresses, pillows, and blankets were stacked in another dorm, and the painters were just beginning to varnish the brick walls in another dorm. The workers assured the sisters they could complete the four dorms, the dining hall, and the staff rooms before the beginning of school on Monday. The sisters thought a few helpful words would be in order. "Do you realize the children will be sleeping in those beds tomorrow night?" "Do you want me to get a brush and help you?" The fires were lighted!

The sisters were holding their breath, wondering if they could really receive the students on January 31. The sisters and the house girls literally came behind the construction crew with brooms, buckets, and other cleaning equipment.

On January 30, an excited Sr. Jane Marie emailed the following to the sisters back home:

> LOVING … EXCITED … NERVOUS … ANXIOUS … PRAYER-FILLED greetings to you from one who is feeling very much ALL OF THE ABOVE!!! The parents and children will be arriving within the next few hours and we are as prepared as the circumstances permit! The dorms are finished. Beds, mattresses, blankets, pillows, uniforms are all in place. The water will not be connected until a week from Wednesday! We have twenty-liter jerry cans in place to meet the water needs! The kitchen block is about a month from completion. … luckily, we

have the small kitchen store which we will use for cooking on charcoal stoves, a storage of wood, and cooking stuffs! We are using basins for washing pots and dishes, etc. … The dining block is finished! We will eat and meet in that block. The classrooms are being used as sleeping quarters for the men. One is being given back to us in order to hold classes! The shelves are still under construction. The teacher desk has not arrived … BUT … we are welcoming our darlings with open hands, hearts and arms! Classes WILL begin on Monday morning!

The Bishop is coming for Mass with the staff and children on Sunday morning! Of course, he arrives tonight, so we get to entertain him for supper and breakfast, etc. OUR GOOD GOD IS INDEED A GOD OF SURPRISES. … KEEP THE BIG-TIME PRAYERS COMING! (Sr. Jane Marie to the Sisters, January 30, 1998)

THE DAY FINALLY ARRIVES

Sr. Mary Janet described January 31, 1998 as a red-letter day at St. Julie Primary Boarding School. Even in following years, the first day of a new academic year was a time of great excitement. Some children arrived as early as the night before to take up residence in their dorms. It was a time of collecting school fees and countless other details of settling into another term at a boarding school.

Transportation was and continues to be a big problem for the families. Some parents traveled with their children and luggage on bicycles, a few arrived on motorcycles, some walked long distances, and several went together and hired a car or van.

One father and another student's brother brought the boys on bicycles from a village that was most difficult to get to. (When the sisters traveled there by car, the trip of about two hours was over difficult dirt roads.) The bicycles and riders left home in the dark and arrived at school about 11:00 a.m. One sister said she couldn't imagine what it must be like to bicycle with a passenger and luggage all that distance. The sisters admired the love of the parents for their children and all they go through to provide education for them.

What an exciting time it was for us, as well as the parents and children. How I wish you could have seen the beaming faces of parents when they went into the classroom for the 1st time and saw the children seated at their desks dressed in their new uniforms. … Their big smiles and eager eyes indicated readiness to begin. What a joy for all of us. (Sr. Mary Janet to Mary and Al, Bill and Family, Tom and Hazel, Blanche and Family, Leo and Ann, March 15, 1998)

The parent meeting included an explanation of how the Ugandan curriculum requirements would be incorporated into St. Julie's School curriculum requirements. The parents came to realize how much more their children would be receiving educationally at St. Julie School.

Many children did not see or hear from their parents during the three-month school term because of the cost and difficulty or impossibility of transportation and communication. It was hard for these young children to be away from their families for such a long time.

Jointly, the sisters sent an email:

> YES! GOD IS INDEED GOOD!!!! Our school here in the Kibaale District is now a reality! On Saturday we welcomed thirty-nine wonderful children and their parents as our pioneer school family. We had a parent meeting and each parish group selected one member for our executive parent board. During the meeting, the children left in order to change into their uniforms. The parents then went to the classroom where Sister Annete led the children in a newly learned song, "If you're happy and you know it … !" Everyone was thrilled. After the tour of the classroom, the children took their parents to the dorm where they together made up the beds. Immediately following this exercise, the parents and children went to the dining area where they were served a traditional meal of rice, beans and cabbage. After the parents left, the children changed out of their uniforms and became familiar with their new classmates and surroundings. The children gasped in awe that evening as the matron turned on the solar light. The following day the Bishop joined us for Mass at the parish church. Today, the 2nd of Feb. we taught the first lessons in our school." (The Uganda Five to Sisters, Family and Friends of St. Julie School, February 2, 1998)

When the Bishop celebrated Sunday Mass at the parish church, he spoke about St. Julie School. He then invited all to tour the school.

In a letter home, the sisters included some general information about the students and their families:

> Most of the parents of the children in the Kibaale District are peasant farmers who earn their living cultivating local crops such as bananas and coffee and selling the produce. Our children are from the nine parishes of the Kibaale District and were recruited with the assistance of the parish priest. Many of our students are from the families of parish council officers or catechists. The children's ages span from 7-year-old Prisca to nearly 13-year-old Garabuzi. We have observed a large range of academic readiness in our children. (Uganda Five to Sisters, Family and Friends of St. Julie School, February 2, 1998)

Soon provincials in the United States received an update:

> Two weeks of teaching are in the books and the children and teachers are still willing to come back for more! Trooper that Annete is … she offered to take a reading and a math group. So, we have five reading groups and two groups for math. The children are feeling more at home with us as is evidenced by the additional names on the corner of the chalk board, and three children have remained after school for payment of the CONSEQUENCES for not keeping our rules! They helped clean up the room while the rest of the darlings got to go change clothes for after school play! (Sr. Jane Marie to three favorite provincials, February 14, 1998)

BLESSING OF THE SCHOOL

St. Julie Primary Boarding School opened on February 2, 1998, but the official blessing of the school took place on Monday, April 20. Following a solemn blessing of every room, Bishop Deogratias and eight priests concelebrated the liturgy. The students did the readings and also provided liturgical songs and dance.

All the parents and invited (and uninvited) guests were treated to speeches from the Bishop and other dignitaries. Hoima Construction presented the school with a beautifully handcrafted key about the size of a tennis racket. The engraving on one side reads: "St. Julie School Opened A.D. 1998", and the reverse side proclaims: "The Dream Becomes a Reality." All were entertained by the children who sang three selections and performed three traditional dances.

The guests enjoyed a festive meal of matooke, rice, meat, and special sauce prepared by the local women. At the conclusion of the meal, the parents bade farewell, and the children washed the dishes!

THE ACADEMIC YEAR

School began in February and concluded in early December. The academic year was divided into three months of class, three weeks at home, three months of class, three weeks at home, and three months of class.

In the first year, after the first three-week break at home, the students were to return on May 30. Sr. Jane Marie, the head teacher, learned a quick lesson about communication. When the students returned for the second term, sister wanted to have a meeting with the parents. It never occurred to sister that the parents were used to the schools of the district taking the first day of the term for organizing and not teaching. As a result, only three parents and a few students were present. After presenting the material to eight different groups of parents, sister realized she should have sent a reminder letter with the children at the end of the first term.

SCHOOL FEES

The parishes contributed no money to St. Julie School. The diocese gave the land, and the Bishop had made it quite clear that he had no money for the school. One of the sisters remarked, "We are basically on our own." (Sr. Jane Marie email message to Sr. Mary Amy and Sr. Mary Shauna, July 4, 2000)

Aware that most of the parents of the St. Julie School children were peasant farmers who lacked a salary or steady income, the school fees were kept as low as possible, and payments were scheduled in increments at designated times. The parents were making great sacrifices to send their children to St. Julie School. All families were expected to pay something toward the education of their children. Some paid in Ugandan shillings and others paid in kind with a chicken, a sack of beans or firewood. These payments hardly covered the expense to educate the children. The school would not be able to operate without the contributed services of the sisters and a considerable subsidy from abroad.

When parents came to pay the fees, the sisters heard stories of the sacrifices made to provide education for their children. When one mother came to the school to make a partial payment of the school fees, she said,

> "You know, Sister, money is very hard to come by." Sister responded, "Yes, …
> Thank you so very much for the sacrifices you are making to send your daughter
> to our school." After reflecting for a moment, the parent replied, "Ever since we
> heard that our child was accepted to your school, the family had not taken any
> sugar nor eaten any meat. The money is set aside so my daughter will have a
> chance to better her life." (The sisters at St. Julie Convent, Buseesa, Uganda to
> Sisters, Family and Friends, January 22, 1999)

Some parents rode their bicycles in the rain for hours one-way to meet the payment deadline.

A gentleman came to the door early one morning. He wanted to pay school fees. No, he was not the father – the child was his younger brother's daughter. He had come the day before, but the sisters were away, so he spent the night with another brother in Kibaale. He borrowed his motorcycle to come back to Buseesa to make the payment before returning to his home in Kahunde. As he was leaving, he turned to sister, his face beaming, "Sister, thank you for building the school. Everywhere you look it is shining!" The light of appreciation and expectation that shone in his eyes expressed more than his words could tell. (Unknown sender to Sr. Mary Shauna, October 16, 1997)

In one particular situation, because they had heard nothing and received no payments, the sisters thought that a student was not returning for the new school year. The sisters discovered the mother had been in the hospital in Kampala, and when she returned to the village, her husband was not in agreement that the child should be in St. Julie School. The mother was so determined to have her child at the school that she gathered money from relatives and friends and then appeared at the school with her child. (Sr. Jane Marie to Sr. Mary Amy, Sr. Mary Shauna, Sr. Melannie, January 29, 2000).

CLASS TIME

Class each day began at 8:00 a.m. and concluded at 3:30 p.m. with twenty minutes for recess and forty-five minutes for lunch. Subjects included religion, reading, English, math, science, and social studies with time for lunch and recess. The time after school was divided into blocks: Snack time, study time, play time, and family work time. For family work, each student engaged in some type of work that might be part of a regular family. Through the years these included yard or garden work, cleaning, and helping with the preparing of meals (peeling potatoes, sorting beans). When the secondary school came into existence, these students often supervised the younger students in some of these activities.

Classes sometimes included special areas of study or special activities. In their social studies classes, the students had been studying about government and services for the people in their area. Sr. Mary Delrita and her social studies class hosted a guest speaker who helped the children understand the local council system. Later in the month, the students took a thirty-minute walk to Matale, the sub-county headquarters, where they visited the chief officer, the dispensary, and the police station. They then enjoyed a picnic lunch at the meeting hall. Later, in writing class, the students wrote thank you notes to each of the places they visited.

To help the students learn about the Banyoro tribe history and stories of the people, Nodeliere Francis came to speak to the children. Francis is the muzie (older gentleman) who gave the sisters their *empaakos* when they came to Uganda in 1995.

In another class, the children learned about types of weather and how it affects activities. They also learned about the rain cycle and weather observation. To make the learning more concrete, a rope was stretched between two poles cut from trees. A wind stocking was hung from the rope, and a stone was marked with the four cardinal directions. A thermometer was hung and a rain gauge was installed. The weather chart, posted in the dining room, recorded the pertinent information.

The Ugandan syllabus for physical education recommended that students change uniforms for physical education class. Girls and boys were given colorful shorts and white tee shirts to wear. There was much giggling and reticence among the girls until Sr. Margaret Mary explained that, although in the village most girls wear only dresses, shorts for physical education classes were common in the city.

SATURDAY MORNING ROUTINE

On Saturday mornings the children had a routine. They did their personal laundry – washed it by hand and laid it to dry on the grass. Later some clotheslines were installed for their use. The students also did general cleaning, including their dormitory. The floors were washed, and every child made an extra effort to have his or her personal belongings in order. If students had time, they helped in the kitchen or gave their service in other ways.

THE GARDEN

Planning for the garden had begun about the time of the planning for the school. The plants needed to be well established when the students arrived. Bananas, beans, sweet potatoes, papayas, and mangoes were a few of the cultivated plants.

Since most of the cooking was to be done on wood fires or on wood burning stoves, a grove of eucalyptus trees was planted. This would provide a continual supply of firewood.

It was an enormous endeavor, and with each additional field more laborers were needed. Initially, Sr. Margaret Mary coordinated the work and participated in the labor, but eventually Kagaara Willy, from the area, was hired to oversee the farm work.

WATER

With the establishment of St. Julie School, more water tanks were constructed on the school site. Students took their jerry cans to the water tank to refill them. The first school year was barely in session when the groundskeeper informed the sisters that the water supply at the school was completely gone. Alternate water sources included the convent water tanks, the borehole, and the unprotected spring nearby, and a protected spring over three miles away.

In April, the large brick and cement tank outside the convent was leaking and needed to be emptied and repaired. This deprived the sisters of water in the bedrooms and bathrooms. Fortunately, the utilities in the guest block were fed by another tank. By June, the only water source was the unprotected spring nearby.

The "water hole," as the sisters referred to the natural spring some distance from the house and school, served as a source of water for many families in the area. Occasionally when the water tanks were low, the sisters sent students to the water hole for water that could be used for cleaning. The students filled jerry cans and lugged them up the hill to the convent.

The sisters wrote home:

> There is no end to our "water woes." We thought we would have to send our boarders home because we had no rain, and we already had been rationing our water, but our rainy season came, and hopefully all our water tanks would fill up quickly – or so we thought. Our new tank near the kitchen block at school had a hole in it. … How sad! Then the large brick and cement tank outside the convent had a leak. (Buseesa Five to Sisters, Family, Friends, May 17, 1998)

Finally, the sisters were able to write:

> At this minute, it is raining, and we are just about dancing for joy. It's been quite a while since we've had rain, and our tanks are empty. Everyday Paschal [an employee] has had to go to the protected spring about six kilometers away, so this rain, however long it lasts, will be a blessing. We wish our rainy season would start for the benefit of all the people of our village. (Sr. Mary Annete to Sr. Mary Shauna, June 19, 1998)

SACRAMENTS

Since nearly half of the P-3 students had not yet met Jesus in the sacraments of Reconciliation and Eucharist, and those who had received the sacraments, had received only rote learning, the sisters thought it appropriate to provide the entire class with a proper preparation.

During the second term, Sr. Jane Marie prepared the children for the reception of the Sacrament of Reconciliation. A date was arranged with the parish priest. Much to Sister's surprise, it became evident that Fr. Vincent, as well as the children, expected the children to receive First Eucharist at the time of Reconciliation. After sister explained that the students were not yet prepared for Eucharist and that she hoped they would have a love and desire to meet Jesus in the Sacrament of Reconciliation, Father agreed to postpone First Eucharist until term three.

On October 2, the morning of First Eucharist, the children participated in a prayer sharing experience under the guidance of Sr. Jane Marie and Sr. Mary Janet. During the evening school Mass that was celebrated in the school dining/assembly hall, fifteen of the students received Jesus in Holy Communion for the first time. Later, one of the girls exclaimed, "I was so happy I couldn't stop dancing!" (The sisters at St. Julie Convent, Buseesa, to Sisters, Friends, and Family, November 25, 1998)

SCHOOL LIBRARY

Once it was known that the Sisters of Notre Dame were going to establish a primary school in Uganda, children's books began to trickle, and sometimes flood, into the provincial house in Covington. In time, these many books made their way to Buseesa and presented the sisters with a challenge: In order for the children to use the books, a lending system would have to be established.

Sr. Mary Delrita agreed to assume responsibility for setting up the library. She made some contacts back in the United States, devised a classification system, and organized and processed the books. Sister decided that in order for the children to best utilize the library, a simple lending system would have to be established. As Sister sorted through the books a plan began to emerge: folk and fairy tales would be marked FFT, SCI for science, FAN for fantasy, and so on.

All library cards and pockets were prepared using a manual typewriter. By the beginning of 1998, Sr. Mary Delrita had completed accessing 1,226 library books for St. Julie School! In the ensuing years, hundreds of additional books were accessed and made available to the students. By 2015, Sister had prepared over 4,000 library books for the children.

March 12 was the exciting day when the children could begin using the library. Since the room designated for the library was still occupied by the construction workers, Sr. Mary Delrita set up a temporary library in the school secretary's office. Four students were chosen to be the first into the library. Sister guided them in choosing a book and taught the process for checking out the book.

Within a few days, all the children from P-3 had circulated through the library and had a book to enjoy. In a place where even basic textbooks are not regularly available for each student, the establishment of a lending library was amazing. Sr. Mary Delrita wrote:

> What a joy! To see a child hold a book with both hands, look at it and realize
> "if I just write my name on a little card, I can take it away with me!" What a joy!
> (Sr. Mary Delrita's notes, possibly 2003)

Sister's joy continued:

> I hear, "Sister, after Basasibwaki, I am the one to take that book!" or "Sister,
> I want the book of the gingerbread man." The teachers introduce various
> books and/or characters as they fit into their different classes. This whets the
> imagination and desire, and the children make a bee-line for the library. (Sisters
> at St. Julie Convent to Sisters, Family and Friends, November 25, 1998)

The books, and especially the pictures, were truly invaluable because the conceptual background of the children was so poor. The books helped to open the minds and imaginations of the children to a world beyond anything they have known. The sisters remarked that it was difficult to grasp just how impoverished the children's bank of ideas was. The sisters were always answering the question, "What is this?"

A P-6 student, assisting Sr. Mary Delrita in the library, suddenly asked, "Sister, what is a peach?" The challenges were so stimulating, so rewarding!

In 1999, sister recognized the need to upgrade the classification system. With the help of sisters back home, she learned the Dewey Decimal system. Then began the task of changing all the books and cards in the library.

SPECIAL DAYS

UGANDA INDEPENDENCE   This day was celebrated on October 9. Before the school was begun, the sisters celebrated this day with the construction workers. When St. Julie School began, following the tradition of doing something special for our construction crew, the children entertained the workers with song and dances. They sang the national anthem, "O Uganda", and hosted the traditional snack of popcorn and a sweet drink.

When this special day fell on a Saturday one year, some of the children with the matron and cooks, marched to a nearby village. They did their traditional marching, song, and performance for the people of the village. Everyone seemed to enjoy the performance and the children's presence made the day special.

THE OLYMPIAD   In November 1998 this event was held at St. Julie School. After much practice, the students were ready. The events resembled the international Olympic competition including an opening ceremony at which the "athletes" carried flags from ten nations as well as the Olympic symbol and the torch. Competition consisted of throws, jumps, and runs. At the awards ceremony, the athletes received ribbons for their achievements.

The sisters used this opportunity to help the children expand their knowledge of the world. Sr. Mary Delrita provided lessons explaining the origin, symbols, and spirit of the games. She also included some map work. Sr. Margaret Mary prepared the program and worked with the students in the PE classes. The students made paper flags of the ten countries and constructed the Olympic torch from a mailing tube and colored bits of scrap paper.

SPECIAL DAYS FOR BISHOP DEOGRATIAS

A memorable event in these early years was Bishop Deogratias's visit to Kentucky and California in 1997. While in Covington, the Bishop visited Prince of Peace, a nearby elementary school where he spoke with the students. He also had the opportunity to visit with the local bishop, Bishop Robert Muench, and tour the cathedral. Late one afternoon, the Bishop met the families of Sr. Mary Janet and Sr. Mary Delrita.

PARENT EXECUTIVE BOARD

In March, the Parent Executive Board—consisting of one representative from each of the nine parishes having children in the school—was established. At the first meeting officers were elected. The PEB provided consultative input to school policies, created a liaison between school and parish, and assisted in giving information to parents.

FIRST STUDENT COUNCIL

In October of the second year for St. Julie School, preparations were made to introduce the entire student body to the concept of a Student Council. Those students who wanted to run for an office met with the head teacher, Sr. Jane Marie, and learned about leadership and the areas of responsibility. Students filled out papers indicating the office they sought and the reasons they wanted to be chosen. Ten other students had to sign the paper in support of the candidate. The papers were then signed by the head teacher and the homeroom teacher.

A few days later, the candidates presented their speeches. The students exhibited great self-confidence as they addressed the other students. All those present were overwhelmed by the progress the children had made since the beginning of the school two years ago. The following day, the election was held and St. Julie School had its first Student Council.

MEDICAL ISSUES

With so many children gathered in one place and away from home, the sisters and staff had to be vigilant for signs of disease and injury. Already in mid-February of the first year, the sisters noted that many children were sick in the morning, but were generally up and around by noon. The sisters thought it was the newness of everything and the fact that the students were being worked fairly hard. Additionally, the students were used to a school with little teaching and a very unstructured day.

A week later at the faculty meeting, a discussion centered around the reason so many children were going to bed with this and that ailment. The conclusion: There was too much free time, so the students thought about home. In addition, the students did not know how to utilize free time, and they did not know how to be children with time to play. They were accustomed to digging, fetching water and firewood, helping to cook, and caring for younger siblings.

TOP Building a home with sticks and mud
MIDDLE Home in the Buseesa area BOTTOM Classroom at Buseesa Primary

TOP Filling jerry cans at the water hole MIDDLE Borehole near convent
BOTTOM Filling jerry cans from the water tank

TOP Workers on the mission farm   MIDDLE Market along the road
BOTTOM Meat at an open market

TOP Dormitory at St. Julie Primary MIDDLE St. Julie Primary and rocky hill
BOTTOM Bishop Deogratias and primary students

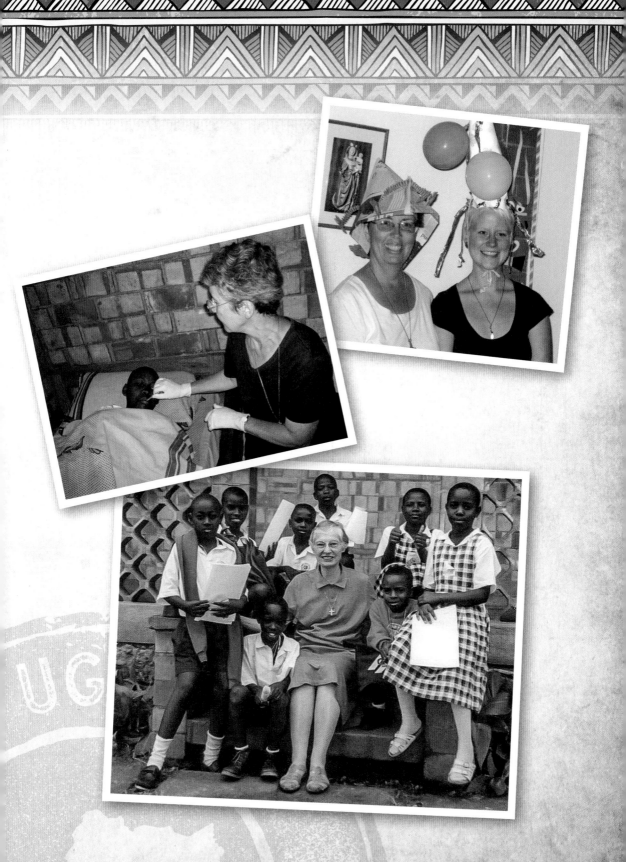

TOP Sr. Mary Colette and Daniela Fangmann (volunteer) enjoy a good time
MIDDLE Sr. Mary Bernadette caring for a sick student BOTTOM Sr. Mary Karlene and students

TOP Meal time at the primary school MIDDLE Students wash their own clothing
BOTTOM Students enjoy reading a book from the school library

TOP Students enjoy swinging on the bars MIDDLE Boys play soccer using a ball made of plastic bags
BOTTOM Sr. Mary Janet and little Deogratias (Chapter 6)

TRADITIONAL ARTS: Dancing, String Instrument, Weaving, and Drums

Once the diagnosis was made, a treatment plan was put into place. Teachers signed up to teach games the children could play in their free time. A snack and play time were added to the schedule, and the "sickness" quickly disappeared.

REFLECTIONS ON THE FIRST SCHOOL YEAR

At the close of the third term, the sisters reflected on all that had been accomplished at St. Julie School that first year.

> Back in February, some of our children were struggling with the basic sounds of the alphabet and simple addition facts. Now, all of them can read at least at the second grade level, and they are all mastering their multiplication and division facts. Some children have gained up to twelve pounds and grown four inches. Our school has budding poets, athletes, artists, musicians, scientists, and theologians. Our children are very comfortable with the challenge to uplift the Kibaale District. (The Sisters at St. Julie Convent, Buseesa, to Sisters, Friends, and Family, November 25, 1998)

Sr. Mary Annete, the newest member of the missionary group, and the one who arrived about two weeks before the opening of the school, wrote:

> I'm loving it here, and I still continue to feel very much at home. It's a little over five months, and God has been very good. Our children are too precious; I can hardly wait until you see them. By the time you come there will be two classes, and we'll already be planning for the third. What wisdom in only having one more class next year. We all get very tired with the strain of trying to make ourselves understood and to understand them. Their English, however, is coming along very nicely. They call out to us from the road as they pass by, and while they know we are in chapel praying, "Good-bye Sistahs … see you tomorrow. … God bless you!" (Sr. Mary Annete to Sr. Mary Shauna, June 19, 1998)

Sr. Mary Delrita wrote:

> It's becoming clearer and clearer that English is NOT English. There's British which some understand and American which most do not understand. This is an important distinction to be aware of. We hear someone speak "English" and think "good, we can communicate," then discover we can hear them but they don't catch what we are saying. (Sr. Mary Delrita to Friends, March 13, 1996)

In another letter, the sisters wrote:

> We are finding language to be a challenge. Many of the children have been exposed to very little English, so it becomes a draining task for them to try to follow English instruction all day. As teachers we realize more and more how important it is to build basic concepts and language experiences. (The Buseesa Five to Sisters, Families and Friends, March 17, 1998)

SAINT JULIE SCHOOL SONG

1. Saint Julie School, our model school, we cherish and we love.
   With heart and mind we all can sing: *God is good, He is so good.*
   How good is God. How good is our good God.

2. We come together, sing and dance. We learn and we work,
   And all we know and will announce: *God is good…*

3. The poor, the needy, and the weak we want to serve and help;
   All children in the world shall feel: *God is good…*

4. To follow Jesus is the goal and radiate his love.
   Be leaders and to tell the world: *God is good…*

5. For friendship in Uganda let us stand and strive.
   The message we proclaim to all: *God is good…*

Words and music by Sr. Maria Bernarde and Teresa

8

DAILY LIVING ON HOLY GROUND

The first years were times of major adjustments for the missionaries. Among these was the adjustment to a new culture with its own language and customs, concern about food and water, and the limitations of transportation and communication. In the establishment of many new ministries, the initial challenges and adjustments diminish in time. This was not to be the case in Uganda. Some challenges were always there, and others just took a new form.

COMMUNITY LIVING

Community life is always challenging no matter where one lives. In Uganda, there was constant change with new sisters coming and some leaving and then returning from a home visit. In May of 2001, Sr. Maria Bernarde arrived from Germany and in September, Sr. Mary Paulynne from California. Both sisters enriched the education program at St. Julie. Other comings and goings included volunteers, Sisters of Notre Dame visitors, friends and relatives of the sisters or the volunteers, and lay staff. All of this called for great openness, flexibility, give-and-take. The blending of new people with those who had been there was not without joy and pain.

When the number of the sisters in the community changed, responsibilities in the house, in the school, and on the farm had to be adjusted. One of the sisters remarked that one thing she had come to recognize is the fact that a sister on mission must expect to be in a state of transition much of the time.

Each sister brought her strengths and weaknesses, and at times relationships were tense. The multiple tasks and responsibilities that each sister had to carry put a strain on her and on the community. At times, the sisters gathered to discuss situations and reached some kind of resolution. They had their tears, apologies, and reconciliations. The sisters put much effort into being sensitive, caring and understanding of one another.

Each evening after supper the sisters enjoyed some type of relaxation. This usually included card games or some type of board game. A letter described one special evening.

We are trying to work on taking some time each week to have fun together. The last thing we did was a little crazy but it was fun. We listened to a tape of '50's and '60's music and danced, then ended up with refreshments while we played "hangman." There aren't a lot of amusement options here in Buseesa so it takes some creative thinking." (Sr. Mary Janet to Sr. Mary Margaret, Sr. Mary Amy, and Sr. Mary Shauna, June 11, 1996)

Since some of the sisters were from Kentucky, it was traditional that the Kentucky Derby be celebrated each year. A tradition at the Kentucky "Run for the Roses" was that decorative hats were worn. Thus, in Buseesa, the participants also created and wore decorative hats. A board represented the racetrack and had both a starting gate and a finish line. Bottle caps with the name and number of each horse were used. With the roll of the dice the "horses" moved forward. Prizes were awarded to the person with the most creative hat and those whose horse came in first, second, or third place.

Bishop Deogratias was a familiar visitor at St. Julie Mission. On one visit, he asked if the sisters could be more involved in the parish, such as with the women's development, as they did with the women's group. One of the sisters responded that the sisters were being stretched about as far as they could be to keep the school going. They told the Bishop that it seemed impossible at the time, but they would be alert to opportunities to do whatever they could.

UGANDA MARTYRS PARISH IS ESTABLISHED

With an already large church population and the potential for growth a strong possibility, on January 26, 1997, Bishop Deogratias officially established the Buessa church as a parish. It would now be called the Uganda Martyrs Parish. The ceremony was held at Mutugu, the farthest outstation of the parish. The sisters left Buseesa in their new vehicle, making tracks on either side of the footpath as they traveled through the bush. At the Mass, children were confirmed and one couple was married. Included was the ceremony for signing the document for the parish and a document for the official establishment of the Sisters of Notre Dame convent in Buseesa. After Mass, lunch was served, gifts were presented to the Bishop, speeches made, and representatives from each outstation entertained the guests.

The Buseesa parish included the parish church and thirteen mission stations called outstations. The number of outstations increased through the years. The parish priest, who at that time had no assistant, visited each outstation a few times a year for Sunday liturgy. Thus, there were Sundays when the parish in Buseesa had a communion service led by the chief catechist.

BISHOP DEOGRATIAS BYABAZAIRE

In 2005, the sisters and students were saddened to learn that Bishop Deogratias would not be present for the celebration of Confirmation. The Bishop suffered from diabetes, and in his great zeal for the Church and his diocese, he didn't always take the best care of himself. Earlier, while attending a conference in Kampala, he became ill. He was hospitalized for weeks and cautioned by his doctors to take time off. He responded positively to this warning and appointed Fr. Robert Mugisha to represent him at Confirmation.

In the ensuing years, the Bishop was hospitalized several times and suffered a severe case of malaria. He was diagnosed with hydrocephalus, a stroke, and diabetes. In 2009, because of his deteriorating health, and at his request, the Bishop was relieved of his duties as Bishop of Hoima. In 2010, Pope Benedict XVI appointed Bishop Lambert Bainomugisha as the Apostolic Administrator for the Diocese of Hoima, pending a permanent appointment of a new bishop for the diocese.

In August 2012, the sisters visited the ailing Bishop Deogratias. The Bishop gave them a warm hug and was very happy to see them. They visited for about an hour. The sisters had prepared a photo album for him that showed the beginning and growth of the mission. Sr. Mary Delrita had mounted the photos and added captions. The sisters thought the Bishop was very touched. The sisters found him greatly aged and quite feeble. He walked and spoke very slowly, but the sisters thought he remembered things and knew well who they were. Before they left, they asked the Bishop for his blessing. He made a simple sign of the cross and laid his hands on each of their heads. In the letter describing the event, Sr. Mary Janet wrote, "I can't tell you what this meant to me! Somehow I just felt God's love and goodness for all of us. I still get teary when I recall that moment."

On February 9, 2014, at the age of 74, Bishop Deogratias Muganwa Byabazaire passed away. He was ordained in 1969 and consecrated Bishop of Hoima in 1991.

Bishop Deogratias always had a keen eye and an open heart for the poor and the less fortunate. It was said, that during his service as bishop he sponsored at least 300 students with school fees. Many of these students became priests, sisters, and successful women and men. The Bishop lived a simple lifestyle and by the end of his life had given away all of his personal property to assist those who were in need.

The Mass of Resurrection was celebrated in the cathedral in Kampala and in the Cathedral in Hoima. Many bishops, priests, religious women, and lay persons attended both celebrations. Bishop Deogratias was buried in a chapel erected just outside the Hoima Cathedral.

Deogratias Muganwa Byabazaire
1941 – 2014
May he rest in peace

THE FARM EXPANDS AND EXPANDS

One sister wrote that in the beginning of the mission, a farm was not included. However, the sisters realized the need shortly after their arrival in 1995. A farm was needed to provide food for all at the mission. Secondly, the farm provided an outreach and a contact with the village people. And thirdly, the farm offered employment for local people.

In January 2002, Martin Hilgers, a volunteer from Germany, arrived in Buseesa. He assisted on the farm and tutored students in math in P-7 at St. Julie Primary. When his volunteer months were nearing an end, Martin requested that he be considered for the position of farm manager. His offer came at a time when the sisters were experiencing a number of failures with the farm. They realized their inability to continue managing two schools plus a farm about which they had little knowledge or experience. Martin was hired as the Director of Development and Management for two years.

Martin had many plans for the development of the farm. Some of the plans he was able to implement, and some met with resistance. Because of many improvements and developments, the diet of the children improved. Martin worked with the farm workers, even holding workshops with them. The workshop results were especially helpful as many suggestions for improvement mirrored his ideas. Martin trained a new manager before returning to his home in Germany in September 2005.

As the student population of St. Julie Mission increased, there was the stark reality that this meant the farm also would have to grow. Local people were hired to assist with the work of the land and the animals. Women were especially eager to be employed since many of them were the sole provider of their family. (Some husbands had more than one wife and family.) Some of the women arrived carrying their youngest on their back. The sisters saw a baby lying in the field under an umbrella for protection from the sun while the mother worked. It was these women who urged the establishment of a nursery for children from ages three to five.

When Sr. Mary Kristin and Sr. Mary Shauna visited in 2007, they joined the prayer group Sr. Immaculate, who was able to speak Runyoro, conducted with the farm workers. There were introductions, the praying of the rosary, and a litany. Two of the women had their babies with them.

CROPS   Bananas and coffee trees had been planted the first year. In later years, clonal coffee trees were planted as these had high yield. It was hoped that the trees would be a source of income that could help with the expenses of the school.

Later the sisters added other fruits and vegetables. Most crops were perennial plants that were propagated by removing shoots and suckers from old plants; few crops were started from seed.

While in the chapel one morning, Sr. Mary Janet heard what she supposed was a truck in front of the convent. She thought it might be a lumber truck to pick up the timbers cut from the forest. Later she was told that it was a tractor that the priest hired to plow the garden for the parish and St. Peter Secondary School up the hill. Sister checked it out and found a small tractor doing a great job turning the soil and preparing it for planting, which would have taken many people many hours, perhaps days.

Sr. Mary Janet thought grapes would make a good addition to the mission. Upon her return from a trip to Italy, Sister brought some cuttings from the grapes at the Sisters of Notre Dame Motherhouse in Rome. The cuttings seemed to like the soil and climate of Buseesa, and in time began producing grapes that Sister was able to make into delicious jelly.

In addition to crops, animals were included in the farm area. Meat was generally served once a month. On a meat-menu day, 50 rabbits, three goats, or one pig would be slaughtered.

Visitors noted that

> There are many more animals kept here than it would appear at first glance. Joan showed us their 57 goats, 82 free-range rabbits, 2 cattle, 64 pigs/piglets, and 500 chickens that lay 7 flats of 30 eggs each day. (Ed Kohinke, Engineers without Borders, Greater Cincinnati Professional Chapter, June 2013)

CHICKENS   The sisters had a healthy population of chickens almost from the very beginning. In 2001, the Hoima Construction Company completed the construction of a new chicken house. It was a brick structure with two rooms for the birds, two storage areas for feed and other needs., and an isolation area that the sisters hoped they would never need.

RABBITS   The diet, especially in villages, is very deficient in animal protein. With students coming, the sisters began to search for a good yet inexpensive source of it. The government and agricultural specialists had been encouraging the raising of rabbits for meat. Rabbits multiply quickly, are relatively inexpensive to house and feed, and rapidly reach a size that they can be eaten.

The sisters engaged a man to build the rabbit hutches, and prepared to purchase some rabbits. On one trip to Kampala, the sisters obtained the initial breeding stock of four rabbits, a gift from Mukiibi Benigna, a member of Parliament and representative for women's concerns in the District. She had paid $60.00 for the rabbits. The vehicle was filled on the trip home, so Sr. Margaret Mary offered to keep the rabbits in front with her. The male rabbit was in a box at her feet, and sister held the three females in a box on her lap. Shortly into the trip, sister began to scream and laugh. The box she was holding began to "leak" as the terrified rabbits experienced the first lap of the rough ride home.

Within a few weeks, the first litter was born, but the little rabbits died. Soon, other rabbits were born, and the rabbit project was well on its way to providing some animal protein for the sisters and students.

Mukiibi Benigna visited the school in November 1998. She was interested in a plan to breed rabbits for meat, so she offered to supply the school with exotic rabbits to be obtained from her contacts. A few months later, she was in the area and wanted to check in on how the sisters were and how the rabbits were doing. She was very impressed with the beautiful rabbit house and seemed satisfied with the care the rabbits were given.

The next year, Mukiibi Benigna came again to check on the rabbit project. At that time, she expressed a concern about education for girls on the secondary level. Sr. Jane Marie assured her that plans for secondary education for girls coming from St. Julie Primary would be made in the future. It would be almost impossible for them to find a school that could match the quality of education they had been receiving at St. Julie.

For many years, the sisters continued raising the rabbits, but circumstances eventually led them to depend less and less on these small, furry creatures. Stealing was a problem and some rabbits died of disease. Once the pastor's dog invaded the rabbits' sanctuary and attacked a number of the rabbits, causing many others to die of fright.

COWS   In addition to the chickens and rabbits, the sisters had a great desire to provide milk for the students. A veterinarian provided guidance in the preparation and purchase of a cow. He offered practical suggestions on the building of a cowshed and the type of grass that was needed. Special grass was planted but quickly died because of drought. Later, other grasses were planted. A young man was hired to build the cowshed, but day after day it appeared that little or no work was being accomplished.

Through social services in the Hoima Diocese, the sisters were able to purchase a cow for $900.00. It was a two-for-one deal because the cow was pregnant. Schools in the United States provided the funds for the purchase of a cow; and in January 2000, the first cow, Kahunde, arrived. The men had a difficult time unloading the very frightened cow, but eventually they maneuvered her safely into the shelter.

Two weeks later, when the sisters were returning from the District Health Office, they discovered that Kahunde was loose and not too eager to be captured. To complicate matters, a new puppy was chasing the cow and making her even more nervous. After securing the puppy, the workers were able to capture Kahunde and return her safely.

Shortly thereafter, through Heifer International, the second cow, Ruth, arrived; and one of the workers was placed in charge of the two cows. In a few months, the farm boasted not only two cows but also two calves.

The birth of a calf was an exciting moment. One evening when Sr. Mary Delrita was in her room she heard the caretaker of the farm animals calling her. The cow who was about to deliver was having some trouble. Sister joined the caretaker and headed to the cow pasture. There was Ruth with the hooves of the calf already appearing. Judging from all appearances it looked as though all would go well, but Sister decided to remain. To her surprise some of the boys from the dorm were there because they heard the cow mooing late that night, and they knew she would be delivering soon. Every once in a while, a soft voice was heard from one of the boys, "Please God, let everything be OK," or "Help her, God." After the calf was born, a voice could be heard again, "Thank you, God!"

A year later, one of the calves died of a tick-borne disease. Within a short time, all the cows died, and it was decided Buseesa was not a good place to raise cows.

PIGS   Two promised piglets and a half a sack of feed were delivered to the convent one evening at 7:00. Since it was getting dark, the small creatures could not be taken to their new home up the hillside. The only confined place the sisters could think to house the piglets for the night was in the back of the pick-up truck. The next morning the piglets were transported to their new home. One of the piglets was not responding well and eventually died. The survivor, Petunia, was later joined by more of her species.

Farm animals, like people, enjoy their moments of freedom. A few months after Petunia's arrival, while Sr. Jane Marie was interviewing a prospective teacher, and the Dominican sisters were measuring students for their uniforms, the pigs escaped from their pens. The chase was on until one by one the pigs were captured.

GOATS   Sr. Mary Janet related a similar experience with other farm creatures:

> I walked down the path to begin my day at school. As I got near school and came to the garden area where the sweet potatoes were planted, I saw that a number of our goats were munching the plants. They had gotten through the gate that had been left open. I all but ran the rest of the way and got someone to help me chase the goats back into their area. (Sr. Mary Janet to Family and Friends, February 24, 2006)

BEES   When Martin was farm manager, he began raising bees. A young boy of the area came to give advice about the raising of the bees. While Sr. Mary Janet was on a home visit, she learned all she could about this new interest.

One evening sister went to harvest the honey. Wearing her protective hat and carrying a lantern, she set out. When she arrived at the school, she found the gate was locked. She called to the men she anticipated being there, but there was no response. Then she saw a fire in the forest area, and she assumed the men were there. To get into the school property she could go all the way around and through a bushy garden, but sister decided to climb the gate that is about six feet high with barbed wire on top. She was somewhat afraid but determined. Fortunately, one of the workers arrived and helped sister over the gate. Three men dressed in their bee suits and looking like astronauts were ready to collect the honey.

> We went from hive to hive, five in all, opened them, and took the honeycombs dripping with the rich, sticky honey. We filled two big barrels with the honeycombs. I helped by operating the smoker, putting the stuff in barrels, and at times managing the light. … We worked from 8:00 p.m. to 11:00 p.m. At one point, we had to go back to the fire to add more fuel for the smokers and also to get another barrel. I fell into a big ditch trying to cross on a narrow board. Julius had to pull me out.

> When I arrived home a worried Sr. Cristina met me at the door. I still had bees on me and one stung me as I opened the door. I did get stung quite a few times through my socks, and some bees managed to get into my shirt sleeves. I don't think I will try this again but I surely have a much greater appreciation for the work that our men do and do without any complaints. We were all covered with sticky honey, black jacks and other sticky things from the forest, mud and dirt. Thank God we did have a successful harvest. (Sr. Mary Janet to Sr. Mary Margaret, January 23, 2012)

FACTORS AFFECTING THE FARM   The weather was an important factor in the growth on the farm. Extreme wet or dry seasons were responsible for the loss of some crops. But the weather was not the sole problem on the farm.

In 1997, eighty eucalyptus seedlings were purchased to replace the ones eaten by termites. Several neighbor boys explored the surrounding forest to locate the termite hill. A large colony lodged under the overhang of a huge rock was discovered. The boys broke it down and destroyed the termites.

In 2001, a government worker arrived with his rifle to go into the forest around the school gardens and shoot the monkeys that stole the bananas that were used for food for the students. It seemed a harsh way to solve a problem, but the worker promised to kill only a few. He assured the sisters that would frighten the others away. He killed ten monkeys and brought five tails to the sisters. (These are used as part of the dress in some of the native dances.)

ENOUGH WATER: A FREQUENT AND SERIOUS PROBLEM

Water continued to be a challenge and a concern. Initially, rain was collected in plastic tubs and stored in jerry cans. Later, rainwater was collected from the roof of the convent and school and traveled via pipes to brick holding tanks.

CEMENT AND BRICK TANKS   In April 1998, when a large brick and cement water tank was leaking and needed to be emptied and repaired, the sisters gathered every basin and barrel they could locate to save water from the leaking tank. These containers lined the hallway, disappearing one by one as the water was used.

PLASTIC TANKS   Because of the leakage in the brick tanks, they were replaced with plastic tanks. The population in the mission continued to increase, and more tanks were added. In December 2004, twelve 24,000-liter water storage tanks were delivered. Six tanks would be used for drinking, cooking, and personal needs; two for the older teacher housing; two for the new teacher housing; and two for the site of the secondary school.

The tanks cost about $2,725 apiece (that included a 25% discount.) The sisters had already asked the plumber to get someone to build the base for the tanks. He promised to do the negotiating so the sisters were not charged "white people" prices. By 2015, more than 80 tanks dotted the grounds of the convent and school.

Early in the afternoon, one of the workers brought to the sisters' attention, a crack in one of the 24,000-liter tanks at the teachers' housing. Sr. Mary Rita immediately contacted Crestanks, the company from which the tanks were purchased. Sister asked that someone be sent to examine the cause. The general manager in Kampala promised someone would come as soon as possible, probably the next day. By evening the tank exploded. Thankfully, no students were around. Some teachers witnessed the event while arriving for staff meetings to be held the following day.

Crestanks offered no explanation why tanks had exploded: once at St. Julie Primary, once at Notre Dame Academy, and twice in the same location at the teachers' housing. This was very frightening because of the approximately eighty tanks on the property, many were located near and around areas where the students pass or play. The force of the water coming from an exploding tank was enough to kill someone nearby.

A few months later, someone noticed that there was a trickle of water leaking from the tank next to the secondary administration building. The tank was directly in front of the tank that exploded a few years previously. Sr. Mary Rita called Crestanks. In an effort to limit the danger if the tank exploded, sister began to drain the tank that was about half full. Within two hours, the tank exploded. As in the past, this happened during the second evening family work time, leading the sisters to believe that the problem was related to the time of day and cooling. Crestanks continued to have no explanations why the tanks exploded.

One evening, one of the large plastic water tanks at the end of Notre Dame Academy's laboratory building developed a crack. Sr. Anita Marie warned the students to stay away from the tanks. About twenty minutes later during the evening study period, the tank burst. A loud sound reverberated through the buildings. Students screamed and ran at first. After seeing the damage, they quickly settled down. Another large tank located between the laboratory and administration buildings exploded in November, and again vast amounts of water were lost. All were thankful to God that no one was injured by either explosion.

Crestanks finally replaced the water tanks. It was assured during a face-to-face meeting in Kampala, and in numerous emails that it was only because the sisters were "valued customers" that the tanks would be replaced at no cost other than installation.

The cause of the explosions was totally unknown until an article about the exploding tanks appeared in the August 2016 issue of *Drumbeats* (Covington's mission publication). One of the Engineers Without Borders who had been in Uganda wrote that they had determined that possible causes for the explosions were: (1) The plastic used in the tank was of unequal thickness; (2) One tank was cut when the nearby grass was being cut with a machete. Later, cement tanks were gradually replacing the plastic tanks.

BORE HOLE   The original bore hole provided water until 1997 when it ceased producing water. In May 2015, the depth of the hole was increased and the pipes replaced. Then the sisters were able to pump water and use it for watering the garden and cleaning the house. They were able to share the water with their neighbors, especially during the dry season.

WATER HOLE/PROTECTED SPRING   Since the water hole provided water for local residents, the situation was always a concern for the sisters. Finally, a pipeline and a cement cover on the nature spring created what was called a protected spring. When heavy rains came, the water came gushing out of the pipe. The water was cleaner than the water that sat in the water hole, and it was much easier to fill jerry cans at the protected spring.

FARM WATER TANKS   One tank for the farm was built underground. This tank was about six meters deep and about five meters in diameter and held precious water for the animals. Another one of this size and two small ones were built above ground. All of these tanks collected water from the animal shelter roofs and stored it for the animals' use.

WET/DRY SEASON   The dry months sometimes seemed to last forever, and lack of water became a major problem. During dry seasons, those back in the United States frequently received messages about the water situation. Sr. Mary Janet wrote:

> PLEASE TELL GOD ABOUT IT. THANK YOU.
> We are in such a bad state with water. The kids are rationed to five liters for bathing and laundry. They collect jerry cans in the morning and with the help of maintenance water is drawn from the borehole. P-4 – P-7 carry the cans from the hole. I feel sorry for the kids especially P-4 little ones as they struggle with the cans from the borehole. I think they are getting 10 from there. Our kitchen needs twenty jerry cans a day. You can imagine what this means. We did have a good rain yesterday but sooooooo much more is needed. (Note from Sr. Mary Janet, March 2012)

RAIN ARRIVES   The arrival of long-awaited rain is greeted in special ways by the children as the following stories reveal. During one dry season, the children, the sisters, their families, and the sisters of the home provinces had been praying for rain. When the rain finally came, it was with hail and wind. The children, however, could only run out excitedly and try to catch the hail on their tongues and in their hands. They ran through the rain and tried to collect it in their basins for bathing. One sister commented, "It was wonderful to see the absolute delight with God's gift that children can celebrate."

On another occasion, the teacher told her class to tell God of the great need, and beg him to send the rain. Very shortly after the prayer, thunder resounded, and the clouds quickly moved across the sky. The rain then came in great abundance. The children spontaneously burst into song: "Thank you God for being so good, being so good to us!" Everyone was cheering, excited and grateful to receive the precious gift of rain.

In the later years, the sisters noted that the wet and dry seasons were shifting. In fact, the arrival of each season that had been so predictable became more and more unreliable. This affected the crops and also the water level in the tanks. In some years, the low water level was of special concern when it coincided with the beginning of a new academic year.

HEALTH ISSUES

The sisters took great precaution concerning their health, but sometimes that did not seem to be sufficient. Their letters and emails refer to heavy colds and sisters being run down due to over-work or stress, pneumonia, malaria, falls, and other incidents. There were the occasions when they recognized the need to take some extra time for rest.

In an undated letter, Sr. Mary Bernadette, who was serving the health needs of the sisters, staff, students, and farm workers, listed some of the more common ailments: malaria; respiratory and gastro-intestinal infections; a variety of wounds, many from parasites; other first aid needs; and bacterial infections unique to the area. AIDS was usually undiagnosed or not discussed even though family members may have succumbed to the disease. Although this is a very Catholic area, the ancient witch doctor mentality, and curses, still influence the lives of many.

EBOLA OUTBREAK   In October 2001, there was an outbreak of Ebola in the Gulu District of northern Uganda, about 140 miles from Buseesa. Forty people died from the virus. It did not affect the Kibaale District where Buseesa is located.

On July 19, 2012, news of an Ebola outbreak in the Kibaale District filled the radio, television, and newspapers. There was absolute panic everywhere. The mother of one of the P-4 students, who was a nurse at Kagandi hospital, died. She had become ill with "a strange disease," and died unexpectedly. Shortly thereafter, her four month-old-child died. Two of the sisters and some of the teachers went to the burial. It was later determined that the woman and her baby son were victims of Ebola.

WHO (World Health Organization) and the CDC (Center for Disease Control) reacted immediately as they had previously with other outbreaks in Uganda. Schools in the district closed, and gatherings were cancelled. In order to keep the students, teachers, and workers safe, Sr. Anita Marie and Sr. Cristina Marie placed both schools under lockdown on July 30, allowing only workers to come on and off campus without special permission. Although difficult to enforce, it was received well by almost everyone, including the parents. An announcement was put on the radio stating that parents should come and get their children. Teachers quickly completed reports and organized the children to leave. Parents came all during the day but were not permitted into the compound. Children were called, signed out, and then released to a parent or another appointed person. Once they left the compound, they were not permitted to return.

Three NDA students and two St. Julie students were unable to go home because they were related to a woman who died of Ebola. The family feared possible contamination. These students stayed in the formation house and used the time to study and help the sisters. Thankfully, fears of the contagion never materialized, and these students went home ten days later.

HEALTH ISSUES: SISTERS AND VOLUNTEERS   The year 2003 could almost be described as the year of illnesses and accidents. Late one afternoon, Sr. Mary Annete came from the garden to check on the water boiling for drinking and cooking needs. In her effort to move one of the pans of boiling water, the pan slipped, and boiling water spilled onto her leg and foot. Sister was wearing boots, and unfortunately, the water flowed into one of them. Sister frantically pulled it off, but the damage was done. She managed to hobble to the main house, and her calls for help brought the other sisters.

Sr. Mary Delrita, the nurse, was in Kampala, so the sisters scrambled to administer whatever first aid they could recall. They used the healing sap of aloe vera from their yard and also applied ice and cold water. Since Sister could not climb the steps to her bedroom in the formation house, she was assisted to a bed in one of the guest rooms. With the aid of the satellite phone, the sisters eventually were able to contact Sr. Mary Delrita. Sister assured the sisters they applied the correct first aid and suggested a few other things to help Sr. Mary Annete through the night. Very large blisters revealed the extent and depth of the burns.

When Sr. Mary Delrita returned the next afternoon, she immediately went to check on the patient and examine her wounds. Because the burns were third degree, and the danger of infection was a great concern, Sr. Mary Annete was confined to the makeshift hospital room for a few days. Even when she was permitted up, Sister's activity was limited.

A volunteer wanted to visit a family in Muhorro. Although not feeling well when she left Buseesa, she went because transportation was available. A day or two later, the sisters received a call from the priest in Muhorro informing the sisters that the young woman was very ill and needed to return to Buseesa. Sabastian, the sisters' driver, left immediately, traveled north, and returned with the volunteer. The young woman was then able to be cared for in Buseesa.

Later that same month, another volunteer became ill with a fever that was diagnosed as malaria. When her condition did not improve, the sisters brought her to the convent guest room. With this arrangement, Sr. Mary Delrita was able to monitor her condition more easily. When treatment efforts failed, Sr. Mary Delrita took the young woman to see a physician in Kampala. They returned to Buseesa with medication. It was another week before the volunteer was able to get up and resume her activities.

HEALTH ISSUES: STUDENTS   Most of the illnesses Sr. Mary Delrita addressed were minor needs of the children: stomachaches, headaches, runny noses, and sore toes. The sisters thought many of these were a cry for love and attention. The sisters considered how difficult it was for seven to thirteen -year-olds to be away from home and family for three months at a time. Most did not see or hear from their parents during this time because of the cost and difficulty of transportation and communication.

In a boarding school of several hundred children, accidents are inevitable. A P-3 boy suffered an eye injury, and despite treatment, the swelling did not go down. Sr. Mary Delrita was able to contact his parents and accompany them and the child to the hospital in Kampala several hours distant.

When one of the students fell on the playground and broke her arm, Sr. Mary Delrita accompanied her to Kakumiro to the doctor for the bone to be set. The girl was put to sleep with IV medication, and the bone was repositioned by feel as there was no X-ray available. For each return visit, the doctor was away. After the prescribed number of weeks, Sr. Mary Delrita finally removed the cast; the arm had healed well.

On another occasion, one of the students was making his way to the convent when he was bitten in the ankle by a snake. He was carried to the convent where Sr. Mary Delrita began to treat him with the traditional local means. As a precaution, the boy was taken to the local clinic to assure he was in no immediate danger. The father was soon able to take his son home.

While Sr. Mary Delrita was in the United States on a home visit, she received an urgent email: A student had a fever and was given the usual medication. Later, the girl had a painful lump on her neck and was crying. The sisters took her to the clinic. "When they looked at her at the clinic in Bujuni ... and I mean only looked at her without any tests, they gave her a penicillin injection and asked us to give her three to five more." Sr. Mary Annete explained what the child had previously been given and feared an overdose. She said, "I've given injections in the past and could give it ... but I'll go on what you advise ... Please let me know." (Sr. Mary Annette to Sr. Mary Rose Paula for Sr. Mary Delrita, August 14, 1998)

The curse of bedbugs in the dormitories of both schools descended upon the mission during term one of 2015. In addition, fruit bats were nightly making their presence known by means of voluminous droppings on the school and convent verandas. Cockroaches were prevalent in the kitchen areas and in the rooms of teacher housing. Fumigation seemed in order. The sisters hired a company from Kampala to do the job, paying a high price for the service.

Despite promises and a contract to the contrary, the unwanted visitors did not depart. All through the second term, the students and matrons of both schools battled bedbugs on weekends with boiling water, mattresses removal, and spraying. At the end of the term, the company that had failed to produce the promised results returned.

COMMUNICATION

Communication, which in the first years was limited to Uganda or United States mail and the fax machine at the office of the Hoima Construction Company in Hoima and in Kampala, improved gradually.

RADIO CALL   After the illness of two sisters in the first year, the sisters installed a radio call system. A large antenna was erected in the convent courtyard. The sisters were connected to the Bishops' channel. The Missionaries of Africa broadcasted each morning from 8:00 until 8:30. Sr. Mary Janet recalled that the remainder of the day, the radio produced "squawking noises."

PHONES   Later the sisters acquired a solar phone. Its use was best at night when the transmitting satellite passed over the area. There was a delay in the transmission of the voices that made the calls a frustrating experience. Eventually cell phones came into use across the nation.

A very unexpected sight in Uganda is the large number of people who utilize cell phones. The phones are relatively inexpensive and a convenient way to keep in touch with others. The sisters' use of cell phones is quite challenging. Through trial and error, it was discovered that reception was best on the road in front of the convent and in the center of the soccer field. The high, rocky hills surrounding the mission limit accessibility.

INTERNET SERVICE   Considering the sisters' location, it seemed that email was impossible. But due to the knowledge, creativity, and determination of two young men and a wealthy gentleman, Bushnet was established in Kampala in January 1997. It was designed for organizations working in the remote areas of Uganda. The sisters discovered they could be linked to Bushnet via their high frequency radio and thus, they became Bushnet's second customer.

In mid-1997, the installation of a computer facilitated communication between the sisters and their home provinces. Unfortunately, the fee both to send and receive mail cost about fifty cents a page. Each subscriber had an electronic mailbox located on the hub. The hub established radio contact with each subscriber at a pre-arranged time, and anything in the out box went out, and anything sent to the sisters came in at that time. Sisters in the USA were cautioned not to send attachments and photographs as this used up the allotted megabytes. When this occurred, the monthly fee jumped to the next higher category, and this became the set fee.

Today with a new internet server, emails can be sent and received at any time, but if the allotted megabytes are exceeded, the fee increases. Because of this limitation, pictures are generally not exchanged.

POSTAL SERVICE/ SHIPPING   In the first years, the United States postal service was utilized to send materials to Uganda. Later, a worldwide delivery company provided the service, carrying packages that arrived in Kampala in a few days. Later materials were sent through another company. It was much less expensive, but since transport was primarily by boat, it often took about four months for the material to arrive. A decision was made that any materials, (e.g., pencils, notebooks) that could be purchased in Uganda would no longer be sent from the United States. Through the years, more and more items could be purchased in Uganda. On rare occasions, boxes were sent from the United States, and any person traveling to Uganda was asked to take items for the mission.

In May 2001, coming home from Kampala, the sisters stopped at Hoima House where packages from the United States were delivered. They had always checked, and this time they had a real surprise: one of the boxes was a Christmas box sent by the sisters in Carrollton, Kentucky, in 1997!!! They wondered where it had been all this time.

TRANSPORTATION

The Land Cruiser purchased in 1997 served the community wonderfully well over its six years. It had taken many ruts and bumps, accidents, and long trips. But eventually, it was determined that the vehicle was no longer safe, and the cost of repair was becoming prohibitive. It seemed to be in the shop more than it was on the road. All the sisters joined in the data collection process and sought information about the most cost-effective vehicle from as many different, knowledgeable contacts as possible. Finally, it was determined that another Land Cruiser would be best. With unpleasant memories of the first purchase, the sisters undertook the necessary steps to secure a new vehicle. The day finally arrived when the sisters were told they could come to Kampala to pick up the new vehicle. Everyone was happy with it and felt much safer in the new Land Cruiser.

Through the years, transportation continued to be a major challenge. In some cases, the challenge was the vehicle, and in other years it proved to be the roads and the weather.

Edward Kohinke, a member of the EWB-GCP (the Greater Cincinnati Professional Chapter of EWB [Engineers Without Borders]) wrote a blog in June 2013, describing the roads and giving glimpses into the culture and everyday experiences of the local people. Mr. Kohinke gave a vivid description of the roads and the sights along the way.

The road was crowded …

> Our driver, a man named Friday, expertly negotiated the chaotic mixed flow of vans, motorcycles (boda bodas), bicycles, pedestrians, and jaywalkers without the aid of pesky painted lane lines. The boda bodas almost always carried a passenger and enough cargo to fill a small pickup truck (couches, set of four car tires stacked, a bundle of thirty-foot rebars getting dragged along. … We did get into a traffic jam due to a boda boda accident … but luckily the only fatality seemed to be a watermelon splashed across the road.

> Open-air markets lined both sides of the road, like a single-aisled Home Depot and a Super Walmart that went on for miles. Workers fabricated their goods on location. We passed building materials, water tanks, furniture, produce, slabs of beef hanging from hooks.

They drove

> past trash heaps and slums and squatter camps, across papyrus marshes, and finally on the road to Mubende. Endless rumble strips rattled the windows and the teeth, and huge speed bumps forced the van to crawl through every town along the way. Though our van was like most others on the road, our seven pale white faces drew more and more stares the further we went. … Trenching for

roadside conduit ran for at least thirty miles, broken into segments being hand-dug by different work crews standing waist-deep in the deep red clay earth.

ROAD CONDITIONS   The road conditions with numerous potholes, deep tire ruts, and slippery surfaces required a skilled driver behind the wheel. For short distances, the sisters usually drove the van or truck, but generally hired drivers to navigate the longer trips and the crowded streets of Kampala. Sometimes, no matter how skilled the driver, accidents happened or the vehicle broke down. Even the sun could prove to be an antagonist.

One late afternoon, the sisters were returning home. The sun was at a low point and sister could hardly see. The wheels got caught in a rut and the vehicle swerved again and again. Being a bit unbalance due to the uneven distribution of cargo, the vehicle turned over on its side. Local villagers came to the rescue and got the vehicle upright. About three kilometers from home, the vehicle had a flat tire. Fortunately, the two priests from the parish came to the sisters' rescue.

On another occasion, Sr. Jane Marie and Sr. Mary Annete were taking Sr. Mary Shauna to the airport when the tires of the vehicle went into one of the deep ruts in the road. When Sr. Jane Marie tried to maneuver the vehicle out of the rut, it was suddenly sucked into the dirt wall on the side of the road. Sr. Jane Marie sustained injury to her head, leg, and abdomen; and the other two sisters had some bumps and bruises.

Within minutes, Mukiibi Joseph, a member of Parliament who was passing by, stopped, checked out the situation, and transported Sr. Jane Marie and Sr. Mary Shauna to the Dominican sisters' house in Kakumiro. The Dominican sisters offered some first aid and took Sr. Mary Shauna to the airport. Sr. Francesca, OP accompanied Sr. Jane Marie to the hospital in Kampala. After being checked in a quick fashion and with only a few questions by the doctor, Sr. Jane Marie was released. The two sisters went to ARU to stay for the night.

Meanwhile, Sr. Mary Annete remained with the vehicle for three hours until some help could arrive. Many villagers came, vehicles stopped to offer help, and a message was sent to Buseesa. Sr. Mary Annete recounted the incident: A man went home, changed his shirt, and returned to sit at the roadside with his little boy the entire time. He told the story of the accident to everyone who walked by. Sister wasn't worried because she knew God was there, but as it grew dark, she began a prayer to St. Anthony: "St. Anthony, St. Anthony, I am lost and can't be found."

A priest who was on his way to give a retreat in a neighboring village offered to take Sr. Mary Annete to the Dominican convent where she remained overnight. A

Ugandan doctor heard about the incident and came to check on sister.

VEHICLE PROBLEMS   Two sisters were returning from Kampala with a large supply of materials: seven bags of sugar, each weighing 100 pounds, seven big bags of wheat flour, and two new solar batteries, which were so heavy that two men had difficulty moving them.

> I think we had too much weight because we had a major flat … in the middle of nowhere! What to do! The badly torn tire was smoking and I was afraid of a fire. We threw water on it. … I thought about what my brother Leo taught us in auto mechanics but I was not exactly dressed to crawl under the truck to loosen the spare. Some young men came to see what was going on. They didn't seem to know what to do. I had to laugh when Annete proposed quite seriously that we call the gas station. The boys … before long … were under the truck to loosen the spare. I had real misgivings about their know-how, but what were we to do! After some trial and error … they did succeed. … It cost us about $25.00 which was a small price to allow us to move ahead. … I think every trip on our roads is an act of trust in God's care. (Sr. Mary Janet to Sr. Mary Kristin, March 27, 2002)

WEATHER PROBLEMS   Sr. Mary Janet, Sr. Mary Annete, and Sr. Jane Marie began the trip to Muhorro for another interview and testing session for new students for St. Julie School. The sisters were not aware that Muhorro had had ten days of rain.

> Suddenly, the roads became slippery without any signs of mud. The car veered and slipped and turned on its side … the driver's side (right) … my arm smashed the window on my right and yes … Annete and I were wearing our seat belts. … The taxi driver who was following me came immediately to our rescue. He said, "Sorry, sorry. And you were not even going fast!" … He got many men to help us set the vehicle on its four wheels, and he got us out of the mud. They checked the engine and said all was well. (Sr. Jane Marie to Sr. Mary Amy and Sr. Mary Shauna, August 7, 1999)

The sisters were able to complete the journey and return to Buseesa by evening. There was considerable damage to the right side of the vehicle, but the sisters sustained only aches and pains from their bodies straining against the seatbelts, and Sr. Jane Marie's right arm had some cuts. Again, the good God protected the sisters on the roads where the most unexpected does happen.

CROSSING INTERNATIONAL BOUNDARIES   One of the first times the sisters traveled from Buseesa, Uganda, to Arusha, Tanzania, they decided to drive. The route took them through Uganda, through a small section of Kenya, and then into Tanzania. When the sisters reached the Uganda-Kenya border, they were required to go through customs. In addition, they were required to export their car from Uganda, and import it into Kenya. The same ritual was followed at the Kenya-Tanzania border. After this experience, it was decided to take the bus for all other trips into the other East African countries.

PUBLIC TRANSPORTATION   Public transportation, too, proved to be a challenge. Taxis (large vans) were usually filled beyond comfortable capacity. Departure time at the gathering area seemed to depend on the whim of the driver. A letter from one of the sisters described travel from Kampala, Uganda, to Tanzania to the ceremony for the reception of new novices.

> We traveled from 4:00 p.m. in the afternoon until 12:00 noon the next day. We had to change buses in Nairobi. We had border checks out of Uganda into Kenya, out of Kenya and into Tanzania. … The buses were not exactly Greyhound but endurable. On one of the buses two sisters had the same ticket seats as two other people and so the sisters ended up sitting in the back. It was surely an educational experience. It began that way in Kampala when we arrived to take a certain bus line, but the seats we thought we had reserved were given away because we had not confirmed them. So, we ended up on a different bus line. … (From Sr. Anita Marie to [no person named], n.d.)

On a trip to Kampala, the sisters sought out a taxi for the return trip home.

> We got in this taxi about 10:05. It is now 11:20 and we are still sitting in the hot sun in the taxi park waiting for enough passengers to make the journey worthwhile. … It is now 11:45. We got out of one taxi and into a different one. Maybe this one will move soon. … It is now 12:50 and we are still sitting in the Kampala taxi park waiting. It's a way of life in Uganda. Waiting is <u>so difficult</u>! We still have four hours ahead of us. 12:55 Praise God, we're on our way! (Sr. Mary Janet to Sr. Mary Margaret, January 11, 1996)

On another occasion, the sisters planned to visit a school on the east side of Uganda that required about six and one- half hours of travel. Sabastian, the driver, took the sisters to the Mubende post office where they boarded the bus for Kampala. Upon arriving, they went to the bus park to get their next bus. When they arrived, they stated their destination, people pointed them to the bus headed there. People on the bus also helped them get off at the right place.

SPECIAL CELEBRATIONS

The special religious celebrations at the parish church and at the school multipurpose room continued to reflect the faith of the people and the local culture.

BAPTISM   At one Sunday Mass about twenty babies were baptized. The deacon had one white piece of cloth that he used to touch the babies' faces. The Christ candle was an old-looking kerosene lamp. The baptismal "font" was a plastic basin. The deacon and servers carried the basin and a plastic pitcher of water from child to child.

WEDDING   One Wednesday, the sisters attended a wedding Mass as part of a weekly charismatic gathering. One of the farm workers and his wife had been together for a number of years, but only now were they able to afford the wedding ceremony. This was not uncommon. After Mass, the couple's five children, members of the family, and friends accompanied the bride and groom to their home with singing and dancing. A meal in the afternoon was followed by socializing and music; speeches and gifts were presented.

CHRISTMAS   A sister wrote that the holidays were usually challenging for them. "We are, in a sense, more alone than ever. Our area is very deserted and quiet." She explained that the celebration of Christmas in Buseesa was so different from her home culture and devoid of many of the customs cherished at home. She concluded, "The adjustments we have had to make in community have been very difficult for all of us. Culture shock is something you don't even realize you are really suffering from." (Sr. Mary Janet to Sr. Mary Shauna, December 27, 2002)

While visiting the sisters in December 2014, Sr. Mary Shauna had the opportunity to celebrate Christmas with them. They celebrated the Christmas vigil Mass at the parish church. On Christmas Day, they set out two-by-two to three of the twenty-six outstations. These small Christian communities were miles apart and served by only two priests.

The sisters left the convent at 9:30 a.m. and drove through the bush, dropping off each pair of sisters carrying the Blessed Sacrament to their respective outstations. They returned about 3:30 p.m. Sr. Mary Shauna described her experience at one of the outstations:

> When arriving at Rusandara, Sister Teopista and I were greeted by the catechist while two other men took drums to the hillside to call the Christians to church. The children were the first to arrive followed by their mothers and fathers, most traveling by foot and some on bikes. Sister Teopista, a first-year temporary professed sister, led the service, read the Gospel, and gave the reflection all in Runyuro.
>
> The singing and dancing were extraordinary especially after Communion. The joy of sharing Eucharist was registered on everyone's face and expressed in the singing and dancing. (Sr. Mary Shauna, "Christmas in Buseesa Uganda", SNDKY website, December 25, 2014)

NEW YEAR'S DAY   2013 The festive Mass for New Year's Day was packed with ladies decked out in their Christmas outfits – traditionally made of material with reflecting designs. The choir was full of holiday enthusiasm; one young boy played five drums at one time! One of the Notre Dame Academy graduates directed the music.

During a song after Communion, a young girl began to dance in the middle aisle. Soon she was joined by one of St. Julie Primary's former teachers and another woman. One of the sisters commented that it was so sincere and spontaneous with "lots of clapping."

PALM SUNDAY 2003   The celebration of Palm Sunday seemed to the sisters to be something very close to the event over 2,000 years ago. The parishioners and students came carrying palm branches they had cut from the forest. Some tied fresh flowers around the palm, while others had their palms braided. All proceeded to line Buseesa road and prepare for the blessing of the palms. The priests and catechists led the procession to the church with all singing and waving their branches.

HOLY THURSDAY 1999   Because the priests went to the cathedral in Hoima for the Chrism Mass, and there was no Mass on Holy Thursday, the sisters drove to Bujuni, a neighboring parish. For the sisters, it was another experience of poverty. The church was so old and in such bad condition that it had to be torn down. The people had not been able to raise enough money to rebuild, so the Mass was held outside under a shelter with no walls and only wooden logs supporting iron sheets as a roof. The wind was blowing and heavy rain hitting the metal roof sounded like thunder. The washing of feet was more than a symbolic ritual because a number of the men had walked barefoot over the dirt roads.

HOLY THURSDAY 2003   Holy Thursday was mostly impromptu. Father looked at the choir and said, "Now we need to sing a Gloria," and someone intoned a Gloria. Then he said he needed some volunteers for the washing of feet. Some benches were moved around, and fourteen people came up, six of them children.

GOOD FRIDAY 2003   The veneration of the cross was especially devout. People formed two rows and approached the cross where they knelt, bowed to the ground, prayed for some time, bowed to the ground, and got up. It took quite a while, but the people just sang and sang. Sr. Anita Marie sang along, but she had no idea what she was singing.

HOLY SATURDAY 2003   The Easter Vigil was always a moving experience, especially witnessing the lighting of the new fire – not a small one but a huge outdoor bonfire.

The people entered the dark church. One of the priests lit a lantern and hung it rather high from a hook in the middle aisle. The first reading was read by a lady with curlers in her hair. There were no baptisms since baptisms were performed at other times during the year. At the conclusion of the service, everyone walked home in the pitch dark, but all the sisters had their torches (flashlights).

The next year when it was time for light, the church was suddenly bathed in it. Fr. Francis had acquired a generator and three electric bulbs to illuminate the church. Truly, the light of Christ had come into the world. The symbolism was powerful.

Ordinarily, the sisters did not take the children to the parish church for the vigil because of the dark and the length of the service. One year, Fr. Peter offered to come to the school for a short version of the vigil. The ceremony began with the fire that was lit outside the hall. There were candles for everyone.

> What a sight! About 300 children and adults processed into the darkened hall with lighted candles as we sang with gusto "Go Light the World." They held their candles high and swayed to the music. It was such a moving sight as I thought about the impact Jesus' life and victory has had on our world.

> How I wish you could have been with us last evening as our children celebrated Easter Vigil in our school hall. The roof almost came off with their joy and enthusiasm. They sang, swayed, shouted, and at the end our little ones stayed and danced the alleluia as only African children can do. (Sr. Mary Janet to Family and Friends, April 8, 2012)

EASTER 2004   On a regular Sunday, many parishioners were required to stand outside because the church was too small to accommodate the entire parish. On Easter Sunday, the crowd was even larger, so the parish came to St. Julie's multipurpose hall for the 10 a.m. Mass. By pushing back all the tables and using all the benches and chairs from both the dining and the assembly spaces, the sisters thought they had sufficient seating. Wrong! Throughout the service, the sisters had to gather every available chair from both primary and secondary classrooms and office space. They put mats on the floor in front for the little children. In this way everyone eventually was seated for the celebration.

CORPUS CHRISTI   Students from Notre Dame Academy prepared decorations for the celebration of the feast of Corpus Christi. They spent the day gathering flowers, ash, bits of brick, and other materials to create beautiful pictures of Eucharistic symbols and words for the liturgy. They made their designs along the path over which the Blessed Sacrament would be carried in procession. The dirt-packed path from the road to the church was covered with large squares of inspirational designs and words. It took hours to complete such an intricate work.

Inside the church, flower-decorated banana stalks stood in the corners. Up above, zigzagged across the church and attached to the tops of the windows, waved cords of United States used-car dealership triangular pennants.

The Eucharistic celebration began at 10:00 a.m. and by 10:30 a.m. Father had begun his thirty-five-minute homily in Runyoro followed by a ten-minute translation of the key points. At the presentation of the gifts, adults came forward to place their shillings in the basket. With a packed church of about 400 and another 100 or so standing outside, this part of the service took about twenty minutes.

About 1:00 p.m. the Eucharistic procession began from the church and circled around the property. As the streams of worshipers processed, some women walked immediately before Father and placed clean mats on the ground to reverence the Eucharist.

JUBILEE CELEBRATIONS   The celebration of the jubilees of profession of the sisters are days of great joy and special witness to the younger sisters and the people of the area. Some sisters returned to their home provinces to celebrate with their religious community, their relatives, and friends. But they also desired to celebrate with the people in Uganda.

Sr. Anita Marie, who was to celebrate her Silver Jubilee (25 years), wasn't sure about such a celebration, but she finally agreed.

> Since the time of a silver jubilee is really special, and since I thought it would be important for the young girls (and boys) at both schools to think seriously about such a call, I agreed. Then it was also decided that it would be a good witness for the parish to join in. (Sr. Anita Marie to many people, November 22, 2004)

The Mass was held in the multipurpose building that is larger than the parish church. The liturgy was celebrated in both Runyoro and English and included singing and dancing by the students. One of the students translated the renewal of vows into Runyoro and helped Sr. Anita Marie practice it.

When it was time for sister to renew her vows, the hall was totally quiet. She recited her vows in what she thought was imperfect Runyora and repeated them in English.

> The secondary girls wrote cards and they mentioned the sacrifice of my family in my following religious life and in coming to work with them here. It was really beautiful how sensitive they were to the real cost of following the Lord. (Sr. Anita Marie to many people, November 22, 2004)

During their years in Uganda, Sr. Mary Colette also celebrated her Silver Jubilee. Sr. Mary Delrita, Sr. Mary Janet, Sr. Maria Bernarde, Sr. Mary Rita, Sr. Mary Judith, and Sr. Mary Ruthilde celebrated their Golden Jubilees.

These days sometimes brought special surprises, special gifts from God. On the day that Sr. Mary Delrita celebrated her jubilee, the wife of the sisters' driver Sebastian, gave birth to a baby girl. She was named Vivian in honor of Sr. Mary Delrita whose baptismal name is Vivian.

ANNUAL RETREAT

The Constitutions of the Sisters of Notre Dame state that each sister makes a yearly retreat of seven days. The sisters ordinarily made their annual retreat at the Carmelite Retreat Center in Mityana. When the sisters from Buseesa made retreat here they brought their own retreat material as there were no preached, guided, or directed retreats available.

FINANCES

Since the sisters receive no salary, all monies to sustain the mission come from generous donors in the United States and Germany. In the United States funds are raised through activities sponsored by the sisters, organizations, and schools. There are also many individual donors who give generously especially at times of special need, such as a new vehicle, additional classrooms, or dormitories.

Keeping track of these finances proved to be a daunting and frustrating responsibility. Money in United States dollars was wired to Uganda and had to be exchanged for Uganda shillings. The exchange rate varied from one transfer to another. Separate accounts had to be kept for the convents in Buseesa and Mpala, the farm, as well as St. Julie Primary, Notre Dame Secondary, and both Buseesa and Mpala nurseries. This included the salaries paid to staff persons in each of the areas. Through the years, the method of keeping records changed format, and new forms and categories required adjustment. Each month a financial report was sent to the Covington province finance office. For large expenditures, a special request had to be submitted to the province or general level, depending upon the amount being requested.

Another ongoing challenge was a balanced acceptance and use of things from the west. The sisters needed to work out how to achieve this balance without offending willing donors. They made every effort to procure and use locally available materials especially in the school. They also recognized that it was not good to just give things to children and others, as they did not want to develop any unrealistic expectations in the people, especially the poor.

PASSPORTS AND WORK PERMITS

Every time the sisters went to get a work permit or a passport, the experience was one that could be chronicled in a book.

By 2007, the sisters had been in Uganda for twelve years. Every three years it became necessary to renew work permits. This year, Sr. Mary Janet and Sr. Mary

Delrita needed this renewal. Sr. Mary Judith, Sr. Mary Colette, and Sr. Antoinette Marie needed to apply for the first time. When Sr. Mary Janet went to Immigration in November 2006 to begin this process, she learned that fees had increased. A Ugandan work permit cost $3,000. This was unbelievable. The sisters contacted Bishop Deogratias for an appeal. It took about six months to bring about national legislation that lowered this outrageous sum to $375.00 for missionaries and others working for charitable organizations.

Three candidates began collecting documentation required for passport applications needed to travel as postulants to Tanzania in April. In Tanzania, they would begin their novitiate formation. In January, they began making trips to the immigration office in Kampala. These many trips were filled with frustration. Time after time the postulants were told that something was wrong with their paperwork or pictures, or that the papers weren't ready. This meant more trips to Kampala. Finally, by God's gracious care, on one of these trips, Sr. Antoinette Marie and the three postulants met someone they knew who worked in the government. They told him of their situation and he worked to get the much-needed passports for the postulants. He called three days later when the passports were ready to be picked up.

By 2012 things had not improved. In utter frustration, Sr. Mary Rita wrote to someone who had previously assisted the sisters with the immigration office.

> But now, I am sorry to inform you, we have again undergone several horrendous experiences that I think you would like to know about. It took us exactly forty-four trips into Kampala to secure Sister Ruthilde's work permit and our Ugandan sisters' passports. Sister Ruthilde is from Germany, a country that has been very generous and supportive of Uganda. Our nine candidates going to Tanzania … are native Ugandans. There is no conceivable reason why this process should have taken so long AND been so expensive. … a priest from Kampala went to assist and was seriously insulted by the office staff. (Sr. Mary Rita to Sasagah Godfrey, Ministry of Internal Affairs, April 4, 2012)

Sister explained that the staff lost files on several occasions, and the sisters needed to begin everything over again and pay again. Sister concluded by describing Uganda as a "country outstanding for its hospitality and gracious manners"– the opposite of what she experienced with this government office.

DANGEROUS FIRES

The threat of fire is such a reality that the sisters, staff, and students needed to be alert at all times. Sounds that resembled crackling were probably from a nearby fire. Especially in the dry season, fire spreads rapidly through the dry brush and even through the precious gardens. When there is a fire everyone springs into action. There were no pipes or hoses to carry water to the scene of the fire. The following are some of the fire stories the sisters in Uganda related in their letters:

ELEPHANT GRASS   A fire erupted in the field of dry elephant grass (very tall grass) near the convent. The flames, fanned by the high winds, licked the tall reeds and quickly consumed the brush and trees. It was a frightening and worrisome situation, and the sisters and children ran into the bush ahead of the flames to pull away the dry grasses or beat the fire to extinguish it.

The children were so unaware of the danger of being surrounded by fire that the sisters offered special prayers invoking the protection of the Guardian Angels. As one child felt the intense heat and watched the fierce flames, he asked if this is how it was when the Uganda Martyrs were killed. He obviously knew well the story of these courageous martyrs. Much of the area was damaged, but the sisters realized what a good garden space it could make for the school. What appeared a tragedy would soon become a blessing.

HILLSIDE   One evening after prayer, Sr. Cristina Marie went to check on the fire burning on the hill behind the convent. Sister reported that the fire was a stone's throw from the chicken house. All went immediately to fight the flames. Some went for precious water from the water tanks that were already low. Others grabbed branches from trees to beat the flames. One sister tried to beat the flames with a banana tree that had fallen, but it was so dry it fell apart. She then went to fetch a machete to cut a branch from a tree with green leaves. She had to whack it forcefully and finally cut it. Sr. Maria Bernarde tried to call the farm workers at school and went to the rectory for help. They had quite a crew beating and pouring water. The cassava burned as well as some of the trees. When they finished fighting the fire that night, the sisters were full of black soot and dirt.

BY GOVERNMENT SCHOOL   One morning the government school across from the convent started a fire to burn their garden. (A common practice.) They planned to burn the area to make a new banana plantation. The fire burned all day. Although the fire seemed to be under control, at 5:30 p.m. it jumped the fire breaker the man had just completed. All the sisters, along with the children, went out and tried their best to put out the fire. They managed after some time to contain it and finally put it out. It was a blessing no one was hurt, but one worker was nearly attacked by a very large snake. It brushed his leg, but with the help of those around him, the snake was killed before it did any harm. The sisters were told that fire makes the snakes "run."

HOT AND WINDY   Someone had set a fire on the hill behind the school. It was hot and windy, and the fire was leaping high in the sky and coming very close to the piggery, the dorm building, and the gardens. Many of the workers were fighting the flames by beating them with branches from the bushes and trees. The fire did some damage to the garden, but it was stopped before damaging the buildings. In the dry season there is always trouble with fires because people clear their land by burning (which is against the law). The fires add to the difficulty in this dry hot season because much smoke seems to stay in the air and makes it hard to breathe. Many of the children and even adults suffer from coughs and dry eyes at this time of year.

EARTHQUAKES

Being located near the Rift Valley in East Africa, the sisters should not have been surprised by an occasional earthquake. At 2:40 one morning, they were awakened to the rumbling and shaking of the earth beneath them. They had often had tremors, but this was more severe than usual. Later they learned that the quake registered 4.4 on the Richter Scale, and the epicenter was just west of them in Lake George. Fortunately, there was no damage from the quake.

On the night of February 5, 2004, the sisters experienced a rather sizeable earthquake. Even the sisters from California who were used to such natural occurrences commented that this was remarkable. The loud rumble as well as the relatively prolonged quaking was noted by almost everyone; however, some sound sleepers slept through it.

During another night, a powerful earthquake shook the buildings, and there were at least three large aftershocks. The sisters could hear the children crying and calling out from the St. Julie dorms down the road. The matrons were on hand to calm the children. Some of the sisters living in the convent were also frightened. However, the sisters from California were not so disturbed as they knew just what was happening. All calmed down. There was no damage to any of the buildings and no one was injured.

SECURITY

Because of some security issues, it was suggested that the sisters get a dog. "Police" arrived on September 6, 1998 and was put on patrol in the farm area. On August 17, 2003, "Caesar" took up residence in the convent courtyard, where he was usually locked up because he barked when students came to help in the kitchen or garden.

REBEL ACTIVITY   In July of 1997, the sisters were told about some rebel activity. It appeared that the rebels had sent scouts into the area to see if it was worth their time and trouble to come and loot. Several scouts were arrested and plans were extracted from them. The sisters kept their curtains on the outside of the compound closed. The pastor suggested that they not run the generator at night so they could better hear noises from any intruders. Since security was not so solid in the area, extra police were sent there.

In March of 2000, there were rumors of rebel activity, so some people left their homes. One woman sought refuge in the school, and others in the church. No official warning was received, and it was surmised that thieves came to the village to scare the people so they could make off with some of their goods.

In June of that year, the local police force came and patrolled the periphery of the compound. The officials were concerned that a heated election might create problems in the area. In August, an officer came to inform the sisters that he would leave the police at the school site. There were reports of some looting in villages. Also, guns and police uniforms had been taken, and one policeman had been killed. However, the officer felt the sisters and students were not in immediate danger.

Police presence was intensified in October when the sisters were again alerted to the closeness of rebel activity. The sisters tried not to alarm the children but encouraged them to stay in the compound and not wander off. The sisters also devised a plan of action for taking care of the children in the event of immediate danger.

In a letter of December 14, 2000, to Sr. Mary Margaret, Sr. Mary Annete wrote:

> All is quiet in our area again and we thank God for that. It's very hard to sort out rumor and actual trouble. … who are just thugs and robbers and are there really rebels near. We don't take it lightly, but always keep our children and their safety of great importance.

SEPTEMBER 11   Early in the morning the pastor came to the convent to express his sympathy over the tragedy that occurred in the United States. This first news came as a shock to the sisters, and they tried to tune into the radio to learn more, but the information was sketchy. They remained shocked and prayerful, thinking of the many who had died or who were in terrible suffering.

Later in the evening the sisters received email messages giving some of the details. Articles in the *New Vision* also gave some information and commentary. Over the next days the sisters continued to receive email messages from Sisters of Notre Dame all over the world, expressing their shared grief and solidarity with all American sisters, and indeed, with all Americans.

On October 19, Sr. Mary Annete went to Kampala for a warden meeting conducted by the United States Embassy. Security issues were discussed, especially in the wake of the September 11 catastrophe.

ELECTION RIOTS   In 2006, there was great tension concerning the national election. This eventually erupted into violence in Kampala and elsewhere.

HOUSEGIRLS AND IRON SHEETS   The sisters' first experience with stolen property was the disappearance of iron sheets destined for the roof of the convent. The sheets were stored under lock in the garage. A villager informed the sisters that their house girls had stolen twenty-four iron sheets from their garage and sent them to a village where one of the girls lived. Having gathered details of the theft, the priest brought the information to the sisters and urged them to contact the police the next morning. The sisters counted the sheets in the garage the next morning, confirming the loss. The police were called and the girls interrogated. The sheets were recovered, but it was a devastating time for the sisters as they had totally trusted the two girls. The girls were detained at the sub-county jail until the next day.

Having been released on bail, the girls returned to the convent, busied themselves cleaning their rooms, and under the supervision of the sisters, packed to leave. Since all the iron sheets were accounted for and retrieved, the girls were pardoned, and there was no trial. It was a sad day in Buseesa.

PLASTIC BARRELS   Over the Christmas holidays, several large plastic barrels that are used on the farm were taken from the compound. The barrels are expensive and this was not the first time some were taken. The sisters were told that their employees stole the barrels, and sold them to a local official in a neighboring village. They reported the theft to the police and shared with them the information they had received about the suspects. Two of the farmworkers were apprehended and arrested. When the police looked for the local official accused of buying the stolen items, he could not be reached because of a reported "illness." Later he denied any guilt. The two men apprehended were detained in jail for several days. The jail was a terrible, windowless room in a mud-walled building. The room had no furniture, not even a bench, and only the mud floor to sit on.

When the sisters went to claim the stolen barrels, only one plastic barrel and one metal one had been recovered. They quickly realized how hopeless the situation was and suspected perhaps some bribery on the part of the police with the local official. Thus, they decided to drop the charges. The two men were probably guilty of stealing other things. A third man ran off in fear after the arrest, and unfortunately, he went with some of the farm tools.

FENCE AROUND SCHOOL   To provide security for St. Julie School, a chain-link fence surrounding the school compound proved to be too costly for the budget. The sisters chose to purchase three gates and make the fence with local thorn trees and barbed wire. The thorn trees have long spines and grow thickly together, preventing access by intruders. Five hundred fifty thorn trees were planted in a few days.

Bananas (matooke) on the tree

9

NOTRE DAME ACADEMY BEGINS AND GROWS

St. Julie Primary was barely underway when the sisters began thinking about the possibility of a secondary school. What would happen to the St. Julie Primary students when they completed P-7? There were opportunities in the area for boys, but few for the girls. What about the possibility of a Notre Dame Academy Secondary School for girls?

When Bishop Deogratias visited at the conclusion of the first academic year, the sisters expressed a concern. They requested that a search be made for more land if there was to be a secondary school in Buseesa. The Bishop suggested that the sisters survey the land by actually walking around to see the 100 acres of land the church presently owned. He spoke to the local chief who agreed to walk with the sisters and show them where the church property boundaries were.

It seemed that when the decision had to be made about starting the secondary school, there was no question in the minds of the provincial administrations (at least in Covington) that the community would not sponsor a coed secondary boarding school. Therefore, the secondary boarding school would be for girls, principally for those who had gone to St. Julie Primary. There was extreme "unhappiness" on the part of the missionaries that secondary education for boys would not be provided.

PLANNING FOR NEW NOTRE DAME ACADEMY

In December 2002, the first class would graduate from St. Julie Primary. It was time to address making Notre Dame Academy Secondary School a reality. From July 1 to July 25, 2002, five secondary teachers arrived in Uganda to become acquainted with the ministry of secondary education in Uganda: Sr. Mary Rachel Nerone, Sr. Mary Rita Geoppinger, and Sr. Anita Marie Stacy from Covington, Kentucky, and Sr. Marie Paul Grech and Sr. Antoinette Marie Moon from Thousand Oaks, California. The twenty-five days the sisters spent in Uganda were filled with much traveling, many appointments and contacts, and multiple opportunities to learn firsthand what was involved in secondary education.

The sisters wanted their days to be as profitable as possible. They developed some questions and asked Sr. Jane Marie to review them to make sure they were appropriate for presenting to the head teachers of the schools they would visit. They then met with all the sisters and learned much about the culture. When they visited Bishop Deogratias in Hoima, the sisters had some prepared questions, especially about teaching religion, considering the Ugandan culture especially in the Buseesa area.

During the next several days the sisters visited schools in various areas of the Hoima Diocese as well as in Kampala. All those they met were most helpful and willing to share what they could. In one school, Sr. Anita Marie and Sr. Mary Rita spent a morning learning about the science curriculum and checking out textbooks. The sisters received a schedule of what was taught in physics, chemistry, and biology for each of the three terms. They stopped at a bookstore and purchased samples of textbooks.

The sisters learned that:

- A typical day went anywhere from 7:30 a.m. to 4:00 p.m. This was followed by a structured after-school program that included supervised study until 10:00 p.m.
- A typical classroom had sixty-five students, and some had many more.
- The classrooms consisted of four walls, a chalkboard, and maybe a cement floor.
- Not even the wealthiest boys' and girls' school provided a textbook for each student.
- The library was a room where sets of textbooks (about five to ten of each publication) were housed.

During a visit with the District Education Officer (DEO), the sisters received an overview of the Ugandan educational system in the Kibaale District. He provided information about starting a secondary school, and the sisters learned about curriculum, textbooks, faculty, and finances.

Near the conclusion of their visit, the sisters wrote that they had probably seen more schools in their short stay than the sisters who had lived there for years. They learned that the Ugandan secondary system was significantly different from anything they were familiar with in the United States. In Uganda they had visited the gamut from the wealthiest to the poorest schools. At the conclusion of their visit, the sisters established some recommendations for the new Notre Dame Academy Secondary School in Buseesa, Uganda.

In October, Sr. Mary Rita and Sr. Cristina, OP, traveled to Kampala to purchase material for the uniforms of the new secondary school girls. Any trip to the open markets, located down back alleys, was very challenging. The sisters found themselves bargaining, holding tightly to their purses and at times not knowing who was the owner of the shop or if someone was pretending to be the owner.

GOAL OF NOTRE DAME ACADEMY SECONDARY SCHOOL

Notre Dame Academy in Buseesa, Uganda, was a school for "Women Who Make a Difference." The primary aim was to give each girl a holistic education that prepared her well for life. This included not only excellence in the secular subjects but also religious experiences. To this end, the school sponsored daily prayer in the classrooms, weekly student-prepared Mass, and retreat experiences yearly. Every Sunday evening the liturgy prefect conducted an optional students' prayer meeting. It was always deeply edifying to see so many girls attending and praying so devoutly for the hour or so that the prayer lasted. (Sr. Mary Rita, *Newsletter*, July 22, 2009)

CONSTRUCTION OF NOTRE DAME ACADEMY SECONDARY SCHOOL

The Hoima construction crew arrived in Buseesa in January 2001 to begin work on the formation house, the new chicken house, and the multipurpose building that in two years would be used by students at St. Julie Primary and the girls at Notre Dame Academy. Construction on the multipurpose building moved at a slow pace. Since it was to be a large building, the construction crew made extra effort to be sure it had a sound foundation. They had brought a portable cement mixer on site. It was a great improvement to mixing the cement by hand. Previously, even the cement columns that strengthen the foundation had to be made by hand. Each column contained steel or iron reinforcement pieces that had to be cut, bent and formed by hand from long bars of metal. By July, brick walls were rising from the foundation.

Sr. Mary Rita and Sr. Anita Marie—both from Covington—arrived in October 2002 to direct the preparations for Notre Dame Academy. Their earlier visit provided much information on which to base their decisions. Some of their plans were temporarily halted when in December, the sisters received the following:

> I do think that before any more building projects begin, those in process need to be completed. In other words, SNDSS will not start to build until further notice. (Sr. Mary Shauna and Sr. Mary Rachel to Sr. Mary Rita, December 1, 2002)

It was decided that for the 2003 academic year, perhaps St. Julie Primary could share with the Academy some dorm space as well as the block that formerly served as the St. Julie Primary dining room. The primary school dining room had moved to the new multi-purpose building. By 2004, the number of Academy students would double and it seemed apparent that a dorm building would be needed. Additionally, St. Julie was planning to accept P-1 and P-2 students in the near future. To accommodate this, St. Julie would need more classrooms. There were already plans to expand the library to provide the resources for both schools.

Finally, in June 2003, preparation at the site for the Notre Dame Academy building began with the slashing of the high grass. The sisters were assured of a dormitory building by February. Fr. Heinz said ALL would be finished by May, but the sisters were betting on August. Later, subsequent buildings would be constructed. The sisters felt they would be using the primary school facilities for two years.

A year later, the new dorm building was completed. The Academy students were delighted as they located their new beds in their new dormitories. Then the girls helped to clean and prepare the rooms that would eventually be used as classrooms, a science laboratory, and a school office. It was estimated that the construction of the classroom block itself would take another full year. In the meantime, three dorms would be occupied, and the four remaining rooms would be used as the school until the entire secondary school was complete.

With the opening of the secondary school, the sisters found themselves facing the need of additional teacher housing. When the first teacher house was built, they were not considering a senior secondary school for girls. They also did not know that they would have a steady stream of volunteers from Germany.

Finally, by early 2006, construction was completed. Sr. Mary Janet wrote:

> We are delighted with our two new buildings, which have been under construction for about a year and a half and are now finished. We have a fine two-story classroom building with six classrooms for the high school and also a two-story teacher house with accommodations for our staff and guests. We are so grateful to all of you who have helped to make these buildings a reality for our mission. (Sr. Mary Janet to Family and Friends, February 23, 2006)

STUDENTS FOR THE NEW SECONDARY SCHOOL

As the sisters continued their conversations about buildings and space, they needed to set in place plans for the classes at the school.

The sisters sent a letter to each of the priests in the eleven parishes that had children in St. Julie School, explaining that Notre Dame Academy would be taking up to twenty-five girls in the new S-1 class. Each pastor was provided with three recommendation forms with instructions about the secondary school entrance test on December 28. The letter also requested that the forms be returned by December 15. The sisters would come to meet with the pastors at their convenience. The letters went out in November, but no one responded. They would soon learn how typical this was in Ugandan communication, and in no way was it indicative of the priests' lack of interest.

Sr. Mary Rita and Sr. Anita Marie began their visits to the various parishes. The visit of five parishes each day was very tiring, but the sisters were energized by what they saw, heard, and experienced. One thing they gleaned from their visits was that the parishes to the west of Buseesa were poorer than those to the east. It was noted that the people of these western parishes really valued the opportunity the sisters were offering and at a price they couldn't resist.

At 8:40 a.m. on December 28, six people had already arrived at the school – unheard of in Uganda! Twenty-six girls (ranging in age from twelve to seventeen years of age) and their parents or sponsors arrived, and much to everyone's surprise, the testing began promptly at 9:00 a.m. as scheduled and continued until 3:00 p.m. The testing became a community endeavor. Sr. Mary Annete remained at the house to direct people to school. Sr. Mary Delrita directed the adults to what the sisters jokingly called the Hospitality Room. As the parents sat on wooden benches from the students' desks, she entertained them with reading materials and answering questions. The girls were directed to Sr. Mary Janet to begin the written tests. Sister noted the beginning and ending time for the math and English tests for each student. When the tests were completed, the students were assigned a number and asked to wait in the Hospitality Room. When a girl's number was called, she went to another room to meet with Sr. Anita Marie to discuss the math test, and then to Sr. Mary Rita to go over the English test. The tests were simple enough that the sisters could tell at a glance how well or how poorly the girl did on them. The plan was also to engage the girl in conversation as much as possible to check her communication skills.

The student and her adult companion then met with Sr. Mary Paulynne who explained the school fees and the work-study program. One of the workers and an aspiring secondary teacher served as a translator for the parents, and if necessary for the girls, to make sure they really understood. The work-study was a totally new concept, and the parents and parish priests were so grateful for the possibility.

Parents were to pay 60,000 Uganda shillings and the student was able to earn 60,000 Uganda Shillings each term. There was a one-time down payment of 10,000 Uganda shillings to secure the student's place.

During the events of the day, all the sisters were watching and listening for the girls' comprehension and use of English. The sisters were impressed with their command of English and how easy it was to communicate with them.

The next day, the sisters compared notes and chose eight girls for acceptance and placed four on the waiting list. This gave them latitude for the St. Julie Primary girls who hadn't as yet committed.

TEACHERS

In general, it was difficult to find teachers who were willing to come to the bush area. Sometimes one would agree, but then left after a day or a week, having found another teaching position.

Math and science teachers were especially difficult to find. The sisters were anticipating a major problem in filling the position of a biology-chemistry teacher. They had found some possibilities, but the individuals did not want to come so far out into the bush. A bio-chem student who was very professional and seemed as if she would do a wonderful job was not interested in the bush country.

THE DOORS OPEN

On February 3, 2003, the doors of Notre Dame Academy Senior Secondary School officially opened to receive twenty-two girls for the S-1 class. Sister Mary Rita and Sr. Anita Marie were disappointed when only a few girls appeared the first day. But again, they soon learned that this was standard procedure in Ugandan secondary schools. It took about a week before all the girls arrived.

Before the school year actually began, each student was given a list of things to bring. When Sr. Mary Judith arrived for her sabbatical, she found herself laughing over the list: five cups of beans, one hoe, one slasher (grass cutting whip), one spoon, two drinking cups, one plate, three passport photos. Sister concluded an email with the comment, "How does that strike you for high-school readiness?" (Sr. Mary Judith to Sr. Mary Shauna, February 9, 2004)

One of the sisters wrote that the first week of school was great! The students were most willing to accommodate to the situation of the new school. Since none of the secondary school buildings was completed, part of St. Julie Primary was needed. The S-1 students were squeezed into one of the dorms of the primary school. The students helped in the shifting of beds, mattresses, and personal items.

Because the results of the national Primary Leaving Exam (PLE) had not been issued, it was not possible to begin classes. Until then, a month of student orientation was begun. The girls were introduced to the spirit, philosophy, policies, and procedures of Notre Dame Academy Senior Secondary School.

Once the PLE results arrived, each girl and her parent(s) came for a personal interview with Sr. Mary Rita and Sr. Anita Marie to discuss the student's continuance in the program. The assessment was based on the PLE and also the student's attitude and accomplishments during the month of orientation. If the student was accepted in S-1, the initial 10,000 Uganda shillings was applied to the parent's 60,000 Uganda shillings debt for the first term. If the girl was advised to discontinue, the 10,000 Uganda shillings payment was applied to her upkeep during the orientation month. Uganda requires a passing grade on the PLE to enroll in a senior secondary school.

WORK-STUDY PROGRAM

In addition to working on study skills, English and math, the girls were introduced to the work-study program. One-half of the school fees (tuition plus boarding) would be paid by their parents; the remaining half was to be earned by the girls for their work in the classroom, on the compound, and at the job assigned them. An explanation letter was sent to all the sisters.

> The work-study program is an integral part of the secondary program. It allows the young women to take ownership for their education and helps to form responsible women who will contribute to society in the future. These young women will also be contributing to the smooth operation of the school both primary and secondary. It is true that their tuition will be lessened and that we will always need to subsidize from outside sources. (Sr. Mary Kristin, Sr. Mary Shauna, and provincial council members to Sisters in Buseesa, February 24, 2003)

The month of February provided an opportunity to learn and practice the work-study requirements. A solid work ethic, self-respect, and personal accomplishment were emphasized. Every student was encouraged to set goals for herself and to develop a plan of action for accomplishing them. There was opportunity to work closely with their teachers to learn what was expected and how they would be assessed. The work supervisors discovered that, despite the fact that the process was foreign to these Ugandan students, they were doing a good job of it.

IN THE CLASSROOM

The teachers for this first year at Notre Dame Academy included Sr. Mary Rita and Sr. Anita Marie. When Sr. Mary Judith from Covington, Kentucky, arrived in 2006, the science department was greatly strengthened and enriched.

The sisters discovered that the screening process seemed to be quite effective, and the students performed according to expectation. The students ranged in age from twelve to fifteen. One of the sisters commented:

> You have to experience them and their culture to appreciate the challenge of it. But they have a serious European curriculum (thirteen to fourteen subjects) with a stringent Ugandan leaving exam that is way out of sync with what happens in the classroom or what they are prepared for. (From: unknown to Sr. Mary Shauna, April 17, 2003)

The sisters were able to acquire a few more textbooks so that there was one book for every three students, which was considered quite good.

The course of studies, based on the European model, was quite intense. S-1 and S-2 students took thirteen required subjects per week: English, math, biology, physics, chemistry, history, political science, commerce, geography, agriculture, physical education, music, and art. In their third and fourth year, ten subjects were required. At the end of S-4 they must sit for exams in eight of these subjects. This was most challenging for students, particularly for those from the bush area.

The students were very basic in their grasp of language and subject matter. Sr. Mary Rita started with an introduction to grammar and literature that she thought was grassroots. Sister revamped the lessons to adapt to the situation. The sisters discovered that science was even more of a challenge.

Sr. Mary Rita wrote that she was most energized by teaching, especially teaching literature to students who had very little life experience on which to build and no exposure to the world of literature. Sister was grateful that many in the S-1 class had been students at St. Julie, and they had good reading skills even though these were still at an elementary level. This helped greatly in improving the skills of the entire class.

Emails during the first term (three months) indicated that the sisters had some very unexpected, and sometimes frustrating, experiences and learnings.

> Sr. Anita and I have much to learn about the culture in general and the uniqueness of the Ugandan teen in particular. While in some ways the growing pains of teenage girls are the same everywhere, they are undoubtedly expressed in ways that are both new and unusual to Anita and me, who collectively have over fifty years of secondary experience. (Sr. Mary Rita, to unknown person, May 31, 2003)

On February 9, 2004, Sr. Mary Judith wrote to Sr. Mary Shauna:

> Equipment was a major source of frustration. Everything was in short supply; the students weren't all that responsible with the things and texts they were given to use, and it was an uphill climb in every class.

Sr. Anita was frustrated with so much of the procedural things. Science was a detailed discipline, and details were not a strong suit in this culture.

At the end of a term, exams proved to be an excellent exercise for all because they clearly demonstrated to teachers and students alike how much had been accomplished in a relatively short time. The teachers were of the opinion that the girls had learned solid study habits as well as a substantial amount of the required curriculum.

At this time, parent-student report card conferences were held at three centers to make it easier for the parents to attend. Unfortunately, because of the difficulty of securing affordable transport, many of the parents and/or girls did not come for their conferences. This was disappointing since most of the girls had done a remarkably good job in each of the four areas of their work-study, scholarship, conduct, and job. It would have been a pleasure to pass on this good news to the parents.

INTERACTIVE LEARNING   Notre Dame Academy fostered leadership skills by providing interactive opportunities in and outside the classroom. Friday night debates and Saturday night seminars were examples. Each week a debate topic was assigned, and girls were appointed to the various roles of responsibility, such as chairperson, principal speaker, or judge. All students were required to attend. The teacher moderators tried to give every girl a chance to fill each of these positions over the course of the year. The Saturday night seminar featured one academic discipline per week. In the course of the term, a seminar was conducted in each of the twelve major subjects. The S-4 teacher and class were responsible for the organization and presentations. The subject matter, however, covered the syllabus from S-1 to S-4, so all students were expected to take an active part in the event.

Teachers tried to make the seminars more practical. For one math seminar, the math teachers had the students measuring water tanks and buildings for a practical application of their math skills. The commerce teacher required students to collect actual invoices and receipts, and interview businesspersons about such transactions. Thanks to a grant received for solar computers, all the girls had access to a computer to facilitate learning in every subject and to acquire another practical skill.

SCIENCE AND MATH   There is great need for students to perform well at the S-4 level of testing at the O level. (Ordinary level, S-1 – S-4) At the next level of education, called A-level, (Advanced level, S-5 and S-6) most of the students drop the sciences since they have either failed or believe that continuing in the arts is easier. However, in Uganda there is need for nurses, doctors, and science teachers.

The individual classrooms served the needs of most subjects. An exception was the sciences. Performing experiments using regular tables and carrying in even the simplest of equipment, offered major challenges for the teachers of these subjects.

At Notre Dame Academy the sisters were trying to use demonstrations and experiments in science, not only to make science appealing, but also to help the students understand and be successful in science. Most Ugandan visitors to Notre Dame Academy were impressed with the science equipment that was very simple by American standards. One of the hardest items to produce for the classroom demonstrations was HOT water. Since there was no electricity, keeping water really hot was quite a task. Teaching physics, with a very specific curriculum that is not always related to the students' everyday experience, proved to be a real challenge. One of the sisters commented that she could hardly wait to get to the chapter on electricity!

Finally, the new science building was to be a reality. But, as with all the other building projects, the completion date kept changing. First it was December 2006, and then the end of June 2007. Fr. Heinz, who was responsible for the construction of all the other buildings on the property, acknowledged that the science building was the most challenging of all his projects. His company had built few labs and none quite like this one.

The science building consisted of two complete labs, each equipped for physics, chemistry, biology, and agriculture. By first world standards, the labs were little more than big rooms with tables. But for the sisters and students in Buseesa, the labs were a place where students could work freely with accessible water from a tank and propane gas transported from Kampala; it was a dream come true.

Mathematicians and scientists are notably scarce in Uganda despite almost limitless job opportunities. With few exceptions, the students were terrified of the sciences and had no desire to continue with their study. Notre Dame Academy was working to reverse the trend. As much as possible, the teachers wanted to provide a hands-on experience for every student. The new science labs would help to make this more possible.

COMPUTERS   From the beginning years of St. Julie Primary, the topic of computers was raised. At the time, monies were being used for payment of the rectory and the convent. Plans for St. Julie Primary were in the making, and an estimated cost was projected. Funds first needed to go for bricks. In addition, there was no electricity in the area.

With the building of Notre Dame Academy, Sr. Anita Marie was so excited when she learned that the school was awarded a grant to equip a computer room. Sister had experience with computers and was sure that students, who could not continue their education because of poor academic scores or lack of school fees, would especially profit from learning to use a computer.

On a home visit to Covington, Kentucky, Sr. Anita Marie called several computer retailers to find out what computers would be appropriate in Uganda. Back in Uganda, she visited stores in Kampala asking about prices for solar panels. Solar panels rather than electricity were determined to be a better fit because Buseesa did not yet have electricity, and the electricity in other areas was shown to be unreliable. It was decided to purchase laptops since desktops, although more durable, would consume too much energy. Contact was made with Bushnet, the sisters' former Internet provider, to seek recommendations. Bushnet knew a company in the United States that was designing low voltage computers that would work directly from batteries powered by solar panels. The sisters were directed to a solar company and a computer company, both in Kampala.

Finally, the computer room became a reality. The decision was made to teach keyboarding and basic skills first, as the students would need these to be marketable. Even the native teachers were interested in learning to type and use the computer.

In 2010, Sr. Anita Marie, as overseer of the computer lab, graciously allowed some of the students to work with and practice on a computer in their free time. But soon word came from the village that a computer had been stolen from Notre Dame Academy. Sr. Anita Marie was incredulous and went to check the computer lab. A computer had been unbolted from the table and passed through a screen of a back window that had been cut out. Being solar powered, the computer was substantially useless to anyone but the mission. The thief was never apprehended, and the computer lab became off limits in free time.

In April 2012, the technical director for Mountains of the Moon University in Ft. Portal asked about the possibility of using the Academy's computer lab for an extension course in the Kibaale district. The week was a great success, and there were many more interested than could attend.

GEOGRAPHY FIELD EXPERIENCE   Annually, the S-3 students made a geography field trip to become more familiar with the resources and geographical features of Uganda. They took note of industries, markets, and any special land formations. One trip was east toward Lake Victoria and Queen Elizabeth National Park. Another time they visited Makerere Research Farm. They then traveled to the fish reserve and the national zoo. Another year, the students traveled northwest to the lakes around Hoima that included some arduous travel by foot.

In more recent years, the students traveled to the western part of Uganda to Lake Katwe Salt Works where salt is harvested, a process that has taken place for over 500 years in basically the same manner. The students also visited the fishing port and spent the night at Queen Elizabeth National Park.

One year at the park, as a group was preparing supper and the others were in the hall where they were to sleep for the night, an elephant came charging into their lodging. Fortunately, the park authorities were able to divert the large animal, and all were safe.

On another occasion, a bus was provided for the trip. The passenger door on the bus did not close properly and opened after each bump in the road. Nevertheless, the students continued on their journey. On the way home, the headlights failed. The driver pulled over at some desolate spot where Sr. Anita Marie and another teacher went to look for help at a service station. Meanwhile the bus driver and the conductor disappeared. They did not respond to any phone calls. Finally, the security guard at the service station said he knew of a lady nearby who might be of some help. The woman agreed to let the two teachers and forty students use three small rooms, but they needed the mattresses from the bus that were in a locked compartment. More phone calls yielded nothing. Finally, a text message was sent, and the conductor came and unlocked the storage area. Sr. Anita Marie recalled that they were so close in the small rooms that the girl next to her hit her in the face several times when she moved during the night. But all were most grateful for the night's lodging.

That did not conclude the adventure. In the morning, one of the girls passed by a dumpster on the way to the latrine and was bitten by a monkey. No matter where the sisters went, there were always stories to tell.

VISITING DAYS AND PARENT CONFERENCES

Students at St. Julie Primary and Notre Dame Academy Secondary enjoyed visiting days during each of the three school terms. These visits were often combined with parent-teacher conferences.

Great anticipation surrounded the visiting day as well as a certain sadness on the part of children who had no visitors. Groups of students congregated in the primary and secondary areas and waited excitedly for the arrival of parents, sponsors, or guardians. Families often brought treats: sweeties (candy), sodas, clothes, and funds that students could use for canteen purchases during the next months.

Faculty and parents assembled about 11:00 a.m. for information about the calendar and the school program. It was also an opportunity for parents to ask questions. By noon the house was packed, and the meeting usually ended by 2:30 p.m. Individual parent-teacher conferences followed. In many cases the students had to translate since the teacher and parent did not share a common language.

A REGISTERED SCHOOL

It is no small feat to complete the process of registration of the school. Normally one full year is required between licensing and registration, and as far as officials are concerned, there is no rush to complete the forms and receive approbation. The sisters wanted to establish Notre Dame Academy as a testing center so that the S-4 girls could sit for their leaving exams in Buseesa and not have to travel to some other center. Many trips to the district offices in Kibaale as well as to the ministry of education in Kampala were needed to complete the elaborate process required for registration. There were always many problems and delays in getting the needed signatures, stamps, and forms. But all was finally completed one week before the deadline.

On March 9, 2006, Notre Dame Academy was licensed and registered as a senior secondary school in Uganda. This made it possible to apply for the Universal Certificate of Education (UCE) testing center status. The paperwork was completed in a timely manner, and the sisters were assured that they would be in the first cycle of inspections for the 2006 school year. The inspectors were scheduled to arrive sometime within the first two weeks of April. These days came and went without any inspectors.

In May the inspectors arrived. They informed the sisters that the teachers' credentials were not adequate and the school could not become a testing center. It did not seem to matter that the teachers' credentials had been checked and accepted by the ministry of education and sports only a few months before. The inspectors did, however, have some suggestions as to how to rectify the situation. With Sr. Mary Rita in the United States for a home visit, Sr. Anita Marie spent a very harrowing three weeks contacting teachers, tracking down documents, making trips to Kampala, and praying unceasingly.

Approval for the license for the testing center finally came through on May 19, 2006. Through a radio announcement, Sister had to gather all the S-4 girls who were home for their holiday, and get them registered for the exams. With only two days to spare before the final deadline for the 2006 testing, Sister hand carried the forms to Kampala. Some were initially rejected because of their cursive signatures, but eventually all twenty girls' applications were accepted.

SPIRITUAL DEVELOPMENT

LIVING ROSARY   On October 7, the living rosary was prayed with the Notre Dame Academy students, the staff, and even some of the garden workers who stopped to join the group gathered under the large mango tree. It was a touching sight as each group completed its Hail Mary and brought flowers to place at the foot of the statue of Mary as a token of love and devotion. Since Mary was patroness of Notre Dame Academy under the title of Our Lady of the Rosary, this day and its accompanying prayer ritual, became an annual event.

RETREATS AND SHARING ACROSS THE CONTINENTS   The retreat shared between Notre Dame Academy, Covington, Kentucky, and Notre Dame Academy, Buseesa, began in 2002. The retreats were an attempt to help the girls step back from the busyness of their everyday lives as students and look at what really mattered in life. The retreat bridged the continents and highlighted the fact that secondary students across the world had many of the same desires, hopes, and dreams. The retreats concentrated on those things that unite us.

The girls in both schools had been paired and had written letters about themselves and their lives to their "sister." Part of each retreat was the sharing of letters the girls had received from their "sisters."

The shared retreat went beyond what would ordinarily be called a retreat. One year a main emphasis was on getting to know each other's culture. Names were of great interest to girls on both sides of the Atlantic. The girls made posters with their name and the name of their partner on the other side of the globe. Another year, girls in Covington made prayer beads, and the girls in Buseesa made small offering baskets for their partners.

Food is of central importance to teenagers, so an attempt was made to prepare and enjoy the food of the others' country. This was met with mixed reviews. Some in America loved posho and beans, and others hated them. Jell-O in Uganda was viewed suspiciously.

In 2005, the girls were given journals and encouraged to use them for prayerful reflection. The next year journal writing continued with more direct questions for reflection. The girls were encouraged to share some of this with their sister partner when they again wrote to her.

In 2014, the two schools shared a joint activity day. Students in each school showed some aspect of their lives. A film showed life at Notre Dame Academy in Covington. In Uganda, one of the Engineers Without Borders filmed the event in Buseesa. S-1 students displayed the garden they had planted in agriculture class. S-2 students demonstrated how to make banana fiber dolls while S-3 students made paper beads and fashioned jewelry from them. S-4 students in full costume did a traditional dance. Students in both schools wrote letters to their sisters. Students at Notre Dame Academy in Covington had sent scrapbooks to Uganda featuring their school and families.

CHARISMATIC RETREATS   In addition to providing the joint retreat with Notre Dame Academy in Covington the students in Buseesa experienced a retreat with the Emmanuel Community, a charismatic group from Hoima. Two young lay persons spent three days with the girls talking about being a Catholic Christian. Both the young man and the young woman modeled beautifully what it meant to be on fire with the love of God. Continuously these leaders reminded the students "God is good, all the time." This mantra that the girls enjoyed chanting expressed completely the message of our spiritual mother, St. Julie. It was truly a time of spiritual renewal for all involved.

In the following years, leaders from the charismatic group led the retreat. One year after a talk on the sacrament of Reconciliation, the girls had the opportunity to celebrate the sacrament. These retreats were always a time of special blessings.

SEMINARS AND EXAMS

SEMINARS   Each Saturday evening, the senior secondary girls held an internal seminar on one of the ten testable subjects studied. These become excellent skill-building opportunities.

A refinement and upgrade of this process took place when the history and commerce teachers arranged the external seminar in their disciplines. This meant inviting students from surrounding secondary schools to participate in the Saturday process. Students from all the local schools prepared and presented specific, assigned questions covered in the respective syllabus. All the students were encouraged to supplement, comment, and debate specific points. In 2007, 153 students accepted the invitation to attend the history seminar. Only thirty-five students attended the commerce seminar. Nevertheless, both were a valuable experience for everyone attending.

MOCK EXAMS Because the Ugandan system of education was so test-based, it was imperative that both St. Julie Primary and Notre Dame Academy Secondary arrange for and administer practice exams in preparation for the Primary Leaving Exams (PLE) for the primary and the Universal Certificate of Education (UCE) for the secondary.

In preparation for these tests, the teachers at Notre Dame Academy administered two practice exams, called mock exams, each of which extended over two weeks. Teachers from other districts corrected and graded both of these exams. The results gave students an idea of how they would perform on the national exams.

Notre Dame Academy scheduled two sets of external mock exams. One set of mock exams was sponsored by the Mityana Diocese. Later, these students participated in the UPISSA exams (Uganda Private Independent Secondary School Association).

The students were very serious about the mock exams and benefited from the practice sessions. The exams were a good preparation for the big exams in November.

In 2007, nine teachers from Notre Dame Academy traveled to another secondary school to mark the UPISSA mock exams. An estimated forty schools took part in this exercise. Approximately three hundred teachers graded the papers. Marking began on Monday, and the last group, chemistry, finished on Saturday.

LEAVING EXAMS–A HARROWING EXPERIENCE The Universal Certificate of Education (UCE) for S-4 and the Primary Leaving Exam (PLE) for P-7 were harrowing experiences. The secondary tests (UCE) were based on a student's entire eleven years of education. Students spent much time studying and preparing for these exams, for on their results rested the individual's opportunity for further study as well as the overall success and reputation of the school. The entire month-long nationwide testing schedule extended from mid-October to mid-November.

The process of the UCE for the S-4 candidates began with a three-hour briefing on the testing manual. This was followed by several weeks of testing. Each day, three times a day, the head teacher was required to drive to the Kibaale police headquarters to secure the tests. At 8:00 a.m., a police officer unlocked the official, double-padlocked truck in which were stored the morning tests. These were sealed in plastic envelopes, securely wrapped in heavy brown paper, and marked with the name of the specific test and the date and time of testing. Once the head teacher had signed for the parcel, attesting to the fact that it had not been tampered with, he or she was free to take it to the respective center. This process was repeated at noon when the morning tests were returned and the afternoon tests were given out and then returned after the afternoon testing.

Every student was required to take ten tests. English language, mathematics, biology, chemistry, physics, and agriculture are required. Most of these subjects have more than one session of testing. The other four exams are electives.

The testing room was set up according to precise specifications: There had to be 1.2 meters between each desk; there could be no written materials in sight (all charts, maps, and the like, had to be removed from the room); seats had to be assigned and a card with the student name and UCE number had to be attached to the desk; the room had to be locked when not in use for testing.

Before students were admitted into the examination room, their student identity card was checked, they were searched for any possible writing on their bodies or concealed cheat sheets, and seats were then assigned. Seats were changed with every test.

Investigators were assigned to a specific center to monitor the tests and to make sure that the regulations were followed to the letter. There was also a scout who was to show up unannounced at the testing center from time to time to make sure all were doing their jobs.

EXAMINATION RESULTS   Each year the parents, teachers, and students waited with great expectancy for the results of the UCE testing, which were expected to be announced by the end of January or early February.

The results for the students were given in five divisions, with Division 1 being the highest and Division 5 being the lowest. The results of some years' testing are as follows:

2009	11 students in Division 1	2010	13 students in Division 1
	14 students in Division 2		19 students in Division 2
2011	12 students in Division 1	2013	19 students in Division 1
	15 students in Division 2		19 students in Division 2

In its years of UCE testing, Notre Dame Academy scored in the top one hundred out of over two thousand secondary schools nationally. Undoubtedly, the goal of the teachers, parents, and students was being attained. The sisters heard good reports from the community and from the students attending A-level schools (Advanced secondary level of S-5 and S-6).

DEBATE TEAM

Notre Dame Academy was invited to participate in a debate—the topic being on whether Kenya, Uganda, and Tanzania should form a federation. (Actually, the competition's goal was to see how well the participants knew English.) Eight schools participated. There were to be five student speakers; eight more students could come as observers, as well as two teachers. The team left about 10:00 a.m. and returned about 6:00 p.m.

As the taxi returned to the school, there were shouts and joyous cries. The sisters rejoiced to find out that Notre Dame Academy finished FIRST in the competition! All were proud of the students and the school. Students at St. Julie Primary were also proud, for it was in these classrooms that the students had begun their study of English. The school won a very nice world wall map, and the students' prizes were copybooks or math kits.

NETBALL TEAM

On March 20, 2004, Sr. Mary Rita had received a letter announcing a meeting for the district athletic competition that the Notre Dame Academy girls were expected to participate in on March 26. The school was scheduled for a netball contest (similar to basketball in the USA) on the following Friday. This necessitated quite a bit of scrambling and a great amount of hard work. A team of fourteen girls was quickly organized, and they practiced daily. The team placed second in the first competition but did not fare well at the next level. All at the school were proud of them for their effort, cooperation, and sportsmanship.

In 2015, the netball team was successful at the local and zone levels. Unfortunately, on the way to Masindi for the regional level, the truck transporting the team suffered a broken axle. The girls had to find alternate transport to Masindi and home after the matches. The team succeeded in obtaining fourth place, an excellent showing for such a small school. (Sisters of Notre Dame, Buseesa Annals, March 25-28, 2014)

THE WEEKEND IN A BOARDING SCHOOL

The girls debated on Friday night. Even though it was a required activity, the girls really enjoyed it and got very spirited and even passionate in their discussions. On Saturday, a large part of the girls' time was taken up with housework around the compound, work-study jobs, and personal care. The girls washed their own clothes and cut one another's hair.

Each Saturday there was a testing program that lasted about three hours. The girls took two one-and-a-half hour tests in the afternoon. This was done in the secondary schools all over Uganda. It was one of the many ways to prepare the students for the S-4 leaving exams. The entire educational system was structured around these tests. On Saturday night each dorm took a turn planning an activity. There was singing and dancing, or card games, or a short play.

On Friday and Saturday, the lights were out by 11:00; on weekday nights, it was 10:30.

On Sunday, Mass was either in the church or in the multipurpose room at the school. If no priest was available, a communion service was held. The students were free the remainder of the morning. There was a supervised study in the afternoon for those who needed to catch up in their studies. All were encouraged to come; those who were falling behind, for whatever reason, were required to be there.

CANTEEN   The tiny, basement store located below the dining hall was a favorite of all ages, not only students, but teachers and farm workers as well. Here, for very reasonable prices, one could purchase everything from pencils to toothpaste, razor blades, jerry cans, flip-flops, and bath soap. The sisters purchased these items in Kampala on their periodic trips for supplies and sold them at cost to those who otherwise had no place to obtain them.

When the outdoor gong was struck, announcing the opening of the canteen door, the sisters and student helpers who staffed the store prepared for an onslaught. Keeping order in the line was an almost impossible task, as each wanted to be first to select items or just be there to see what others were purchasing. The wobbly table that served as the store's counter was constantly in danger of collapse as students pushed, leaned, and hung on to it. "Canteen" was a joyous word around St. Julie's, perhaps a little less so for those whose job it was to stock, keep order, clean, and sell the myriad items.

WORLD YOUTH DAY

An unimaginable surprise arrived from the Liebfrauenschule, a secondary school in Mülhausen, Germany. In 2005, five girls from Notre Dame Academy, Buseesa, were invited to come to Germany for World Youth Day in Cologne! The trip would include two additional weeks where the girls would have the opportunity to visit Notre Dame ministries in Germany.

In order to be eligible, the girls had to be at least seventeen years old. They were to write an essay about why they would like to be chosen as a Notre Dame Academy representative at this event. The consent and support of their parents who would have to pay for the required travel documents, was also required. When the twenty essays were completed, all the sisters voted on them, also taking into consideration their knowledge of these girls.

The five lucky winners set off on the evening of August 8, accompanied by two German volunteers who were returning home after a year of service at the mission. Everything was new and exciting for the Ugandan girls.

The first week spent with German families was eye-opening. The second week at the conference was overwhelming and filled with a powerful sense of the church and world youth. During the last week the girls visited the convents and the various ministries of the sisters. All returned with deep gratitude for this once-in-a-lifetime opportunity.

ST. PETER SECONDARY SCHOOL, BUSEESA (FOR BOYS)

With the building of Notre Dame Academy Secondary School for girls, the sisters were frequently asked, "What about the boys?" There are secondary schools for boys in other areas, but until recently, there were none in the Buseesa area.

Several years ago, when Fr. Francis Komakech was pastor of the Buseesa parish, he began St. Peter's Secondary School for boys. He hoped that this secondary school could meet the needs of boys in the area who had probably attended Buseesa Primary and could not afford to pay the significant school fees other secondary schools charged. In 2006, St. Peter's had six students enrolled in S-3, twenty-four students in S-2, and thirty-one students in S-1. During the third term of that year, the school fell on hard times, and the majority of its teachers left the school.

The head teacher, as well as Buseesa's new pastor, Fr. Paul Tusiimi, petitioned the sisters in Buseesa to take over some of the vacant positions. After discernment, several sisters decided to share their skills until the end of the academic year as a gesture of good will and service to the broader community. Several lay teachers from Notre Dame Academy also expressed the desire to supplement their salaries by teaching part-time at St. Peter's. The students of St. Peter's who had been without teachers for weeks, welcomed as volunteers, Sr. Mary Judith, Sr. Anita Marie, Sr. Maria Bernarde, and Sr. Mary Rita.

Teaching at St. Peter's was a unique experience. The classrooms were completely bare except for a few roughly built student desks and a blackboard. There was no teacher desk or chair, no chalk, no surface on which to put any supplies. But the students were quite eager to learn. Despite an extremely poor background, they wanted education.

Every teaching device, be it only a stapler or ruler, was a curiosity and received attention, sometimes too much. The students covered a broad age range with some of the S-3 students looking like they might be about twenty years old. In these first years, the odds were certainly against success.

APRIL FOOL'S DAY UGANDA STYLE

The ringing of the doorbell very early in the morning caught everyone's attention. When the door was opened, a student explained that there had been a robbery, and some of the construction supplies had been stolen during the night. Sr. Mary Rita, Sr. Mary Judith, and Sr. Anita Marie ran down the road to the school to see what the loss might be. When they arrived, they were surprised to see the girls looking through dorm windows to watch what was happening. They paused, and the culprit looked at the sisters, smiled, and announced, "April Fool!" The sisters were much happier to have been fooled than robbed.

Women carrying bean plants from the garden

TOP Sunday Mass at Uganda Martyrs parish church MIDDLE Sr. Mary Teopista leading a communion service at an outstation BOTTOM Palm Sunday, a little like Jesus' time

TOP Women at an outdoor Mass MIDDLE Sisters in convent chapel (front) Sr. Cristina Marie, Sr. Mary Rita, Sr. Anita Marie, Sr. Mary Judith, Sr. Mary Juliet; (rear) Sr. Maria Bernarde, Sr. Mary Janet, Sr. Mary Delrita, Sr. Mary Rozaria BOTTOM Sr. Jane Marie, Sr. Mary Delrita, Sr. Mary Janet, and Sr. Mary Annette (seated) at the cathedral in Hoima

TOP Sr. Mary Juliet with children in the nursery school at Buseesa MIDDLE Local family by their home.
Christopher is second from the left in the front (Chapter 6). BOTTOM Sr. Mary Sunday and nursery school students

SISTERS WHO SERVED AS HEAD TEACHER AT ST. JULIE PRIMARY SCHOOL
TOP Sr. Mary Colette and students MIDDLE LEFT Sr. Jane Marie MIDDLE RIGHT Sr. Cristina Marie
BOTTOM Sr. Mary Paulynne with her math students

TOP Sr. Mary Judith, Sr. Mary Rita, Sr. Anita Marie (seated)
MIDDLE Notre Dame Academy classroom building BOTTOM NDA students studying

TOP Notre Dame Academy classroom
MIDDLE Sr. Mary Judith with science class in lab
BOTTOM Sr. Anita Marie with students in computer room

SISTERS WHO SERVED AS FORMATION DIRECTOR:
TOP Sr. Mary Delrita and Sr. Antoinette Marie with postulants MIDDLE Sr. Mary Annete and candidates
BOTTOM LEFT Sr. Mary Immaculate, first Ugandan to profess vows as a Sister of Notre Dame
BOTTOM RIGHT Sr. Mary Colette

TOP LEFT Sr. Marla (former provincial superior, Covington, Kentucky) TOP RIGHT Sr. Mary Sujita (former superior general) MIDDLE (front) Sr. Mary Juliet, Sr. Mary Kristin (superior general), Sr. Therese Marie, Sr. Mary Sunday; (rear) Sr. Mary Immaculate, Sr. Mary Shauna (former provincial superior, Covington, Kentucky), Sr. Mary Rozaria BOTTOM LEFT Sr. Mary Anncarla (provincial superior, Thousand Oaks, California) BOTTOM MIDDLE Sr. Mary Ethel (provincial superior, Covington, Kentucky) BOTTOM RIGHT Sr. Birgett Marie (former provincial superior, Germany)

10

ST. JULIE SCHOOL CONTINUES TO GROW

Life at St. Julie Primary Boarding School was never dull. There were always new discoveries about students, about the culture, and about rules and regulations regarding education in Uganda. In the second year, and in each ensuing year, another grade level of students was added until St. Julie School included levels P-3 through P-7. After some years, P-1 and P-2 were added. As the number of students and classrooms increased and changed, so did many other aspects of the school.

CONSTRUCTION

After considerable communication with the district administrator's office, it was agreed that a bulldozer would come to prepare an area of the field to be used as a regular track for the children. Many months passed, and then without notice the bulldozer arrived, and the job proved to be a challenging adventure for several reasons. It was the rainy season and the project involved (1) picking up the driver and returning him to his village at the end of the day; (2) getting ten jerry cans of fuel to be used each day.

After about a week, the bulldozer had to return to the district officer even though the job was incomplete and incorrect. A kind of grass that does not have to be slashed and cut was planted. This enhanced the area and prevented erosion.

It seemed that new classrooms and dorms were constantly needed and constructed. This required obtaining the needed information (building plans, projected costs) and submitting them for approval in the home provinces. Bricks, piles of sand, and workers dotted the school landscape.

In the summer of 2001, the chicken house was under roof and would soon be ready to receive the chickens. The next step would be to tear down the old chicken house to provide space for work to begin on the foundation of the new formation house. The multi-purpose building would be large and have a spacious area with a stage at one end.

The building would serve as a dining room, an assembly hall, a setting for welcomes and entertainment, and a worship space. Here school liturgies and other prayer gatherings could be held. In addition, when an event proved too large for the parish church, services could be conducted in the multi-purpose building.

During the December holidays, men from Hoima Construction were on site working to complete the dormitory that had been scheduled for completion on November 30, 2001. On February 5, the students arrived and occupied the new building. While the inside was complete and furnished with beds, the bathing facility and the outside work still remained to be completed.

REGISTRATION OF SCHOOL

For two years, the sisters were in contact with the District Inspector of Schools (DIS), the District Education Officer (DEO) and the District Health Officer (DHO) in order to become registered as a school in Uganda. After many attempts to get the DEO to visit, he finally arrived on November 23, 1998. He was pleased with what he observed and agreed to send the inspector of health to complete the visitation soon.

In June 1999, the DIS made an unexpected visit to check classrooms, enrollment, and basic construction in progress.

The next month, a Minister of Parliament came for a visit so that he could write with accuracy his letter of recommendation for St. Julie School's registration.

> He was absolutely delighted with all that he saw and experienced with the children. After he spoke with the children, he stated that he was amazed that they could hold a conversation with him in English. (Sisters of Notre Dame Buseesa Annals, July 19, 1999)

Sr. Jane Marie had been reminding the Bishop "almost to the point of embarrassment" about getting a copy of the land title, which was all they were lacking to submit the application for registration. The following week a notice in the newspaper indicated the deadline for application for school registration for private schools was December 30, 1999. If the school was not registered, it could not open its doors in 2000. Opening without the registration made one liable to prosecution! A call to the Bishop resulted in the Bishop stating that he would write a letter that had been an acceptable procedure in the past, and send it with his driver the next day. When the driver arrived with the letter Sr. Mary Janet and Sr. Jane Marie took the completed packet of information (in triplicate) to the office of the DIS. He was not in! The assistant DEO took the packet and said all was in order and he would track down the inspector.

Sr. Jane Marie had asked the Bishop if he thought they should open as scheduled, and he replied in the affirmative. She then asked him if she were then arrested, would he come to get her out of jail. He laughed and said that would not happen.

Sr. Jane Marie had sent a letter to the Ministry of Education in Kampala and related all they had done to pursue registration. There was still no word about the application.

A notice then appeared in the newspaper that the deadline for application for registration had been extended to January 20, 2000.

With only a day away from being officially registered as a private school, the sisters became aware that certain papers were still missing. The Bishop was informed and sent Fr. Peter to help the sisters. After Fr. Peter signed a few contracts for the sisters, the sisters began a four-hour trip around Kibaale looking for the (DHO) to see if he had completed his report. He was nowhere to be found. His assistant came to the school for the inspection. Father Peter took the report to the Bishop who would take it to Kampala the next day.

On November 19, 2001, came the good news:

> We now have within our possession the official registration/license to operate a primary boarding school in Uganda. … This means that we can have our children stay at our school for that famous leaving exam next year. Without the license we would have to register for the test at Buseesa Primary. (Sr. Jane Marie to Sr. Mary Amy, Sr. Mary Shauna, and Sr. Mary Kristin, November 19, 2001)

SCHOOL STAFF

As a grade level was added each year, more teaching staff was needed. Sr. Maria Bernarde Derichswiler, who came from Germany in 2000, assisted in the upper primary grades and prepared students for the music competitions. Sr. Mary Paulynne Tubick from Thousand Oaks, California, arrived in 2001 and served as teacher and later as head teacher. In 2002, Sr. Mary Karlene Seech from the Chardon, Ohio, province came and served as teacher in P- 4. In 2004, Sr. Mary Colette Theobald arrived from Thousand Oaks, California. During her many years in Uganda, Sister served as teacher, head teacher, and director of the young Ugandan sisters in formation. Sr. Mary Ruthilde, from Germany, came in 2007 to assist in the library and in St. Julie School. Later, Sister was one of the first sisters to take up residence in Mpala. In 2010, Sr. Christina Marie Buczkowski from Thousand Oaks, California, was assigned the position of head teacher at St. Julie Primary. As the Ugandan sisters became certified, they assumed responsibility in the classroom. In addition, many Ugandan teachers taught students in various levels in the school. When volunteers from Germany and the United States arrived, many of them assisted in the classroom, and at times taught classes, thus assisting the classroom teachers.

DIFFICULT JOB

Every principal has moments that she will never forget. Sr. Jane Marie wrote to Sr. Mary Janet who was visiting in the United States. Sister explained that the father of a student boarded a taxi from his home heading to Kampala to buy some goods for his shop. On the way the taxi was attacked by robbers. They shot the father and stole the taxi. The father died a short time later. Sr. Jane Marie continued:

> So, now I had to tell Namale that her father was killed by robbers. She sobbed on my shoulder and I just hugged her and spoke softly to her about how her father was a good man, he loved his family and was good to them and that he is now with Jesus … he has no pain. I tell you Janet I really do not like having to give this type of news to the children. (Sr. Jane Marie to Sr. Mary Janet, June 24, 2002)

CURRICULUM

In 2000, the sisters obtained three copies of the new Ugandan Primary Curriculum. They couldn't believe it: They were expected to teach business education and entrepreneurism two periods a week in each grade beginning in P-1! Agriculture was to be taught four periods weekly in each grade!

TRADITIONAL ART   One of the Ugandans taught the children traditional art which included broom-making (out of twigs and grasses) and the weaving of mats (from grasses) and baskets (from long strands of banana fiber cut from the main stem of the banana leaves), all useful skills for everyday living. One sister said that she got a jolt when she saw the way even young children handled knives to do everyday chores. Native singing and dancing were also part of the curriculum.

PEN PALS   There were often requests from individuals and schools in the United States to have pen pals in Buseesa. Many advantages support such an endeavor. But sometimes those in the USA failed to realize that the project required the students to write in a second language and to write in a format with which they were not familiar. Probably none of the students had ever seen a letter. There was also the challenge of what to write in the letter. Sr. Mary Janet wrote, "Pen pal letters are killing us. … we need as much time as possible for class."

CULTURAL STORY   One of the reading texts used in the classroom contained a story about Halloween. Having no idea about this unusual day, the children asked many questions. Sr. Jane Marie did her best to explain the custom celebrated in the United States. The reading lesson ended, but the idea remained in the minds of some students.

Months later on October 31, the bell at the convent was pulled, and voices rang out, "Trick or Treat! Trick or Treat!" Upon opening the door, the sisters discovered some students in their Halloween costumes. They had smeared ashes over their faces and had taken branches from trees and had them sticking out all over them. These students definitely deserved a treat, a "sweetie" – a piece of candy.

MAKE-BELIEVE

In a country where the harsh realities of war are not far from the minds of the adults, the realm of the imagination has more or less been extinguished. One of the greatest challenges for the sisters was to introduce the children to the wonderful magic of "Once upon a time."

As a special reward for bonus points earned in the first term, the school community was to view the movie, *The Lion King*. To prepare for the great event both grades enjoyed the story during the literature period.

> We somehow were able to fit seventy-six students and seventeen staff members in the sunroom at the convent, where we all viewed the feature-length cartoon on a thirteen-inch television screen. … The following day Sister Jane received two reminders that we need to work to introduce the world of make-believe. She asked our main gardener how he had enjoyed the film. "Very much," was the reply, and it was immediately followed by the question, "In America, do they have special places where they teach the animals to speak English?" Another worker commented, "I was amazed to find the animals speaking English and we could understand them!" (Your Uganda Four to sisters, families, and friends, June 13, 1999)

PRIMARY LEAVING EXAMS (PLE)

Students completing P-7 (the last primary grade) took the national Primary Leaving Exams (PLE) to determine their eligibility for secondary school. For those who failed, their education ended at P-7. The several tests were administered over two consecutive days at test centers determined by the government.

The first experience of these tests was in 2002. The days were filled with excitement and nervous tension. St. Julie students would take the PLE. Everyone in the district was looking to see how the St. Julie students would perform. The exam was taken at Buseesa Primary School, and only the head teacher was permitted to be present. There were strict rules to follow prior to entering the testing site. Sr. Maria

Bernarde, the P-7 class teacher, walked the students to the testing site encouraging them along the way. All the other students prayed that the students would do well on the tests.

The the following years some of the anxiety was diminished somewhat in regard to procedures, but the PLE continued to put an enormous pressure on students and teachers alike. The results of the testing were not released until January, right before the new academic year. The test scores were given in levels. Level 1 was the highest, and Level 5 was the lowest. The St. Julie students generally scored in Level 1 and Level 2, the highest ratings. One year, three students scored in Level 3: all girls who had failed the math section. This alerted the staff to the need to work more with students in this area. The secondary school began to put more emphasis here also. Students, parents, and teachers were proud of the accomplishment of these primary students.

| 2007 | 7 Division 1 | 2009 | 11 Division 1 | 2011 | 3 Division 1 |
| | 9 Division 2 | | 17 Division 2 | | 19 Division 2 |

One year at the end of January, an announcement was made on the radio that head teachers were to come to the Kibaale District office at 10:00 a.m. to pick up the PLE results. Because of the parish Mass, the sisters did not arrive until noon, where they found a group of head teachers who had been waiting. The offices were locked and no one was around. After waiting a while, they went to Karaguuza to find the person in charge of distributing the results. Upon finding his house they learned that he had gone to town. The group moved to the market area, and after a further search, they finally found the person.

For the first time in 2004, St. Julie Primary School was asked to serve as a testing center for the primary leaving exams. This required some adjustment of rooms and furniture at the school, but the convenience of not having to travel elsewhere to test compensated for this.

LOVE OF MUSIC AND MUSIC COMPETITIONS

Music is such an integral part of life in Uganda, that within two months of the school's beginning, two men were engaged to teach drumming and dancing to the students. Father Peter, a former pastor, had purchased three sets of *ebinyeges* for the boys. The girls used bath towels around their waists for their part of the costume of the native dance. In June a set of four drums was purchased from a local village drum maker. Performances, celebrations, and welcomes could now be accompanied by drums and dancing.

When it was Sr. Mary Annete's turn to teach music, she instituted a rhythm band. Musical instruments consisted of triangles made of mango juice cans with pencils to strike the cans, rattles made of bottles filled with beans, and cymbals made from pieces of pipe. In a short time, the students were performing skillfully to recorded music.

MUSIC COMPETITION   Music competitions were a greatly anticipated event each year. Sr. Maria Bernarde and others worked for months preparing. The students loved to sing and dance, so all the preparation was a happy experience for them. Competition began on the local level; winners advanced to the district and then national levels.

At one competition, there were seven types of presentations included in the primary level. The dramas and traditional dances required costumes and props. Fabric was purchased, and one of the matrons sewed many, many gomesi dresses (traditional dress of the Ugandan women) and other required costumes. Later, it was discovered that the addition of monkey skins added points to a presentation in the traditional numbers. Because of their cost, the sisters did not purchase any skins. Had the sisters known earlier about the additional points, they could have had ten monkey skins for free from the official they hired to shoot the monkeys who were eating the farm crops. The colobus monkeys have long black hair with streaks of white and long graceful tails. The boys performing in the traditional numbers wore grass skirts over their shorts, *ebinyeges* tied on their legs, and monkey skins around their bare backs and shoulders.

The competition included playing traditional instruments, sight-reading, and singing from the Ugandan music notation. Drums were most important and were featured in almost every number. A homemade xylophone was utilized for some of the "melody." The sisters heard the unending sounds of these instruments from both St. Julie Primary and Buseesa Primary from June through August. Sometimes the drumming started as early as 7:00 a.m. and extended until almost 10:00 p.m. Throughout the preparation and competition, the children demonstrated earnest enthusiasm and boundless energy.

For one competition, the pick-up truck and the Land Rover transported the students, teachers, all necessary materials, including jerry cans of water, and barrels of rice and cabbage for lunch. What was to have begun at 9:00 a.m. got underway about 12:30 p.m. as the judges failed to come on time. Since seven schools were to present seven acts each, there were forty-nine presentations, none of which were short and simple. The dramas and dances were especially long and elaborate.

By 6:00 p.m., the sisters became concerned because in one hour it would be dark, very dark. There was no electricity, nor did they think to bring flashlights. The very poor mud classroom assigned to the students was strewn with the students' costumes, props, shoes, clothes, and barrels with food they had brought. The sisters directed the children to find their things while the light lasted. All struggled to pack up and load the pick-up truck with what they could at that point. By 7:00 p.m., the place was dark.

The last number of the competition was not completed until about 9:30 p.m., and the results had yet to be announced. The students were thrilled to receive a second-place rank. They had to make three trips with the pick-up and one with the Land Cruiser to get everyone and everything back to Buseesa with the last group arriving after 11:00 p.m.

A year later, the students at St. Julie School successfully competed in the Ugandan Annual Music Festival, a nation-wide event involving all schools throughout the country. Practice was taken seriously. The students practiced every free minute, keeping Sr. Marie Bernarde and Noeline very busy. The Western Song was greatly improving, and finally, the students were able to sing the entire song.

An update about the progress followed two weeks later:

> Next Wednesday is the fine arts competition. This year St. Julie is hosting the event. Sister Barnarde is working very hard on this, and we should do well. …
> The children are learning a required German folk song in five voices. Quite a challenge, but the kids seem up for it, and Bernarde is determined that they WILL do well. There is also competition in native dance, native instruments, drama, and speech. (Sr. Mary Rachel, Sr. Mary Rita, Sr. Anita Marie to Sr. Mary Shauna, July 7, 2002)

Finally, the results came:

> It was a wonderful experience … just watching and hearing all the traditional dancing, drama, and music. Typically, the day was scheduled to begin at 9:00 a.m. and actually started at 12:50 p.m. … It was a very long day, but we did win the competition and have advanced to the next level that no one knows when it is. (Sr. Mary Rachel, Sr. Mary Rita, Sr. Anita Marie to Sr. Mary Shauna, July 12, 2002)

St. Julie students performed well at the county level and achieved first place. At the district level, the students were awarded first place. In the following years, the St. Julie students continued to perform well and often achieved first place.

ATHLETIC COMPETITION

Annually, the schools in the Buseesa area come together to demonstrate their athletic skills in track and field events. The children of St. Julie School participated for the first time in 2001. Ten schools participated in the events that began around 11:00 a.m. The entire student body of St. Julie participated by either competing or cheering their schoolmates on to victory. The lunch break scheduled for noon took place at 3:00 p.m. The games resumed around 4:00 p.m. and concluded around 7:30 p.m. One of the St. Julie students placed first in discus. Buseesa Primary School placed first; St. Julie came in seventh.

SCHOOL LIBRARY

Over the years, the library has been one of the children's favorite places.

> Some of the students are seemingly insatiable. They are full of questions and look for books and information on all the topics they talk about in their classes. Recess time or their library class time they hurry in, "Sister, where is the book of … ?" (Reflection: Sr. Mary Delrita, about 2003)

When Sr. Regina, an education professor from Notre Dame College in Cleveland, Ohio, visited the mission, she wrote:

> One of the wisest decisions these sisters made was to begin a library. Sr. Delrita should receive some sort of Library Association Award for what she has done here. All the books are donated by friends of the mission … all neatly catalogued and shelved. These children eagerly examine books about concepts that are totally unimaginable to them. They are filled with questions all the time—about sea animals, airplanes (only one has flown over us since I've been here) about buildings with more than one floor, etc. … Basemira—a child who is just learning the basics in English—asked me to find her a book "about take-away."

> The only book we had contained only a few pictures showing subtraction, but I thought they would disappear under all the pointing and rubbing they got from Basemira's determined fingers. What is so thrilling is the fact that this youngster like all the rest, now knows that the library can answer their questions. I have never seen a library period in any American school that was so filled with such focused patrons! (Sr. Regina Alfonso to several persons, July 9, 2000)

SACRAMENTS

St. Julie School celebrated with its first Confirmation group in June 2000. Bishop Deogratias confirmed thirty-three students. Sr. Jane Marie had prepared the students well in their understanding of this sacrament.

First Reconciliation and First Communion were celebrated each year. Students were well prepared for these special moments. At other times the sacrament of

Reconciliation was offered for the sisters, staff members, and students. On one occasion the two priests from the parish provided such an opportunity late in the afternoon. It took three hours and concluded with Mass. By the time all was finished, it was dark except for the light from the candles on the altar and one dim solar lamp.

VISIT FROM THE KING

On April 4, 2005, a retired minister of the Church of Uganda informed Sr. Mary Janet that King Muwenda Mutebi II was expected to visit Kibaale, and that he wanted to visit the school. The King and Queen of the Bunyoro Kingdom were expected to visit St. Julie about noon on Monday. The sisters were to welcome them and their entourage of about 100 people and to serve lunch to all. Soda and beer were also to be served. This was quite a challenge because it was already Saturday and St. Julie's was expected to provide the meal and entertainment. Everyone at St. Julie Mission got busy, and Monday's school schedule was rearranged.

Monday twelve o'clock came; one o'clock, still no visitors were in sight. The decision was made to continue classes. About 1:30 p.m. the King's secretary drove up on a motorcycle and requested to see our arrangements. As the secretary looked it over, he commented how nice it was and then requested a small room where the royal couple could eat: The King does not eat in the presence of his subjects. Things were quickly rearranged and a place was set up in the staff room.

At 1:45 p.m., a noise was heard, and the motorcade zoomed into the compound. There were pick-up trucks with security guards, official drummers, vehicles with the royal couple and distinguished guests. The director informed the sisters that the King could only stay until 2:00 p.m. Totally frustrated, Sr. Mary Janet stated that it was already ten minutes to two. The faculty and students had prepared a meal and a program and their visitors were not going to leave in ten minutes!

The guards removed the mats and chairs that had been placed before the stage as thrones for the King and Queen. They replaced the mats with leopard skins and bark cloth. When the guests arrived, the special royal guards sat at each corner of the throne area. The royal couple took their seats, and speeches and the program took place. All was presented exceptionally well. The King was delighted! The King was presented with gifts. The official drummers and the guards then led the royal couple to the staff room for their meal. The other guests were served in the dining hall. The children all returned to classes.

About 3:30 the motorcade was organized and began to move along Buseesa Road. Later, the sisters received letters in which they were commended for all that was done to make the visit of the King successful.

NURSERY SCHOOL

To better prepare students for primary education, the parish had wanted a preschool, frequently referred to as a nursery school. This had been the desire for many years. Anne Marks, a former volunteer, took a particular interest in this effort and secured funding to build a structure that could be used for this purpose. At the time, the sisters were adamant that this was a parish project and not part of St. Julie Mission. The nursery that began outside under a tree was moved to Anne's house. For a variety of complex reasons, this did not work out. With a new director, the program was move to Fridah's house down the road. Unfortunately, Fridah, the former matron and farm worker at St. Julie's, was living away from Buseesa and did not know that her property was being rented to the parish for the nursery. When she sold the iron sheets and doors on her building, the nursery was left with no place to go.

In 2008, Sr. Mary Colette took pity on the pastor's plight and decided that a nursery school was merely an extension of the educational program already in place. She accepted the responsibility of housing this program and taking over its administration. The facility was first located in the room under the stage in the multi-purpose room, with an outside access on the ground level.

SPECIAL DAYS AT ST. JULIE SCHOOL

UGANDA MARTYRS DAY   This feast, celebrated on June 3, is a national holiday. The parish and its numerous outstations celebrate with an outdoor Mass near the burial site of Denis Kamuka and his wife.

One year, Mass was celebrated under a canopy of palm branches and shiny foil decorations. After Mass, an elder from the parish, Nakatura John, who knew Denis Kamuka personally, gave witness to his experiences and memories of the would-be-martyr.

One of the more memorable celebrations was 2005. As Nakatura John spoke of Denis' virtues, a large snake was seen at one side of the semi-circular group. Instantly a stampede of frightened children and adults rushed to the opposite side of the assembly. (Such is the fear of snakes.) Young children, adults, babies, and a mother and her newborn were knocked down and stepped on. Within two weeks, the newborn died.

In 2007 close to the end of Mass, some children were playing around the parish truck parked at the rear of the assembled worshipers. One of the children damaged the air valve on a tire, which resulted in a loud hissing sound like that of a snake. The sound frightened the crowd, causing a panic and, and as happened two years before, many ran knocking over benches and people. Sr. Mary Janet, Sr. Anita Marie, and Sr. Immaculate were knocked to the ground. No one was seriously hurt. Once again we were all made aware of the potential danger in such a crowd.

INTERNATIONAL WOMEN'S DAY   A remarkable feature of Ugandan life is the International Women's Day that is celebrated on March 9 as a national holiday. It is a free day for the children. Prior to this day, teachers have the opportunity to speak of how Jesus viewed women, why Mary is such a beautiful role model for men and women, and why every woman is worthy of respect. The role of women is very difficult in this culture, so anything that can be done to show appreciation and respect for women is a big step forward.

BUNYORO CULTURE AND TRADITIONS DAY   To help the students at St. Julie to have a better appreciation and love for their Bunyoro culture and traditions, Sr. Cristina Marie proposed to the teachers that a day be dedicated to the Bunyoro culture and traditions. The day was planned relying on the teachers' personal knowledge, and experience. Students from every class level spent two months preparing various programs to present to the entire school family.

The first Bunyoro Culture and Traditions Day began with a program presented by the nursery students. Even before their program began, the excellent costumes and props of the youngest class had already captured the attention of the students. Each class performed songs, dances, and/or plays. A special teatime snack concluded the day. The response to the day was overwhelmingly positive, and students as well as teachers asked for a Bunyoro Day every year.

OLYMPIAD   This was one of the special events at St. Julie in its first year. The event that began as a one-day contest grew to an event that was held between 10:00 a.m. and 1:00 p.m. on three consecutive days. Through the years, more national flags were added, a parade of the athletes was included, and additional types of events gradually made their way into the competition. As the enrollment grew, the students were divided according to age groups for fairer competition.

ANNUAL FUN/PLAY DAY   The day began after the morning assembly around the flagpole. The activities of the day were explained, and everyone moved to different activities such as musical chairs, sack races, parachute movement, and others. After the games, everyone received a prize. Following the activities, the children gathered in the sunroom of the convent to view a video such as *Pinocchio* or *Jungle Book*.

CLEANING DAY   On the day before departure, the students began the good cleaning of the dorms. They dragged their mattresses outside and placed them on the ground for a good airing. The students looked forward to this day because they loved jumping on the mattresses. They also cleaned their basins and jerry cans.

ST. JULIE DAY   Beginning in 1999, the last day of the school year became known as St. Julie Day. Generally, the Bishop came for Mass followed by an assembly with dramas, traditional song, dance, and musical instruments. In the ensuing years, various elements were eliminated or added: presentation of report cards, diplomas, certificates of attendance, a special meal, or a speech by the student council president. Each year parents joined in this special event and then transported their children home.

DEPARTURE DAY   The other children sat waiting for someone to come to take them home. Almost no children were within walking distance. Some children rode bicycles and others rode motorcycles. Often a taxi came for children who lived in the same village. The children packed into the vehicle, which absorbed more passengers than one would think possible.

ST. JULIE OLD STUDENT ASSOCIATION (JOSA)

On August 16, 2008, an association of former students of St. Julie School was inaugurated. Sr. Maria Bernarde had been most helpful to these graduates and to the new association. Several young men from the first class shared their dream of starting this association in order to help the school and to assist those who were former students. After several planning meetings, the former students gathered for the Mass. At the conclusion of the Mass, these former students stood, were recognized by Bishop Deogratias and took a pledge of dedication to their school. The name of the organization is St. Julie Old Student Association (JOSA). "Old students" is a common name for alumni from a school. It was heartening to see how former students have grown in their leadership and faith.

SISTERS' REMEMBRANCES

Sr. Maria Bernarde wrote:

> "The kids are cute, and I love to teach them although I can't get used to their speed of working: more than slow." Sister explained that it was difficult to learn the names of the students, but she was on her way. "And I am quite convinced that we can do a lot for these children and their future. They would not have many chances without us." (Sr. Maria Bernarde to Sr. Mary Laurence, August 10, 2001)

Sr. Mary Janet wrote:

> It is a joy for me to work with the children. Teaching is a struggle because of the lack of language skills and cultural differences. I want so much to open doors of opportunities for these children, to expand their vision, to enlarge their world. I pray that God will be with me and help me." (Sr. Mary Janet to Family and Friends, Nov 10, 1996)

Sr. Regina wrote:

> As the children were on their way to lunch, a few stopped in the library where I was preparing for tomorrow's seminar. Skovia asked me, "Are you the superior of the teachers?" "No," I told her. "I've just taught longer than the others." She asked, "How can you teach longer? You are short." (Sr. Regina is not very tall.) (Sr. Regina to Everybody, June 25, 2001)

One day some youngsters noticed that sister had some purple ballpoint pen marks on her wrists. Sister told them that the next time she washed her hands she would get the marks off. One helpful student suggested that sister put some saliva on the marks. The youngsters watched very attentively as Sister followed the advice. She heard one youngster say to another, "Even white people have saliva!" (Sr. Regina to Sisters at home, March 1, 2003)

From Sr. Anita Marie:

> Here's some interesting info … many of the kids love eating crickets … they are HUGE … they eat them dead or alive and sometimes cook them. The kids are afraid of chameleons because they believe they are poisonous. They also eat white ants. Well, I have not tried any of this diet yet! (Sr. Anita Marie to Sr. Maria Francine, December 7, 2002)

Although not common in the Kibaale District, elephants are found in Uganda

Pineapple is grown in the mission garden

11

MPALA: A SECOND MISSION SITE

In an undated letter to the sisters, Sr. Marla wrote about a visit to Uganda. Accompanied by a real estate agent, she and Sr. Mary Kristin visited several properties and houses near Kampala. The purpose in looking at property in this area was because of its closeness to universities where the young sisters could further their education.

During their stay in Kampala, the sisters met with Archbishop Emmanuel Wamala. They were seeking the Archbishop's approval to found a house in his diocese. He said that the sisters were most welcome, that he had heard very good reports about the school in Buseesa, and that he would assist the sisters in looking for property. The archdiocese had a land committee, and the sisters were to meet with an engineer from the committee. In visiting the property of Ssedugge Palino, the sisters found the land and buildings to fit what they wanted.

With a decision made, Sr. Mary Colette received the keys to the property in Mpala from Ssedugge Paulino. There had been a delay as it was necessary to find suitable security for the property, despite the fact that it is walled and gated. Sr. Mary Colette traveled again to Kampala to facilitate these arrangements and to install a maintenance worker as custodian. His responsibility included securing the property, maintaining the grounds, and caring for the house until there would be sisters living there.

The Mpala property consisted of about nine acres with two beautiful houses. It dropped off and was wooded with a wetland behind the house.

SISTERS TAKE UP RESIDENCE

Even before taking up full residence, sisters spent the night there after a day of business in Kampala or when picking up new arrivals from the airport.

It was a historic event as Sr. Mary Regina and Sr. Maria Ruthilde, accompanied by Sr. Mary Colette and others, left Buseesa to officially open the house in Mpala on April 27, 2009. The truck was packed with boxes, suitcases, and some furnishings from Sr. Julie Convent in Buseesa. Amid many farewells and good wishes, the sisters left for the trip to Lyamutundwe, usually called Mpala by the sisters. (Later, it would also be referred to as Notre Dame Education Center.) Two sisters rode with the driver, while Sr. Mary Colette and a few others sat in the back of the truck with all the furnishings. As if God were sending a special blessing on this new mission site, a heavy deluge of rain fell, not affecting the covered boxes and furniture, but drenching the passengers!

For the next week, Sr. Mary Colette, on holiday from school, remained with some sisters to assist in setting up the house. Numerous trips were made to Kampala to purchase items, such as a refrigerator, a stove, solar lights, and furniture. Purchasing food, cleaning the house, and arranging the furniture were other important tasks. With Sr. Mary Colette's guidance, the two sisters purchased mobile phones, set up a bank account, got a post office box, and began to familiarize themselves with the locality. (Sisters of Notre Dame Mpala Annals, March 27, 2009)

Originally the plan was to establish a house of studies and hospitality in the Kampala area. However, circumstances necessitated changing the Mpala site into a place of formation. Eventually the sisters would live in the newly constructed formation house, and the newly furnished house on the property would become a house of ministry.

After a short time, it became apparent that the formation program as envisioned would not work. Because of illness, Sr. Mary Regina returned to California, and Sr. Mary Ruthilde remained to engage in other ministries. With these changes, it became necessary to rethink and revamp the plan for Mpala.

In addition to the construction, attention was given to the garden and landscape of the property. Sr. Mary Janet and Sr. Mary Juliet came from Buseesa to begin work on establishing a garden. Some of the candidates assisted two workers in beautifying the grounds and growing bananas, cassava, sweet potatoes, Irish potatoes, tomatoes, pineapple, beans, green beans, and a few other crops. Through the years, the garden increased in size and in the variety of crops raised.

The new residence seemed to attract people. Visiting sisters helped in making curtains, setting up the kitchen, and cooking. There were also the volunteers who enjoyed a holiday in Kampala. Sisters preparing to take flight to their home provinces or to make purchases in Kampala often stayed at the house.

In June 2009, Sr. Mary Colette, Sr. Mary Ruthilde, and Sr. Mary Juliet became the Mpala community.

In the *Ugandan Newsletter,* May 2010, Sr. Colette described the progress on Notre Dame Education Center.

> Recently a covered walkway was installed. Some guestrooms, which were already on the property, are being refurbished, and a small road from the gate to our convent is being completed. A fence now surrounds the entire property. Recently three water collection tanks were installed. … Our promised April completion is long past and now July 1 is being proposed by the construction company. In addition to the construction, we are attempting to build up our garden and landscape the property.

In these initial weeks, the frequent sounds were those of the construction workers engaged in building the house of studies and the formation house. During the construction time, the sisters lived in the residential house on the property. Finally, on September 7, even though the entire structure was not completed, the sisters began moving into the new construction. The kitchen and dining section were still not finished, so the community had to go to the residential house for cooking and meals.

When the new construction in Mpala was complete, one important element was missing: the presence of the Blessed Sacrament in the chapel. After writing several letters to the Archdiocese of Kampala, making many phone calls, and extending invitations to Archdiocesan representatives, the sisters finally got approval to have the Blessed Sacrament in their convent home.

On June 21, 2010, the pastor of the nearby Queen of Virgins Parish in Kisubi, agreed to send priests to the convent each morning except Sunday to celebrate Mass for the sisters, aspirants and some neighbors. This was a great joy because for more than a year the sisters walked up a difficult road, took a public taxi, then walked further to attend Mass. The decision for the pastor was not easy. The priests were worn thin since there were more than twenty schools in the parish, and the priests offered Mass at least weekly at them. The sisters were fully aware of the special blessings God was bestowing on them.

Holy Week that year was a bit different for the sisters at Notre Dame Education Center. They and the aspirants attended all services at the chapel of the Brothers of Christian Instruction in Kisubi. Especially meaningful was the service of the stations of the cross in which pictures were nailed to the trees lining the road leading to the chapel. The service ended in the brothers' cemetery that had a life-size crucifix. The stations were a graphic way to remember what Jesus suffered for us. In 2015, the Annals described the posters portraying the stations with African faces and clothing.

PERSONNEL

Sr. Mary Sharan Hendricks from the Patna Province in India, arrived in Uganda on February 6, 2010. Sr. Mary Sharan assisted Sr. Mary Colette with the formation program. With her strong community spirit and her skills in teaching about prayer and Notre Dame life, she added much to the program. Sister prepared to return to India one year later.

An unfortunate surprise awaited sister her last evening in Mpala. She walked out the door of the dining room to go to her bedroom when a large rat jumped onto her skirt. She darted back into the dining room and jumped onto a chair. To see such athleticism from a woman of sister's age was a wonder to the whole community. The rat had followed sister in, and now all the sisters and candidates were shouting and trying to kill it. Finally, the rodent was chased away. This was surely a strange farewell for Sister.

July 28, 2015, was a sad day for the community when Sr. Maria Ruthilde returned to her home province in Germany. Sister had lived in Mpala since its opening in April 2009. Previously, sister had served in Buseesa. She was a strong and joyful presence in the community and to all with whom she interacted in the neighborhood. A health situation necessitated Sister's return to Germany.

GARDEN/FARM

In 2010, two student interns from the Agricultural Training College worked to transform the simple garden into a high-yielding plot of many attractions. Trellises were constructed, compost piles were created, and many beds of varied shapes were dug, fertilized, and elevated for planting different vegetables and fruits. The interns were very committed to avoiding contamination of natural resources in any way and thus insisted on all organic materials. Fertilizers were plant and animal wastes; pesticides were made from hot peppers and spices.

Sr. Margaret Mary Mouch, who served six months in Mpala, described in her blog of 2013 some of the plants in the garden: corn, sugar cane, Irish potatoes, peas, tomatoes, eggplant, peanuts (called G nuts), watermelon, zucchini, cabbage, coffee, and of course, bananas – at least four different kinds of bananas on the property. There were plants that were new to Sister: mango and papaya.

In 2014, a generous donor in the United States provided funds for the purchase of a cow that the sisters named Tyrone. On December 12, the cow gave birth to a calf, and the sisters informed the donor that the value of his gift had doubled.

ACTIVITIES OF THE HOUSE

In the introduction to the Mpala Annals of 2011, the section entitled *A brief survey of ACTIVITIES*, the following was included:

> The sisters are engaged in administering a house of studies for our temporary professed sisters who are engaged in further studies. There is a formation house on site where aspirants and candidates live as they prepare for entrance into the international novitiate in Tanzania. In addition, we run a guesthouse for visitors, especially friends and relatives of the sisters. Being only thirteen kilometers from the airport, our site is attractive to those traveling from abroad.

Mpala often served as the gathering place when the temporary professed came together for conferences or discussions.

NOTRE DAME NURSERY SCHOOL IN MPALA   On February 7, 2011, the sisters initiated a new ministry. Notre Dame Nursery School opened in the residential house on the property that had been used as a rental home by the previous owner. The rooms were remodeled and painted, awaiting the arrival of the youngsters. The pioneer class consisted of fifty-two children mostly ages three and four. Sr. Mary Colette and Sr. Maria Ruthilde were named the co-directors.

Most of the children cried the first day, some for more than four hours! The teachers and Sr. Maria Ruthilde tried to convince Sr. Mary Colette that this was normal for the first day of nursery school. The following days proved them right.

Classes were from 8:00 a.m. to 12:30 p.m.; some children remained for daycare until 4:30 p.m. The purpose of the program was to prepare the children for primary school by giving them a strong foundation in language and pre-reading skills as well as providing a variety of play experiences that are so vital for child development. Most classes were taught in English. Parents paid the school fees, quite different from the situation in Buseesa. Capital expenses were funded through the congregation.

Later, three levels were established: baby class (three-year-olds), middle class (four-year-olds), and top class (five-year-olds).

By 2013, the enrollment increased to ninety-two children. The staff increased, and the nursery school expanded by remodeling the former guesthouse into more classrooms. In addition, an outdoor eating area was built. At the end of 2015, the nursery school had five classes with an enrollment numbering one hundred eighty-four children.

Occasionally, the children enjoyed an outing to a nearby center. One year, the children of Notre Dame Nursery School joined their teachers and other staff members for a tour of the Entebbe Wildlife Centre. The children were excited to see the animals they had been learning about, especially the monkeys who roamed freely through the zoo. On another occasion, the youngest class went to Wonder World, an amusement park in Kampala, while the other two classes traveled to a play park called Time to Play.

In 2013, an end-of-the-year party and graduation were initiated. The children entertained their parents with songs, poems, rhymes, plays, and traditional dances. Certificates and special prizes were awarded. About three hundred children and adults then enjoyed a delicious meal.

On February 28, 2014, Sr. Mary Tina Petrick arrived in the late evening. She had served most recently in Papua New Guinea, a mission sponsored by her Toledo, Ohio province. The community was happy to receive Sister and learn from her many years of mission experience. She became the director of Notre Dame Nursery.

Sr. Mary Tina's first job in the nursery was to set up an office. She cleaned out cupboards, put up curtains, and found furniture for the room. The next day she visited each classroom and planned a teacher meeting so that all the staff could get to know one another.

On September 18, 2014, after a long process, the sisters received word that the nursery school had been granted an operating license. After two years and another long process, Notre Dame Nursery School would apply for complete registration.

CONSTANT COMING AND GOING

As had been done in Buseesa, the sisters in Mpala offered "Come and See" days for women desiring to know more about the Sisters of Notre Dame. In 2010, the sisters decided to have occasional weekends where the women could spend time with the sisters, pray with them, and hear their vocation stories. It was decided to call these more seriously interested women "seekers."

Among the many visitors to Mpala were three diocesan priests from Rwanda. They remained at the Notre Dame guesthouse for several weeks in order to learn English. The priests served in the diocesan seminary near Kigali, Rwanda. Each day they went to Kisubi Brothers University where a volunteer taught them English. Each evening the priests joined the sisters and candidates for supper and conversation. They concelebrated Mass along with the celebrant from Kisubi parish. The priests explained that even though Rwanda is a French-speaking country, all schools, including the seminaries, must teach English.

Because of their location, the sisters did a considerable amount of traveling. After a year of using public transport, the sisters were able to purchase a vehicle. The sisters chose a van that seated fifteen, similar to taxis used in the country. The van was a used vehicle, as new vehicles were very had to find in Uganda. The vehicle was carefully checked by the sisters' Buseesa driver.

The sisters made numerous trips to Tanzania. They brought candidates from Uganda to Tanzania to begin their time of postulancy. Then they brought from Tanzania those who had completed the novitiate and were to pronounce their first temporary vows. (At times, the first vows were pronounced in Tanzania, and then the sister(s) returned to Uganda.) There were occasional gatherings of temporary professed sisters in Tanzania. Sr. Mary Colette was usually the one to accompany these young members. Sister made many additional trips to Tanzania to participate in programs or meetings.

NEARBY VIOLENCE

Being so close to Kampala, the capital city, certainly had its advantages. But Kampala was occasionally the site of political unrest. In mid-September 2009, rioting broke out in the city. The issue was tribal rivalries. Sr. Mary Juliet was on her way to school when she noticed smoke. Her motorcycle driver turned around to help her get away from danger. It took many hours of going through back roads and alleys for them to get out of the main city where rioting was occurring.

Some of the sisters in the Mpala community were going to Buseesa to participate in a first profession of vows. A clash between the government and the king of the Buganda tribe over issues of power gave rise to riots. However, the radio announced relative peace, so the group decided it was safe to travel. They left at 8:00 a.m. and arrived in Buseesa about 6:00 p.m. They described how they ran into many roadblocks. There were police and soldiers with guns; there was much firing of guns and many fires. They passed twenty-five cars on fire and a bus driver being burned. Many people died in the riots and several were beaten. The sisters and the driver had taken refuge in the Archbishop's house for a period of time.

In the second week of October 2013, Sr. Cristina Marie called one day with the news that the students from Kyambogo University were going to strike the following day. The demands of the students were for sufficient furniture, reasonable fees, and timely return of exams. Sister was a student at the university and resided there. She said she felt safe and would stay in her room. The next night Sister called to share that she was safe, but that the strike was going to continue. Students were going to force the religious sisters to take the front lines! Sister and the other religious decided to flee the campus. She stayed with some sisters she knew and returned to the university when everything had calmed down. The demands were not addressed by the administration, yet classes resumed peacefully.

About a year later, as Sr. Mary Sunday was preparing to go to classes at Nkumba University, she received a call from a fellow student. The student warned Sister not to come as a strike had broken out. Students were striking for what they perceived as unfair behavior by the administration and against the dramatic increases in school and graduation fees. Some buildings were destroyed. Police chased strike leaders who ran from the university. Notre Dame Education Center is only about one kilometer from the university, so some of the strikers dashed there, jumped over the sisters' fence, and ran into the low ground behind the convent. Police followed, shooting their rifles. All the commotion upset the eight-month pregnant cow that proceeded to kick down the enclosure fence and ran around the compound. Garden employees calmed the cow and got her back into the enclosure. No arrests or injuries occurred. A month later, the cow gave birth.

TOP A room in the teacher housing building MIDDLE Looking at teacher housing from across the field
BOTTOM Sr. Maria Bernarde, Julia Mollerherm, Kristin Olbering, Martin Hilgers (3 volunteers from Germany)
Sr. Mary Delrita, and young friends from the neighborhood

TOP Formation House in Mpala MIDDLE Sr. Mary Colette and Sr. Maria Bernarde
BOTTOM Sr. Mary Tina, headteacher of nursery school in Mpala

TOP Sr. Maria Ruthilde served in Buseesa and Mpala MIDDLE Children in the Mpala nursery school
BOTTOM Sr. Maria Bernarde at the Julie Old Student Association foundation party

TOP Secondary student filling jerry cans. Note the pipe carrying water from the roof to the water tank.
MIDDLE A water tank that has exploded BOTTOM Primary students washing dishes after a meal

TOP Engineers Without Borders from Cincinnati, Ohio MIDDLE Bob Simon headed the maintenance group each year BOTTOM Maintenance Crew from Covington, Kentucky

TOP Medical crew from California (through BCDC) MIDDLE East Africa Delegation, 2015
BOTTOM East Africa Delegation Council: Sr. Mary Sawmya, councilor, Sr. Mary Colette, first assistant, Sr. Mary Roshini, delegation superior, Sr. Mary Immaculate and Sr. Mary Elizabeth, councilors

THE UGANDAN SISTERS VISIT THE USA
TOP Mary Violet, Sr. Mary Juliet, Sr. Anita Marie, Sr. Mary Sunday MIDDLE RIGHT Sr. Immaculate, Sr. Mary Teopista,
Sr. Mary Olive, Sr. Mary Annet, Sr. Christine Marie MIDDLE LEFT Sr. Therese Marie and Sr. Dolores Marie (Covington)
BOTTOM Sr. Mary Francello (Covington) and Sr. Mary Rozaria

TOP Sr. Mary Teopistia, Sr. Christine Marie, Sr. Immaculate MIDDLE Google view of St. Julie Mission, Buseesa, Uganda (Imagery © 2019 Digital Globe, Map data © 2019 Google) BOTTOM St. Julie Mission, Buseesa, Uganda

12
FORMATION FOR RELIGIOUS LIFE

Whenever the sisters asked the children what they wanted to be when they were older, many answered, "I want to be a sister. … a priest." As experienced teachers the sisters were accustomed to receiving such responses. The sisters encouraged them to think and pray much about what God might be calling them to do in their life. What they were not accustomed to was how the children at St. Julie's showed the intensity of their desire.

> We often find a group of girls kneeling on the grass outside near the convent chapel during our evening prayer time. They were sent by the cooks to collect trays of eggs, and they didn't want to interrupt our prayers.

> Many of the children have asked to join us for our daily 6:45 a.m. Mass. We've diplomatically told them that once they know the English Mass responses by heart, we'll think about allowing them to celebrate daily Mass with us. Their immediate response to our challenge has been, "How can we learn the words if we can't come to Mass and hear them?" (The Uganda SNDs to Sisters, Families and Friends, September 10, 1999)

THE JULIETTES

In July 2000, Sr. Jane Marie organized a group of girls from P-4 and P-5 who were interested in religious life. The group became known as the "Juliettes" named after St. Julie, patroness of St. Julie School and the spiritual mother of the Sisters of Notre Dame.

Sr. Jane Marie met with the girls once a month, usually on Saturday afternoon. The meeting generally lasted about an hour and began with praying the rosary in the chapel at the convent. The group then moved to the parlor where Sister gave them words of encouragement, instruction, and guidance.

There were a number of activities with the Juliettes that brought them more into contact with the sisters. On occasion, they enjoyed playing games and having the sisters tell their vocation stories. At times, the Juliettes stayed overnight with the sisters and joined in prayer and Mass the following morning.

Later, the P-7 girls came to the formation house carrying their mattresses and necessary belongings for an overnight stay. They and the sisters prayed together, shared a meal, and enjoyed some games.

COME AND SEE

Beginning in 1999, the sisters hosted vocation weekends that later became known as "Come and See." These were opportunities for young women interested in learning about the Sisters of Notre Dame. The young women lived with the sisters a few days and become more acquainted with the sisters, their spirit, their prayer, and their way of life.

Members of the formation community and members of the professed community worked with Sr. Mary Annete to prepare the program for the "Come and See" weekend. One year's theme was *The Quiltmaker*, taken from a book telling the story about a quiltmaker. The group designed quilts following various themes: biblical, favorite things, vocation.

Sometimes there was the sharing of vocation stories, an explanation of the stages of formation, reflection, and discussion opportunities. The weekends were never dull and often included crafts, singing, and dancing. Occasionally, a second weekend was planned for younger girls, with the candidates assisting in the preparation.

In a letter of December 7, 2003 to Sr. Mary Shauna, Sr. Mary Annete explained the formation program in Buseesa.

- They had two "Come and See" weekends a year, with one in January having two separate weekends because of the large number, and then another in April.
- In the midst of their teaching schedules, the sisters had visited seven schools.
- Sister was in contact with about sixty young women in various stages of education. This contact was through writing letters.

PREPARING A FORMATION PROGRAM

Within a few years of their arrival, the sisters began to discuss the possibility of accepting candidates who would become Sisters of Notre Dame. The decision was critically important for the mission.

In response to a letter from Sr. Mary Sujita, superior general in Rome, the sisters wrote:

> We understand all you said in your letter regarding candidates. We're excited about receiving candidates and know there is a process and procedure, and we know that we can't accept them now. What we have done over the past year is talk with other religious communities about their experiences … we are also requesting basic information required of candidates in the communities of Africa to help us in the planning whenever that is to begin.
>
> Yes, we agree that pre-candidacy is essential and a very important part of the plan for Africa. The plan for the entire program surely needs much prayer and

thought and planning. An important suggestion we would like to offer is that the sister/sisters preparing to be formators live in Africa for a time first. This way the sister/sisters come with some knowledge of Africa to help form the program. (Sr. Mary Annete and Sr. Jane Marie to Sr. Mary Sujita, n.d.)

From 1997 through 2000, there was discussion at every level about the possibility of accepting candidates, young women who desired to become Sisters of Notre Dame. Accepting candidates would entail the establishment of a program of formation with its various levels: candidate, pre-postulant, postulant, novice, temporary professed. At certain levels, the young women were introduced to: the charism (spirit) of the Sisters of Notre Dame and how it is lived, prayer, community living, the meaning and living of the vows, and meaning and practice of ministry.

The provincial superiors with missions in East Africa formulated directives for accepting candidates from these African countries. The sisters in the respective countries were asked for their input.

In January 2000, the sisters in Buseesa gathered to discuss their readiness to accept candidates for the formation program. Guidelines sent from the Covington and Thousand Oaks provincials aided in the discussion. The guidelines also offered suggestions as to how they themselves could prepare for such an undertaking. With all agreeing that they were ready to undertake such an important venture, the sisters began to address the preliminary aspects of a formation program.

Preparing a formation program was a critical element for the mission. Even in later years, there were discussions on when was the time to accept candidates.

> There were differences of opinion on all levels. The missionaries were "itching" to take candidates given the interest of local women. Sr. Sujita from the general level, as a person with a mission orientation, was ready to take candidates and put down roots earlier than the two founding provinces. We were being cautioned by other experts in the area of missions not to start too soon. We were very young as a mission and still involved very much in establishing our ministries. Inculturation was still very much of a learning process for all involved. (Sr. Mary Shauna's reflection on the formation program in Uganda, n.d.)

From the very beginning, it was established that there would be an East African novitiate in Arusha, Tanzania. The Uganda community would not have its own novitiate in Buseesa because the native sisters needed to get a sense of the Sisters of Notre Dame internationality and charism (spirit). However, the candidates and postulants would be formed in their respective countries.

The significant challenges that Sr. Mary Annete perceived that the sisters would need to face in the next three years were the following:

- Identifying and preparing appropriate formation personnel for the various stages … particularly as they would have temporary professed by 2006.
- Expanding the ministry opportunities for the young sisters, since it is not realistic to say that every sister would be a teacher.
- Especially for those who would be teachers, finding a suitable, safe, and qualified teacher training college for their studies would be important.

There were several women who expressed a desire to become Sisters of Notre Dame and met regularly with the sisters. The sisters anticipated that by the spring of 2002, they would be ready to accept candidates.

In 2012, the congregation developed a mission policy book, "Ad Gentes," that included directives for formation for all countries. Concerning candidates, the policy reads:

If the sponsoring province(s) and general government have agreed that the congregation would be open to receiving candidates, the following criteria need to be met:

- The mission is stable and grounded, ordinarily after at least eight to ten years.
- There is congruence between the understanding of religious life as it exists in the congregation and its understanding/practice in the culture where the mission is situated. In particular, there should be a determination of whether the practice of the vows as generally understood in the congregation is consistent with the local understanding and expectations.
- A vocation and formation plan has been developed in accord with the Congregational Plan of Formation and in cooperation with the mission and the sponsoring province(s).
- Vocation and formation personnel have been identified and trained, and it is foreseen that the sponsoring province(s) will be able to provide for personnel well into the future.

Candidates must be:
- Practicing Catholics for at least 3 years
- Educated at least through secondary school
- Able to pursue university education or specialized vocational training
- Recommended by the pastors or other church ministers who know them and their families

- Known to Sisters of Notre Dame over a period of time (This may be accomplished through an "aspirancy.")
- Willing to be formed in a national or international formation center.

FORMATION HOUSE

The formation house in Buseesa, although connected to the main convent, was to be a separate building that would be home to those in the first stages of formation. The house included a chapel, kitchen and dining area, a community room, dormitories, lavatory facilities, and a room for the director.

What excitement was shown when solar panels were placed on the second wing of the formation house. Finally, there was light in the chapel, dining and study areas, and the sisters could put away their lanterns. Water pipes were finally connected. For some time, Sr. Mary Annete and the candidates had been carrying water from tanks to their house or collecting it from open gutters.

FORMATION DIRECTORS

Although Sr. Mary Annete had been the SND formation director in the Chardon province, she was asked to enroll in a five-month formation course in Rome. This course included religious from developing nations.

When Sr. Mary Annete returned to Uganda in September 2002, a formation plan and the formation house in Buseesa were nearing completion; all was in readiness to receive the first candidates. There were women who had been visiting the sisters, spending weekends with them, and writing letters to keep in contact with them over the past few years

Sr. Mary Annete served as the formation director until 2004. The Annals of 2004 describe the change that would greatly affect the formation program.

> We have been thrilled with the outstanding work done by Sister Mary Annete with the young Ugandan women who have indicated an interest in religious life. Her "Come and See" weekends as well as her personal contacts with individuals and the secondary schools of the Kibaale District have yielded excellent results. There are currently two postulants, three candidates and two aspirants in the formation house in Buseesa. … Sister Mary Annete has been asked to join the formation team in Tanzania where the international novitiate is located. (Sisters of Notre Dame Buseesa Annals, February 14, 2004)

Sr. Mary Annete left for Tanzania on August 27, 2004, and Sr. Antoinette Marie Moon from the California province was assigned formation director in Uganda. Sister came to Uganda to become acquainted with the sisters and the culture. However, Sister was principal of a Catholic high school in California at the time and needed to complete her ministry there. Sister had no background in religious formation and was not sufficiently prepared for this new ministry. Thus, she traveled to Rome to begin taking courses in formation. After completing her studies in Rome, sister returned to Buseesa on July 1, 2006, and assumed her position of formation director for the candidates.

In the interim (August 2004 – July 2006), Sr. Mary Delrita was asked to accompany the young women in the initial stages of their spiritual journeys. Sister resided at the formation house and guided the young women in their day-to-day living of religious life. Sr. Mary Annete had suggested that during this time, the sisters assist and take turns with classes for the candidates/aspirants. In addition, sisters from the United States came to teach classes in Scripture and living as a Sister of Notre Dame. On May 21, 2008, Sr. Mary Renee Nienaber from Covington arrived to fill Sr. Antoinette's Marie's position as formation director while sister went for her home visit in California.

Sr. Mary Colette Theobald from California arrived on July 5, 2004. Her plan was to shadow Sr. Jane Marie for a month, as she would be filling the position of head teacher for St. Julie School when Sr. Jane Marie returned home in March. After a month in Uganda, Sr. Mary Colette returned to the United States for a year to study spirituality in Chicago. The plan was for her to return to Uganda in August 2005 as formation director and head teacher at St. Julie School.

Sr. Antoinette Marie continued as formation director for the candidates until May 2009, when health issues necessitated her return to California.

In April, 2009, because of the continuing changes in the formation personnel for Uganda, the provincial superiors decided that all the young women currently in any stage of formation in Buseesa would go to the formation house in Tanzania. The formation house in Buseesa was then closed.

Because there was no one in the United States prepared to take on the tasks of the formation program, the sisters in Uganda were asked to discern and decide who of the sisters in Buseesa was best suited to take on these immediate responsibilities. Pentecost Sunday was spent in prayer.

> When the sisters gathered at 4:00 p.m., the presence of the Holy Spirit was almost tangible. Each sister disclosed the results of her day of prayer. It soon became evident that all were in agreement. Sister Mary Colette had the necessary gifts to take on this responsibility. (Sisters of Notre Dame Buseesa Annals, May 31, 2009)

This left a huge vacancy at St. Julie School, as Sr. Mary Colette was head teacher there. It was suggested that Sr. Maria Bernarde and Sr. Mary Janet form a team involving some lay leadership to fill this position. Sr. Mary Colette communicated with the provincial superiors and received their wholehearted blessing on the suggestion.

Sr. Anita Marie assumed the responsibilities of vocation promotion. This included giving vocation talks and making initial contacts with interested women. Sister and a few of the temporary professed sisters visited secondary schools and had the opportunity to speak with many interested girls. As women responded, Sr. Anita Marie became the director of initial formation.

STAGES OF FORMATION

FIRST YEARS OF FORMATION   With many of the necessary pieces in place, the sisters began to accept candidates, and accompany them on their spiritual journey. The period of being a candidate lasted two years. This was an opportunity for young women to come to know the sisters and their way of life. They had frequent instructions on prayer, living in community, and the spirit and history of the Sisters of Notre Dame. It was a time of discernment of the call of God. The next step was a period of postulancy for two years. On September 8, 2002, the first Ugandan candidates entered Notre Dame: Amony Mary, Musiimenta Ruth, and Immaculate Nammuga. They resided in the formation house although there was still some work to be completed there.

When it appeared that a woman was sincere in her desire to become a Sister of Notre Dame, and the community recognized her readiness, she was received into the novitiate.

NOVITIATE   The Sisters of Notre Dame had a two-year novitiate program. This was a time of more intense focus on living as a Sister of Notre Dame. For the young women in Uganda, this meant traveling to Arusha, Tanzania, to join the national novitiate that included young women from Uganda, Tanzania, and Kenya. On September 8, 2004, Amony Mary and Immaculate Nammuga traveled from Uganda to Tanzania to begin their novitiate training.

The investment ceremony of becoming a novice took place at the national novitiate in Tanzania. There were fourteen professed sisters and twenty young women in formation present as the six postulants processed into the chapel to ask for entrance into the Sisters of Notre Dame. Each postulant carried a symbol that she had chosen to represent the decision she was making. Sr. Mary Shobana and Sr. Mary Annete, their directors, guided them through the service and presented them to the community. Amony Mary became Sr. Mary Amony, and Immaculate

Nammuga became Sr. Mary Immaculate. This was a great moment of rejoicing and a historic event for the Sisters of Notre Dame in Uganda.

During the novitiate, the novice was introduced to the Constitutions of the Sisters of Notre Dame and received instruction on the vows, their meaning and practice. The profession of first vows was often celebrated in Arusha, Tanzania or in Buseesa, Uganda.

FIRST VOWS Sr. Mary Amony and Sr. Mary Immaculate were the first two Ugandan women to pronounce their vows as Sisters of Notre Dame.

Months of anticipation and preparation culminated in a wonderful day. The three provincials, Sr. Marla, Sr. Mary Kristin, and Sr. Birgitt Maria, from Germany, attended as well as Sr. Mary Margaret and Sr. Mary Amy, the founding provincials. Sr. Mary Annete came from Tanzania with the two Ugandan novices, Sr. Mary Juliet and Sr. Therese Marie. Sr. Mary Kusum from Arusha also attended as the representative of the sisters in East Africa. Invitations were sent to all the priests and religious with whom the sisters collaborated. The young women who had indicated an interest in joining our formation community were also encouraged to attend. All the people of the parish as well as the parents of the school children were invited to join the celebration. Over seven hundred people were present.

The celebration began in the multipurpose building with the Eucharistic celebration at 10:00 a.m. and concluded at 1:00 p.m. The Bishop was the main celebrant; he was joined at the altar by almost thirty priests. Papers with the words to the songs, some in Runyoro and a few in English, were distributed, and all joined in the singing. In preparation for the Gospel, students danced in a procession with some students carrying a decorated chair with the Gospel book.

After the homily, Sr. Mary Amony and Sr. Mary Immaculate came forward and stood with the formation director and the provincial superior. Each sister was asked about her desire to become a sister. She then pronounced her vows to live as a Sister of Notre Dame. These first vows were pronounced for one year.

Following the Eucharistic celebration was a dramatization of the story of the call of Moses, written and directed by Sr. Maria Bernarde. The remainder of the program included songs, dances, instrumental presentations, and speeches. Sr. Marla in her comments said, "This day begins a new chapter in the history of the Sisters of Notre Dame in Uganda!"

The program was followed by a meal. A caterer from Mubende had been engaged. She, with her staff of six, joined the four cooks at the mission. Under the direction of Sr. Maria Bernarde, they produced a delicious meal. The sisters had bought a bull weighing over two hundred kilo and fifty chickens. A father of one the children slaughtered the bull in the field next to the school. One of the workers slaughtered the fifty chickens. The cooks worked all night and all morning to prepare the food. They wrapped the meat in banana leaves and cooked it. It was very tasty. The serving line was long, and it required a good deal of organization to feed everyone. It was about 6:00 p.m. before the cleanup was underway. It was a day to praise and celebrate God's goodness and care.

In the following years, more young women expressed interest in becoming a Sister of Notre Dame and entered the formation program. With the assistance of a formation director they considered their call from God, discerned if religious life was for them, and pronounced their first vows. These vows were renewed annually until the sister pronounced her perpetual vows.

TEMPORARY PROFESSED SISTERS   The years in the formation program gave the women time for discernment and for living the life of a Sister of Notre Dame. It also gave the community time to come to know these women and how they lived the charism (spirit) of Notre Dame.

As temporary professed, the sisters participated in ministry in Buseesa or Mpala or attended a university in Kampala for further education. They helped to plan and assist in the "Come and See" programs. Some participated in vocation promotion by traveling to various parishes or schools to speak about the Sisters of Notre Dame.

The temporary professed sisters participated in formation gatherings and experiences. Since Sr. Mary Colette, formation director for the temporary professed sisters, resided in Mpala, these sisters sometimes traveled to Mpala for instructions with sister. At other times, Sr. Mary Colette traveled to Buseesa.

Some of the instruction/conference themes included input and discussion on topics such as liturgical celebrations, community life, communication, prayer, the spirituality of social justice, ecumenism, a dialogue on Christian-Muslim relations presented by a Sheik from Uganda Islamic University, a discussion on "The Spirituality of Justice and Peacemaking," and a chapter in the book, the *Holy Longing* by Ronald Rolheiser.

Later topics included "Joy in Notre Dame and its importance to Notre Dame Spirituality" and Consecrated Chastity. A leadership workshop included communication skills, cultural differences and how to deal with them.

Since English is not the first language of the Ugandan sisters, a review of basic writing and grammar was given. A basic computer course was offered to encourage the young sisters to use the computer more and to feel comfortable while doing so. Sr. Cristina Marie worked with the sisters on how to use PowerPoint and make presentations.

Sr. Mary Katherine Pierce, IHM was from the Maryknoll program where the sisters had been prepared for the mission in Uganda. Sr. Katie, as she came to be called, met several times with the provincial superiors and the sisters in Uganda to address issues in community and in formation.

In one meeting, Sr. Katie said,

> If well-formed and educated native sisters insert themselves into local needs, there will be growth. The newly professed should return to Buseesa for a time of local involvement. Later they can move to Mpala for university or other schooling. They will benefit from interacting with other African sisters on the campus of Uganda Martyrs University. (Sr. Katie to Kentucky and California provincial superiors and their councils, June 21, 2009)

At the same meeting, Sr. Katie noted that a major theme of formation needed to be empowerment. When new members begin to speak of "we" and "our spirit," it indicates that they feel ownership and a sense of belonging. Such a disposition takes time to develop.

The years of temporary profession were a time of continuing discernment on the part of the community and the individual sister. Some women discovered this was not their call and returned home.

A sister remained in temporary profession for about five to seven years. Then being sure of her call to religious life and with the support of the sisters, she requested permission to pronounce her perpetual vows. With approval of the superior general in Rome, the sister pronounced her perpetual vows as a Sister of Notre Dame. The ceremony was usually held in Buseesa with family, parishioners, students, and many others participating.

The sisters at the mission discussed how to prepare celebrations, such as profession and final vows. Perhaps they could combine first and final vows and jubilee celebrations since the events were so costly and time consuming. In a meeting, Sr. Katie noted that the sisters needed to exercise caution not to diminish the uniqueness of each such event, while still weighing the expense and the work involved.

PERPETUAL PROFESSION   On May 4, 2013, the community celebrated first vows, perpetual vows, and golden jubilees of Sr. Mary Rita, Sr. Mary Judith, and Sr. Maria Bernarde. Sr. Mary Immaculate is the "first-born" in her family of twelve children, and the homilist made a point of reminding all present, that in professing perpetual vows, she is also the "first-born" in the Sisters of Notre Dame in Uganda. Two of the newly professed were from Nebbi in the north of Uganda, and many of the guests were from there, a very long journey. After Mass, when it was time to bring up the gifts to those celebrating, at least thirty people from Nebbi danced up the aisle with pots of flowers on their heads, with a goat (decorated with flowers), and with hand-woven baskets with mangoes, and the like.

Two days later was an all-day celebration at the home of Sr. Mary Immaculate's family in Karaguuza. The Mass was celebrated by five priests, followed by much singing, dancing, speeches, and food. Sr. Mary Immaculate's father gave one of the speeches; he had a big smile on his face. His first words were, "My soul magnifies the Lord . . ." and before he could get any further, the several hundred people in the family's back yard broke into joyful shouts and clapping.

From her visit to Uganda, Sr. Katie noted that formation in Uganda seemed to provide a focus on individual development and a sense of incorporation. She observed that native members in Uganda were given responsibility and treated as equals.

CONTINUING FORMATION FOR ALL

When a mission was blessed with national sisters, it called for a responsible plan for sustainability regarding both personnel and resources.

Education and the on-going formation of the young members took priority over expansion of the mission. The challenge was to strike a balance between initiating projects with compensated ministries and responding to the poor and marginalized where service was gratuitous. Some points included the following:

- From the beginning, programs must include leadership development, thus increasing the capacity of the national sisters to fill responsible positions for institutions and projects.

- National sisters will be professionally trained and prepared to take responsibility for the financial management of the mission: planning, budgeting, preparing, and submitting financial reports with accountability and transparency.

- The training involves realistic coping skills for suppressing of ministries or mission, death of a member, and other related negative happenings.

(The congregational missions policy book, *Ad Gentes*," Rome, 2012, p. 19)

Providing for the continuing formation of these sisters as well as for all the other sisters was a challenge in Uganda as there was not the ready availability of spiritual conferences, seminars, or speakers. The sisters received material from the home provinces and were committed to regular faith sharing and spiritual reading. They had special conferences when the provincial superiors visited each year.

AFRICAN CONFERENCE Every few years, sisters from Uganda, Tanzania, Kenya, and Mozambique met in one of the countries. This provided the sisters the opportunity to come to know one another and to share the happenings in their respective countries. Discussion often focused on their sharing of the common mission and the inculturation of the Sisters of Notre Dame spirituality in the African context.

In her opening address at the African regional conference held in Arusha, Tanzania, on December 28, 2001, Sr. Mary Sujita noted that the gathering had two main objectives:

> First of all, to provide an opportunity for the African missionaries, the concerned provincials, and the general administration to get to know one another and to share their experiences; and secondly, to look into our common missionary concerns especially vocation promotion and SND formation of African women.

Sister spoke of the many challenges of a missionary vocation.

> As you struggle with the new languages, new cultures, new ways of living and ministering, new ways of being Notre Dame Sisters in Tanzania, Mozambique, Uganda, and Kenya, may you grow in deep respect and understanding of our African brothers and sisters and their cultural richness.

> We may never fully understand them and their culture. But we can always love and respect them as people of God as we continue to discover and appreciate the many hidden treasures of their life and culture. … We all need to develop a multicultural awareness and a sense of wonder. … Our people here have their own history, experiences, ideas, values and attitudes which are drastically different from our own. Hence, listening and learning, in love and respect, will continue to be our challenge as missionaries. Let us make every effort to learn and speak the language of the people and enter into their culture, so that we can reach out effectively to the least among them, especially the women.

In 2003, the general level leadership recognized their responsibility to support the on-going formation for those in the mission. Their letter to the sisters stated:

> We also recognize among the group we have some of the original missionaries, a second wave of missionaries, and the most recent wave of missionaries. How can we support all of you in your on-going formation? We would like to propose a renewal program in which all of you could participate. (Summary of Leadership Meeting in Toledo, February 24, 2003)

Sr. Katie made several visits to Buseesa. The focus of one workshop was to help the sisters get in touch with their cultural sensitivity as individuals and as a community, and seriously consider the ways of incorporating national sisters into the community.

In other presentations and guided discussions, Sister addressed and challenged the sisters in the areas of personal growth, community building, communication, and respect and understanding of the culture. Other topics included culture and cultural adjustment, stages of the experience of being foreign, stepping into one's self (self-disclosure, feedback), conflict-handling skills, and suggestions for improvement. Some sessions included the lay volunteers and staff.

The workshop in May 2004, focused on community development. It was noted that living and working in groups is part of our human and communal reality. Effectiveness in group functioning and relationships will either enhance or be an obstacle to this reality. Effectiveness in mission will depend in great part on our effectiveness within the group.

In her visit in August 2009, Sr. Katie led the members of Buseesa and Mpala communities in a process of goal-setting and objective clarification in order to develop a new mission statement. Long-range planning goals were also formulated. The novices and temporary professed sisters had a special session on how to cope with transition.

As one of the outgrowths of a workshop, the sisters invited Haruna Katongole, a retired minister of the Church of Uganda and a highly respected elder in the village of Buseesa to speak with them about the beliefs and way of life of the people of the Kibaale District. The sisters learned about the physical and spiritual concerns of the people, in particular, their deep-seated fear of spirits and charms.

CONGREGATIONAL RETREATS   In January 2014, two retreats were given in Mpala for the sisters in Uganda. Sr. Mary Margaret Agnes Hemmerle and Joanne Kenner, a Notre Dame Associate, both from Covington, Kentucky, came to Uganda to lead the retreat. The retreat, "Becoming Fire Together," was a Congregation-wide retreat designed to help the sisters deepen their Notre Dame Spirituality and provide an opportunity to grow closer.

Sr. Mary Juliet, Sr. Therese Marie, and Sr. Mary Immaculate were selected to travel to Germany and Rome to participate in the congregational spirituality program. This three-week program was developed by Sisters of Notre Dame from various countries. Later, a few sisters from each country were invited to Coesfeld, Germany, to experience the program, and upon returning to their country offer it to their sisters. Approximately one year later, these Ugandan sisters took responsibility for conducting the Heritage Retreat in Mpala.

CONTINUING EDUCATION IN MINISTRY   Continuing education in the area of ministry was also important. The sisters wanted someone with a strong background in education who could come to Uganda and work with the candidates. These young women would someday be in charge of the schools. Sr. Mary Annete suggested Sr. Mary Regina Alfonso, a retired professor from Notre Dame College in Chardon, Ohio, as a possibility. Sr. Mary Shauna supported the idea and reminded the sisters that something needed to be done to help strengthen the national teachers. She suggested that Sr. Jane Marie give Sr. Regina some specifics as to what she could do while in Buseesa. Sr. Jane Marie agreed, and it was decided that Sr. Regina would work with the teachers at the school and with the sisters.

For three summers (2000, 2001, 2004), Sr. Regina came to Buseesa for six weeks to assist with teacher training. She provided seminars for the sisters, volunteers, and teachers of St. Julie School and Buseesa Primary, often separating the two schools because their respective situations were so different. Sr. Regina visited the St. Julie School classrooms for observations. These were followed by a conference time to provide feedback and give recommendations for the respective teacher. Often Sister discussed teaching methods such as using groups, using visual materials, classroom management, and teaching reading in all classes.

Four educational cornerstones are central to all SND education. These are: the centrality of a good and provident God, the human dignity of each person as an image of God, the Notre Dame educator as Gospel witness, and an integrated education for transformation. It was important that these also be shared with the educational staff in Buseesa. In 2003, all the primary and secondary teachers gathered in the NDA staff room for some reflection and sharing on the four cornerstones. The first Sunday of each month, Sr. Mary Rita invited all to participate in this opportunity for professional growth.

To further formation in education, Sr. Therese Marie and Sr. Mary Rozaria traveled to the United States to attend the Notre Dame Educational Symposium held in Dayton, Ohio, in June 2015. They had the opportunity to meet other Sisters of Notre Dame and learn more about various educational theories and practices. They also took the opportunity to visit the four United States provinces.

The Ugandan sisters took courses at universities in or near Kampala while living in Mpala. The sisters received their degrees in areas that varied from education to social work.

In 2015, Sr. Constance Marie Suchala from the Toledo, Ohio, province arrived in Uganda. Sister was the director of Maria Early Learning Center in Toledo. The purpose of her visit was to observe the early childhood programs in Buseesa and Mpala, to give in-service to teachers, and to advise the directors of the Uganda nursery schools on matters relating to school improvement. Sr. Constance Marie remained in Uganda from February 15 to March 8.

OBSERVATIONS AND CHALLENGES FROM THE GENERAL ADMINISTRATION

The yearly visit from one or both of the United States provincial superiors and the occasional visit from the sisters at the general level yielded valuable insight into situations in the mission. Some issues revolved around inculturation, community living, formation, and mission.

After their visit to Buseesa, Sr. Mary Sujita, Superior General, and Sr. Mary Frances, Assistant, wrote to the sisters in the Buseesa community.

> During our time in Buseesa, we surely witnessed the sense of joy and friendship in your community. Personal and community prayer is a priority, and time is taken, as far as possible, for weekly and monthly conferences, recollection, and sharing. In addition to being a well-experienced, talented group of sisters with much potential for creativity and leadership, your life together witnesses the richness of the international and inter-provincial nature of the community. In addition, the volunteer missionaries seem well-integrated into the community and ministry. In spite of a very heavy workload, it seems that quality time is spent at meals and other times of recreation. (Sr. Mary Sujita to Sisters in Buseesa, January 8, 2002)

The two visitors noted the sisters desired to spend time to be together as an SND community, but still being available to the boarders, teachers, and workers. The visitors suggested that this should be evaluated so as not to create unrealistic expectations. Recognizing signs of burnout in some of the sisters they suggested that the sisters educate the children and workers to respect the sisters' times of silence and prayer. The visitors proposed that the sisters decide on a time each day when they WILL NOT be available and post this time near the doorbell with the notice: "Sisters at prayer" or something similar. This also had witness value.

The sisters in Uganda were encouraged to organize regular meetings with the community and also with the school (teachers/staff) for planning, sharing, evaluating together, all important activities and programs. They were to decide on a definite day of the week or month.

Mud and stick house with a thatched roof

13

PERSONS WHO SERVED AT THE UGANDA MISSION

THE DOOR IS ALWAYS OPEN

The years in Buseesa were years of many comings and goings. Sr. Mary Janet, Sr. Mary Delrita, Sr. Jane Marie, and Sr. Margaret Mary arrived in Uganda on July 13, 1995. At their home, they welcomed Bishop Deogratias who was a frequent visitor. The Bishop's visits and his care and solicitude were deeply appreciated by the sisters. In the ensuing years, the Bishop worked with public officials to clarify and resolve issues. Bishop Deogratias' visits were always a joyous event.

Other visitors included the pastor of the parish church, Sisters of Notre Dame who came to minister or to visit, volunteers, and friends and relatives of the sisters and volunteers. There were also the visits of public officials, and of course, the people of the village. It seemed as though there was always someone coming in or going out the convent door.

SISTERS MISSIONED TO THE UGANDA MISSION

The following are Sisters of Notre Dame who served in the Uganda Mission for a year or more.

SR. MARY DELRITA GLASER (Covington, Kentucky, July 1995–August 2011, July 2012 – May 2013) Before coming to Uganda, Sister ministered in healthcare in the province healthcare centers. In Uganda, Sister utilized this knowledge and skill when sisters, students, and even neighbors were in need. Sister assumed charge of the library and was responsible for cataloguing over 4,000 books. Sister served as interim formation director for two years, and as supervisor of maintenance and kitchen staff.

SR. MARY JANET STAMM (Covington, Kentucky, July 1995–May 2013) In coming to Uganda Sister brought her many gifts as teacher and administrator in elementary schools in the Covington Province. In Uganda, Sister assisted in the organizing of St. Julie School, served as a teacher in the school, served as local coordinator in the convent, and for a time oversaw the work in the school garden.

SR. JANE MARIE McHUGH (Thousand Oaks, California, July 1995–March 2005) Sr. Jane Marie taught in the elementary grades in California before coming to Uganda. Sister took the lead in the preparations and organization of the establishment of St. Julie School. She served as teacher, and head teacher (principal) for St. Julie School. Although all the sisters assisted, Sister did much of the food preparation at the convent.

SR. MARGARET MARY SCOTT (Thousand Oaks, California, July 1995–April 1999) Before coming to Uganda, Sr. Margaret Mary Scott served in a parish as a Director of Religious Education. At St. Julie School, Sister served as a teacher. She was instrumental in planning for the farm and in preparing and planting the gardens that supplied food for the sisters, staff, and students. Sister was also in charge of the poultry.

SR. MARY ANNETE ADAMS (Chardon, Ohio, January 1998–August 2004) In her home province, Sister Mary Annete had served as formation director, guiding and directing women desirous of becoming Sisters of Notre Dame. In her initial years in Uganda, Sister taught at St. Julie Primary School. She was instrumental in developing the initial vocation programs, introducing young women to religious life, and accepting the first aspirants. Sister served a formation director in Buseesa. In 2004, Sr. Mary Annete was missioned to Tanzania to become part of the formation team for the African novitiate.

SR. MARIA BERNARDE DERICHSWEILER (Germany, May 2001–the present.) Sr. Maria Bernarde had retired from teaching and administration at the secondary school level in Germany, and felt called to serve in the Uganda mission. At St. Julie School, sister taught the upper primary classes and for a while served as head teacher. Through her efforts, perseverance, and encouragement, the students participated in music competitions and receive high marks each time. Sister also worked with students in the music aspects of the school liturgies as well as programs for visitors. Sr. Maria Bernarde kept in touch with the boys who graduated from St. Julie School and went to high school in another area. She was instrumental in working with these graduates as they formed the Old Student Association.

SR. MARY PAULYNNE TUBICK (Thousand Oaks, California, September 2001–December 2005, November 2013–present) Sr. Mary Paulynne brought her teaching skills and shared these with the students at St. Julie School. In 2005, Sister returned to the United States, and in 2013, Sister returned to Buseesa and served as head teacher at St. Julie School.

SR. MARY KARLENE SEECH (Chardon, Ohio, January 2002–December 2002) Sr. Mary Karlene had requested to spend some sabbatical months with the sisters in Buseesa. Sister aided in various ways, primarily serving as a teacher in P-4 at St. Julie School. Her few months were extended to include the entire academic year.

SR. MARY RITA GEOPPINGER (Covington, Kentucky, October 2002–January 2014) Sr. Mary Rita had served as a secondary teacher and as principal of Notre Dame Academy in Covington, Kentucky. Sister had spent a four-month sabbatical in Buseesa. In 2002, Sister returned and assumed the responsibilities of head teacher and teacher at Notre Dame Academy Secondary School in Buseesa. Sister was one of the sisters who established Notre Dame Academy on a firm foundation.

SR. ANITA MARIE STACY (Covington, Kentucky, October 2002–the present) Sr. Anita Marie Stacy came to Uganda with a secondary teaching background, primarily in math. In Uganda, Sister assisted in establishing Notre Dame Academy Secondary School and became deputy head teacher and teacher of science and math. With her strong math background, she was appointed the Financial Accountant for the St. Julie Mission and worked with the Buseesa Community Development Center for a number of years. Sister also served as director of those in initial formation.

SR. MARY BERNADETTE PENDOLA (Thousand Oaks, California, July 2004–June 2006) As a trained nurse, Sr. Mary Bernadette became the school nurse. She also served as the teacher of health classes at St. Julie School. Sister brought much life and energy into the community along with her professional expertise.

SR. MARY COLETTE THEOBALD (Thousand Oaks, California, July 2005–the present) In 2004, Sr. Mary Colette came to Uganda for a short time to shadow Sr. Jane Marie. When she returned in 2005, Sister served as head teacher and language arts teacher at St. Julie School. Four years later, she assumed the position of director of temporary professed, directing and guiding the young sisters with temporary vows. Sr. Mary Colette was one of the first sisters to be assigned to the new mission site in Mpala in 2009. She served as formation director and later became director of the Notre Dame Nursery School in Mpala.

SR. ANTOINETTE MARIE MOON (Thousand Oaks, California, July 2006–May 2009) In 2004, Sr. Antoinette Marie visited Uganda to become acquainted with the sisters and the culture. Sister returned home to complete her responsibilities as a high school principal, and then participated in a formation program in Rome. In 2006, Sister returned to Buseesa and assumed the position of formation director for candidates.

SR. MARY JUDITH AVERBECK (Covington, Kentucky, September 2006 – November 2007, November 2008 to the present) Sr. Mary Judith had been a science teacher at Notre Dame Academy in Covington. Sister had spent four months of her sabbatical year in Buseesa discerning whether this was where God was leading her. It was a joyous occasion when she returned to Buseesa to serve as a teacher of chemistry and biology at Notre Dame Academy.

SR. MARIA RUTHILDE HAFERKAMP (Germany, September 2008 to July 2015) After her retirement from education in Germany, Sr. Maria Ruthilde came to Uganda for six months in 2007 as part of her discernment. She returned a year later and assisted in the library and served as a supervisor at St. Julie School. In April 2009, Sister was one of the first who took up residence in the new mission site in Mpala. Here Sister had care of the house and assisted with formation.

SR. MARY SHARAN HENDRICKS (Patna, India, February 2010 – February 2011) Sister came to Uganda as part of her discernment about becoming a missionary. Sister remained and assisted with the formation in Mpala.

SR. CRISTINA MARIE BUCZKOWSKI (Thousand Oaks, California, August 2011– December 2013) In California, sister served in the ministry of education. In Uganda, sister was the head teacher at St. Julie Primary School and served as Maintenance Supervisor.

SR. MARY TINA PETRICK (Toledo, Ohio, February 2014 to the present) Sr. Mary Tina had served many years in the mission of Papua New Guinea. The community in Mpala was most happy to welcome Sister and learn from her years of missionary experience. Sister became the Director of the Notre Dame Nursery School in Mpala.

PRIESTS STATIONED AT UGANDA MARTYRS PARISH, BUSEESA, SERVING ST. JULIE MISSION

Rev. Mugisa Aloysius	Rev. Paul Ziwa
Rev. Isingoma Peter	Rev. Asiimwe Stephen
Rev. Vincent Kirabo	Rev. Kisembo Godfrey
Rev. Paul Barugahare	Rev. Wassawa Peter
Rev. Francis Komakech	Rev. John Nicolas Gonzaga
Rev. Baliabugga Mattio	Rev. John Baptist Ryabunyoro
Rev. Tuhairwe Godfrey	

VISITING SISTERS OF NOTRE DAME

In addition to the sisters who lived and served in Uganda for a year or more, there were other Sisters of Notre Dame who came for an official visit and those who came to offer service in some capacity.

Each year, one or both of the California and Covington provincial superiors visited the sisters in Buseesa. The California provincial superiors during the first twenty years were Sr. Mary Amy Hauck, Sr. Mary Kristin Battles, Sr. Mary Anncarla Costello; the Covington provincial superiors were Sr. Mary Margaret Droege, Sr. Mary Shauna Bankemper, Sr. Marla Monahan, and Sr. Mary Ethel Parrott. Sr. Melannie Svoboda and Sr. Margaret Gorman from the Chardon, Ohio, province and Sr. Birgitt Maria from the German province also visited as they had sisters in ministry in Uganda.

The visits or "visitations" of the provincial superiors were always greatly anticipated because they were an opportunity for both groups to share what was happening in their respective spheres. The visitors experienced the prayer, community, and ministry of the sisters. They had the opportunity to visit with the Bishop and join the Eucharistic celebration in the local parish on Sunday. Time was set aside for a spiritual conference and an opportunity for each sister to meet with the provincial. There was the sharing of news, mail, and packages from home. During the visitation, hopes, concerns, and plans were discussed.

Other special visits are those of the superior general from Rome. The first such visit was in December 1996 when Sr. Mary Joell visited. She was able once again to meet Bishop Deogratias, visit a local village family, and celebrated Mass with the parish community.

Sr. Mary Sujita, a native of India and the superior general, first visited Uganda in May 1999. This was an important time for both Sr. Mary Sujita and the local community in Buseesa. The sisters spoke of all that had been accomplished, and identified their hopes and concerns. Sr. Mary Sujita met Bishop Deogratias, visited with the workers, saw the gardens, and shared her observations, challenges, and hopes for the future. Sr. Mary Sujita visited St. Julie School and some of the local homes. Sister also received visitors at the convent.

> Our women's group came and greeted Sister, addressed her in a few words and presented her with a gift. The shawl matched her sari perfectly. … She spoke to them of the importance of women making a difference in their community and encouraged them to keep thinking of other projects to make their lives better. (Sisters of Notre Dame Buseesa Annals, May 23, 1999)

Sr. Mary Sujita was very much at home as she spoke of how much the area reminded her of places in India and even her own home. In an email, one of the sisters wrote:

> She [Sr. Mary Sujita] fell in love with us … and of course, we're a lovable bunch in the jungle of Africa; said she felt immediately such hope and enthusiasm … amidst all our laughter. … you have to have a sense of humor to live here.
> (Sr. Mary Annete to Sr. Mary Shauna, May 29, 1999)

As provincial superior of the California province, Sr. Mary Kristin Battles had visited the mission a number of times. In 2010, she came as the superior general, and also participated in the African Regional Conferences held in the various East Africa countries.

Treasurers from the general and provincial levels visited the mission to spend time with the sisters and experience life in the mission They acquired a better understanding of the financial records, helped to work out the details of the annual financial report, and developed a computer program that all would use for their annual accounts.

Through the years, sisters came to teach scripture/theology courses or offer in-service for teachers. Other sisters came to substitute for missionaries while they were on home visits. Some sisters came as part of their sabbatical and offered their assistance in the mission; others came as part of their discernment about the possibility of being missioned at a further date.

PERSONS WHO ASSISTED AT THE MISSION FOR A SHORTER PERIOD OF TIME

Sr. Mary Regina Alfonso (Chardon, Ohio, province) came three summers to assist the Ugandan teachers. Sister addressed lesson planning and teaching techniques.

Sr. Marie Paul Grech (Thousand Oaks, California) assisted in the formation program during her sabbatical stay.

Sr. Margaret Mary Mouch (Covington, Kentucky) assisted with the candidates in Mpala during her sabbatical.

Sr. Mary Renee Nienaber (Covington, Kentucky) served as formation director while Sr. Antointte Marie was out of the country.

Sr. Mary Regina Robbins (Thousand Oaks, California) offered classes in Scripture and religious and formation topics.

Jeanne-Marie Tapke, (Covington, Kentucky) provided training in leadership for all.

VALUED STAFF

A vitally important component of the Buseesa mission is the corps of villagers employed at the convent, the school, and in the gardens. In 1995, there were two young girls helping at the convent. By 2015, forty-three lay persons were employed, part or full time, as teacher, matron, driver, maintenance, farm worker, or cook at the mission in Buseesa. In the same year twenty-five lay persons were employed in Mapala.

REFLECTIONS

One of Sr. Mary Renee's favorite experiences: Sister took a picture of some first graders, and they all crowded around to see the picture.

> The last child jumped down two steps, and I said, "That was a big jump!" The children understood me to mean that they should all jump, so they started bouncing up and down. What to do next? I decided to ask them to sing a song. With hands in the air, they delighted in singing their school song about God being good.

> Life is still mostly without electricity, so many things are very work-intensive and time-consuming. Can you imagine washing your sheets/towels, towels/washcloths, and all of your clothes by hand, then hanging them on the line to dry? Meals too take much time to prepare. Yesterday after Rozaria had fixed two meals … I just wanted to find a Burger King and pick up something for us. That won't happen out here in the bush. In fact, for a Sunday treat, we had meat. Two of the young women in formation had to walk about thirty minutes one-way to get fresh meat. They take it all in stride—literally.
> (Sr. Mary Renee, June 2, 2008)

Dear loving Sr. Delrita,

How can it be that you are leaving us here in Busesa. Dear Sr. I can't imagine how loving, caring, guiding and listening you were that now you were going to leave us; we your children in Busesa. You really acted as a mother to me by guiding me - thats in the library, caring for me - as a nurse in the sick bay, and anywhere. You taught me puzzles, how to use the library and you taught me Piasy in Primary 5 in 2009; If I still remember that, why not remember you when you leave us and go to Mpala. In fact you were my best Librarian since I started schooling. You helped me know more about library books and their authors.

Excerpt of student's letter to Sr. Mary Delrita

14

VOLUNTEERS COME TO UGANDA

Throughout the history of St. Julie Mission, individuals, groups, and organizations have come to assist, not only the mission, but also the people of Kibaale District. Their visits and presence have greatly impacted the area. Sometimes their visits were brief, and sometimes their visits led to a permanent establishment. These generous people have touched the lives of the people in terms of education, economics, and health. This chapter focuses on these individuals, organizations and groups.

VOLUNTEERS FROM GERMANY AND THE USA

During these years, lay volunteers came for three months to one year to assist in the ministry in Buseesa. Most of the volunteers were from the MaZ program in Vechta, Germany (Missionare auf Zeit – Missionary for a time). A few volunteers came from the United States. These generous volunteers assisted in the classroom and the library, on the farm, in the dispensary or the canteen, supervising homework time and family work time, or wherever they were needed. One volunteer, Martin Hilgers, became an employee on the farm for two years.

From Germany:

Teresa Schlummer	Katrin Schlosser
Martin Hilgers	Kathrin Beyer
Lioba Ross	Judith Kramer
Miriam Lueken	Melanie Wiederkehr
Sabrina Wurth	Anna Marks
Julia Mollerherm	Christine Rolf
Daniela Fangmann	Kerstin Olberding
Ricarda Oberbeck	Elena Quatmann
Mona Sonnen	Filiz Guemues
Hannah Ratterman	Paula Volmer
Melanie Landwehr	Dorothy Siefker
Lisa Runge	Devi Mueller
Christine Gigl	

From the United States:
    Amy Metzger
    Maria Chal
    MeKenzie Elbert

Some individuals from the United States, mostly relatives or friends of the missionaries, assisted briefly in the mission during their visit.

In 2003, Sr. Mary Shauna sent to the missionaries the minutes of a leadership meeting in Toledo. The topic of lay volunteers was discussed.

> We are deeply appreciative of the help we have received through the assistance of lay volunteers. They have been a wonderful asset to all that we are about in Buseesa. At the same time, we realize the challenges that the volunteers bring with them. In particular, we are thinking of the impact on community life. At some point it may be necessary that some guidelines be established. We also think that a formal application process needs to be set up allowing the home provinces to be involved in the decision-making. One of our major concerns is the legal ramifications that fall on us as the responsible provinces. We are asking you to draft some simple guidelines that would include: number of volunteers at one time, ages, length of stay, training necessary, responsible person receiving the volunteers, etc. (Sr. Mary Shauna to Sisters, February 24, 2003)

BUSEESA COMMUNITY DEVELOPMENT CENTER (BCDC)

In 2008, Anguma Ben, a teacher of economics at Notre Dame Academy in Buseesa, asked the sisters about the possibility of starting some type of microfinance program in Buseesa. The request was forwarded to Sr. Mary Kristin, the provincial superior in California. Shortly, thereafter, Nicholas Smith came to see Sr. Mary Kristin. His father and a group of parishioners from St. Julie Parish in Thousand Oaks, California, had visited the mission in Buseesa a year before and had done several fundraisers to help support the mission. Nicholas knew about the mission from his father and wanted to do something to help. He had just graduated from the University of Santa Barbara in International Finance and Development. Sr. Mary Kristin mentioned the request from Buseesa. After some discussion, Nicholas agreed that this project would be something he thought he could help initiate. Soon, Nicholas was off to Uganda.

MICROFINANCE PROGRAM   In 2009, Nicholas traveled to Uganda, stayed with the sisters, and, in collaboration with Ben and Winnie (the secretary at Notre Dame Academy) put the structure for the program in place. Nicholas, Ben, Winnie, and Sr. Anita Marie became the founding board for the Buseesa Community Development

Center (BCDC). The project was independent of the Sisters of Notre Dame although the sisters were instrumental in the beginning. Sr. Anita Marie served as a board member and treasurer for several years.

BCDC began as group-based loan program that offered microloans of between $90 – $400 to rural farmers and shopkeepers in Uganda. The aim of the program is to have entrepreneurs assist one another in funding various business ventures. Money is allocated to the first person in a group. When she or he begins to pay back the loan, a second person of that group is able to request a loan. Within the first two months, BCDC had managed to organize about one hundred people into twelve loan groups.

The process has been a success. The microcredit loans have helped to empower almost nine hundred families in twenty-two villages and have distributed over $300,000 in loans. These loans helped borrowers increase their capacity to earn more income by providing them the necessary capital to invest in income-generating activities. By increasing families' capacity to earn more income borrowers were in a better position to meet their household needs, such as health and education.

Since the BCDC was founded, borrowers have utilized their loans in a variety of life-changing ways. They have built their first brick homes (rather than mud and stick); others increased their ability to pay toward school tuition fees; others augmented their assets, including land and animals, and some improved their health by eating more nutritious meals. In place of collateral in the traditional banking sense, borrowers' loans are conditional on the repayment of their fellow group members. The repayment rate is nearly 99%.

The BCDC program includes an educational component where talks are given to the recipients on how to manage finances, how to do organic farming, and many other practical topics.

MAPPING THE AREA   As part of his doctoral research, Nicholas had the opportunity to map the Uganda Martyrs Parish. This turned out to be an eye-opening experience as it revealed how the deeper one went into the more remote areas, the more impoverished the villages were. Two of the villages were so poor and disconnected that Nicholas and his friend were the first foreigners to visit them. The sisters and their local driver had never heard of these villages.

EDUCATION   One village had a "school" which consisted of one class in a mud and stick room, and the other had two twelve-by-twelve-inch chalkboards nailed to a tree. The government had determined that the hundred families of the area were not enough to build a school. In 2014, the BCDC began construction of a primary school named Deirdre Ann Academy (DAA) that served children from three villages. The new school provided an education to children from nursery to primary levels. The children were provided breakfast and lunch and had access to safe drinking water and latrines.

MEDICAL ASSISTANCE   In February 2014, a group of twenty nurses from the University of California Davis, whom Nicholas had recruited, came to Buseesa to provide health services. Each day, the nurses traveled to various villages and treated residents for malaria, worms, typhoid fever, HIV/AIDS, and a wide range of other ailments. The group saw more than 1,100 people in one week.

In early 2015, a second group of medical personnel arrived. The visitors resided in the teacher housing building at St. Julie Mission, but had their headquarters at BCDC up the road.

Emily Rymland, a nurse practitioner, was a member of the team of nurses who came to Uganda. The experience inspired Emily to begin raising funds to open a year-round health care clinic in the area. With help from BCDC, Emily opened *Em's Health Clinic* staffed by Ugandan health care providers. Em's treats approximately three hundred patients per month and conducts medical outreach into remote villages where there are no other available health care services. Em's treats infectious and chronic diseases, and offers perinatal care, HIV screening, counseling, nutritional teaching, and dental care.

BCDC has also been involved in trying to improve the health of the area by building latrines and securing delivery of clean water.

Information sources for BCDC:

"The Story Behind the Beginning of the Buseesa Community Development Center," Sr. Mary Kristin Battles, SND, September 13, 2013.

Memo: To: 2013 BCDC Donors; From Nicholas Smith, BCDC Founder; Subject: BCDC Microcredit Expansion; Date: July 28, 2013

"Nurse's Inspiration Leads to a Permanent Health Clinic in Uganda" (posted April 4, 2016) https://newsroom.altabatessummit.org/...nurses-inspiration-leads-to-a-permanent-health

Sisters of Notre Dame Buseesa Annals, 2014, 2015

ENGINEERS WITHOUT BORDERS (EWB) USA

Engineers Without Borders builds a better world through engineering projects that empower communities to meet their basic human needs. In 2013, the Engineers Without Borders (EWB) Cincinnati Chapter pledged five years to help the Buseesa community develop two desperately needed resources: water and energy.

Erin Cummings, a graduate from Notre Dame Academy in Covington, Kentucky, and an engineer, linked the Sisters of Notre Dame of the Covington province with the EWB. Together they developed a proposal to provide clean water to the village and tree-saving biogas to the local schools. Once the national EWB board accepted the proposal, five seasoned engineers traveled to Uganda where they spent two weeks making connections and scoping out parameters of the project.

A blog posting by Ed Kohinke, one of the engineers, offered thoughts about the trip.

> Our trip will take us about 7,6000 miles from home to a place that none of us have ever visited or have known much about. We will meet new people from a completely different culture, breathe the air of a totally different climate, and be unable to speak more than a few words of the local language. Yet we are determined to generously offer our problem-solving skills and engineering know-how in some way that could improve living conditions or somehow touch the lives of strangers. Engineers Without Borders and the Sisters of Notre Dame have provided the connection to the needs of this faraway place, and it is a blessing to be capable of doing the work that is asked of us.

As planned, the engineers visited several sites in the immediate locale of Buseesa and a few at a greater distance taking note of what was available and how it might be used to improve the lives of the people.

A review of the grounds at St. Julie Mission indicated that a bio-digester to produce energy would work well. The farm had ample animal waste to use along with the potential of kitchen and crop waste. With more information needed, one engineer interviewed one of the school cooks; another set out with a GPS to map local water sources and to test the water quality; others made a rough topography map of the proposed digester site. They later visited shops that could provide a majority of the necessary building supplies.

In April 2014, four engineers returned to Uganda to take the next step. The main goal of this trip was to interview potential contractors for the biogas project. The team was able to visit a local school where a digester had been installed. They viewed the digester and followed the gas line to the kitchen where biogas burners had been installed. The concrete room was remarkably clean and smoke-free. It was a dramatic difference from the typical wood-burning kitchen where one had to gasp for clean air, and eyes burned and watered from the smoke. Some engineers checked out the soil, rock, and sand; another scouted for water sources.

Rarely does the mixing of a batch of cement inspire such curiosity and gratitude! Children competed for the best view of the foreign white person doing skilled labor in the kitchen already busy with kids cleaning dried beans and peeling dozens of bunches of matooke bananas for dinner. The engineer did a great job of placing a mortar patch around the wire mesh and troweling a nice finish. The blog that day concluded with these words: "The reputation of our entire EWB chapter is now riding on the success of that patch, so it better last through the summer."

A third group of engineers returned in the fall of 2014 to begin implementing the necessary building project for water and gas. They installed a community water pump and set up the school biogas system.

In March of 2015, four engineers worked on two projects based in the Buseesa area. The community well was installed and was put to work almost immediately. Villagers could obtain water from this source instead of walking many kilometers to procure it.

The project of providing biogas for the school kitchen was also set up. However, the expected output of gas was not forthcoming. Even though the local company returned to investigate, the system still did not work well. It was hoped that continued efforts on the part of both the engineers and the local company would improve results.

Information sources:

Engineers Without Borders (Cincinnati) Blogs posted by Ed Kohinke, June 2013, April 2014,

Engineers Without Borders USA (ewb-use.org)

Sisters of Notre Dame Buseesa Annals, 2013, 2014, 2015

JAY BAYER AND FAMILY

Jay Bayer and four of his children, all engineers or studying engineering, arrived on June 11, 2013, for almost two weeks of utilizing their engineering skills. They carefully surveyed the property for future expansion to an A-Level program and addressed countless small problems that could be solved by engineers. They spoke with the classes about the career of engineering, as each of the Bayers specialized in a different engineering field.

MAINTENANCE CREW FROM KENTUCKY, USA

The sisters in Uganda recognized that the buildings at St. Julie needed some repair. Knowing some persons who could assist in this, the sisters began making some contacts. Mr. Bob Simon, a skilled construction engineer in Northern Kentucky, agreed to oversee the project and assemble a crew of others who had experience in engineering or construction. Seven men from two local parishes gathered to plan for the trip and what they would need to take with them.

The group departed Kentucky August 24, 2014, and returned September 6. They had been informed about some of the issues to be addressed, one of these being the replacement of screens. The original screens had been in place for almost twenty years. The poor quality of the screening necessitated the replacement of <u>every</u> screen! The challenge to use screening from the United States was how to transport rolls of screening. A solution was discovered: the rolls of screen were placed in golf bags. This also allowed extra things, like cans of chili, to be placed in the empty space in the center.

In Buseesa, the group worked from dawn to dusk replacing screens and ceiling tiles, painting railings, renewing, and taking care of whatever was needed. As they worked, it became apparent that there was still much more that needed attention. They created a list of jobs and tools needed and began remote planning for future maintenance trips.

Dirt road in Busessa

15

THE HOLY SPIRIT GENERAL DELEGATION

We had a really wonderful day. … We began with a special morning prayer followed by a festive breakfast. At 11:00 a.m. we began the Pentecost liturgy. (Sr. M. Colette to Sr. M. Margaret, May 25 2015)

The ceremonies in Tanzania were simple but inspiring. The focus was the Pentecost Mass in the Formation House chapel with the installation of the new superiors taking place within it. It reminded me of the vow ceremony with Sr. Kristin calling forth each sister and asking if she were willing to assume the responsibilities of her particular office. She then gave each an African Bible and a lighted red candle that was placed on the altar. The chapel was beautifully decorated in the Holy Spirit theme and the formees [sisters in training] sang and danced their hearts out during the Mass. After Mass, we enjoyed a festive dinner in the "upper room." (Sr. Mary Judith to Sr. Mary Margaret, May 28, 2015)

Posted around the gathering space were the good wishes from around the congregation. It was truly an inspiring day for me. (Sr. M. Colette to Sr. Mary Margaret, May 25, 2015)

What was the celebration described? Why were there good wishes from around the congregation? The mission in Uganda was begun in 1995. In November 1992, the sisters from India established a mission in Tanzania and extended into Kenya in 2001. Tanzania/Kenya became a Province Delegation under the India province. In 2012, the India province began discussions with the general government in Rome about the Holy Spirit Province Delegation (Tanzania/Kenya) becoming the Holy Spirit General Delegation under the general government in Rome.

A delegation is a grouping of several local communities that does not yet meet the requirements for a province. … A delegation is dependent on a province or on the general level. (Directives of the Constitutions of the Sisters of Notre Dame, 2004, 95.2)

HOW IT CAME ABOUT

In a letter of January 25, 2013, Sr. Mary Kristin wrote to Sr. Marla, provincial superior in Covington and Sr. Mary Anncarla, provincial superior in Thousand Oaks, informing them that the Holy Spirit Provincial Delegation would become a general level delegation in about two years. She asked them to consider if they wanted

Uganda to become a part of the new unit and to speak with the sisters in Uganda about the formation of an East Africa General Delegation. "This is a good opportunity for them to shape the future of SND in Africa and to make it more African."

At the visitation in April 2014, the two provincial superiors discussed with the perpetually professed sisters the formation of a general delegation in 2015. This opened the possibility of the Uganda mission joining to form a joint East Africa General Delegation. After much discussion, all of the senior professed sisters voted to do so if certain conditions could be met. Although time for deliberation and preparation seemed very short, lack of personnel available to continue to staff the Uganda mission from both the United States and Germany pointed in this direction.

Pros and cons were debated, and the provincial superiors took note of the concerns and suggestions to share when Sr. Mary Sreeja Chittillappilly, a member of the General Council in Rome, who would visit later in the year. With trust in the good God, the sisters prepared to move into this new yet unsettling future.

When Sr. Mary Sreeja arrived in Uganda in May, she met with individuals and groups of sisters both in Buseesa and in Mpala to speak about the new delegation. Sister assisted the sisters to understand what this new delegation would mean and to help relieve some of the fears the sisters expressed.

The two provincials met with their respective provincial councils to discuss the pros and cons of joining the delegation and decided that for the good of the Uganda mission and the young African sisters, they would accept the invitation and join the Holy Spirit General Delegation. The provincials wrote to the sisters in their provinces:

> The General Government has invited our Uganda Mission to join with the SND Tanzania and Kenya Missions to become a new Delegation under the General Government.
>
> We spoke with. … our missionary sisters and our Ugandan sisters, and prayed for the guidance of the Sprit. We decided to accept the invitation to join this East African General Delegation. Being part of the new Delegation from the beginning will give us the opportunity to influence the structures and policies of the delegation and allow us to collaborate in East Africa more effectively in mission.
>
> We are committed to continue to provide financial support and personnel as long as we are able.
>
> Our Ugandan Sisters and the people of Uganda have a permanent place in our hearts. This new governance structure will not change that. (Sr. Marla and Sr. Mary Anncarla to Sisters, July 2, 2014)

The next important step was to meet with each sister in Tanzania, Kenya, and Uganda. Meetings were held to clarify any questions or concerns about the future and to share information. Each missionary sister from India, the United States, and Germany was asked if she wanted to be a member of the new general level delegation or remain a member of her home province. Every missionary chose to be a member of the new delegation, but to continue to follow the guidelines set by their respective provincial superiors for home visits, medical care, and personal needs.

On August 23, all the sisters from St. Julie Mission and the sisters from Notre Dame Education Center met in Mpala. After prayer and a short introduction and some time for reflection the sisters divided into small groups to discuss the following: "What are the non-negotiable of SND religious life?" "What are the hopes and dreams you have for the new delegation?" "What hopes and fears do you have?" "What are some of the policies that will need to be addressed?" The groups then met together and shared their findings. (Sisters of Notre Dame Mpala Annals, August 23, 2014)

In 2014, the general government in Rome voted to establish the East Africa Holy Spirit General Delegation and include Uganda.

The 2014 African Conference held in Arusha, Tanzania, included all sisters from East Africa who would be members of the new unit. The theme of the conference, "SND Vision for Africa," was an appropriate one as an important topic at the conference was establishing a new entity, the East Africa General Delegation. Sisters commented that it was moving to see so many young sisters involved and active at the meetings. In her opening address, Sr. Mary Kristin set the tone of the conference.

> For fifteen years we have been meeting to dialog, support and learn from one another on our journey in Africa. Now we are about to begin a new chapter of that journey: The creation of an East African General Delegation. God has truly blessed us on this holy ground of Africa. We have received good vocations and we have planted the seeds of ministries, which witness to God's provident care for our African brothers and sisters. Africa is a continent of unlimited potential, and by God's grace we are privileged to be co-creators of the reign of God by seeing the possible and liberating potential. … Twenty-two years ago, when the first seeds of Notre Dame were planted on African soil in Arusha, Tanzania, none of us knew how God in his provident care would lead us. None of us could have envisioned today. God has blessed us with a future full of hope.
>
> Tanzania, Kenya, and Uganda, the units that will form the Holy Spirit General Delegation, have a rich history with much diversity. The seeds of Notre Dame in Kenya and Tanzania were planted by our Indian sisters. The seeds of Notre Dame in Uganda were planted by our American sisters with much assistance from

our German sisters. Our younger African sisters who have contributed much to the beginnings of Notre Dame in East Africa come from a number of different tribal ethnic groups. This has been a strength of our presence in Africa. It has witnessed Gospel community where many have become one in Notre Dame. (African Conference, Arusha, Tanzania, December 14–20, 2014)

The days included time for reflection and small group sharing on various points that Sr. Mary Kristin presented. Units of East Africa gave reports on what was happening in their units including their challenges and what was going well. National sisters met with Sr. Mary Krisitin for a day and were able to share their particular fears and concerns. Other sisters broke into groups to design an East African tertian program (a program of preparation for sisters pronouncing perpetual vows) and a teacher-training course. Later, all shared the results of their respective groups. Plans were made for moving together, and suggestions were solicited from the sisters for members of the new delegation leadership team.

On January 4, 2015, the community received the news that Sr. Mary Roshini Poriyathu, from India, would be the delegation superior of the new East African Holy Spirit Delegation. The other members of the leadership team would be announced after Sr. Mary Roshini considered the names suggested by the sisters that were submitted to Sr. Mary Kristin and her council

On January 10, Sr. Mary Roshini sent a letter announcing the names of the members of the new delegation team: Sr. Mary Colette Theobald, Sr. Mary Sawmya, Sr. Mary Elizabeth Wanza Mulako, and Sr. Mary Immaculate Nammuga.

REACTION OF THE SISTERS

In Uganda, the Uganda sisters realized they would no longer be part of one of the founding provinces. Even though only part of the Covington province for a few years, the separation was deeply felt by the Ugandan sisters. (Sr. Mary Margaret Droege meeting with Ugandan sisters in Covington, Kentucky, May 2016, and in Chardon, Ohio, June 2016). On both continents, the sisters understood the reasons for this major change, but the separation was still difficult on both sides.

The news about an East Africa Delegation created mixed emotions among the sisters in the United States. It was difficult for some when they realized that the young Uganda sisters who were members of the Covington province would now belong to the new delegation. There were questions, especially about funding and fund-raising.

In preparation for the establishment of the East Africa Delegation, the sisters in the Covington and California provinces joined in a novena prayer:

Holy Spirit, you breathed passion for the Gospel into the lives of the apostles, as well as into the hearts of St. Julie and our first Coesfeld Sisters. In your goodness, you continue to inspire us to reach out to people everywhere and, in a special way, to those in Africa.

Thank you for the wisdom, courage and love you have given to our Congregation to respond to this mission. Now under your patronage, our Sisters from different lands will walk together as the Holy Spirit Delegation.

We ask you to give life and energy to these Sisters and to those who will follow, that through life and ministry many will experience God's presence and love.

May your plans for Holy Spirit Delegation unfold in goodness. We ask this through the intercession of Our Lady, Notre Dame. Amen.

In her letter of May 11, 2015, Sr. Mary Kristin wrote:

This is a very historic event in our Congregation. It is the first time a unit is made up of sisters from 6 different countries. Members of the delegation come from Germany, India, the United States, Tanzania, Uganda and Kenya.

In the Covington province, the following reflection was read before the Eucharistic liturgy on Pentecost:

They waited
They waited for days
And finally:
A roaring wind
A shaking of the house
Tongues of fire
Everything broke loose
New understandings
Enlivened courage
Eagerness to share the Word

Today, right here, it's Pentecost
We wait
We prayed the novena
It's supposed to happen today

But there's
No roaring wind
No swaying building
No tongues of fire over our heads
At least, none that I observe

Have we been forgotten by the Spirit of God?
Hardly!
But wait!
Open wide; open fully
Remove all obstacles, objections
Anything that blocks the Spirit's movement

In the Rift Valley of East Africa
There's a shaking in the house
A re-ordering of things once thought permanent
There are tongues
Not of fire, but of nations, tribes and languages
Languages joining together, not remaining apart
There is a roaring
Not of gusting winds
But of voices
Voices raised in praise
Voices raised in thanksgiving
Voices begging for all the Spirit's gifts
Wisdom, fortitude, fear of the Lord

Today is Pentecost
A new beginning
For all who have been waiting
A new beginning
Appropriately called
Holy Spirit Delegation

Holy Spirit, fill the hearts of all your faithful ones
Kindle your love in us
That we may help you
Renew the face of the earth. Amen.

On May 24, 2015, in Arusha, Tanzania, on the feast of Pentecost, the Sisters of Notre Dame mission in Uganda joined the Sisters of Notre Dame missions in Tanzania and Kenya to form the new Holy Spirit General Delegation.

Sr. Mary Kristin Battles and Sr. Mary Sreeja Chittilappilly led the installation ceremony of the new delegation leadership team:

Sr. Mary Roshini (India) Delegation Superior
Sr. Mary Colette (United States) First Assistant
Sr. Mary Sawmya (India) Councilor
Sr. Mary Elizabeth (Kenya) Councilor
Sr. Mary Immaculate (Uganda) Councilor

Sr. Mary Annete Adams (United States) was appointed secretary and Sr. Mary Pramila Vanniamparambil (India), treasurer.

The Delegation center was moved to Nairobi, Kenya.

The Roof of Africa, (June 2015, Volume 7, #2) the publication of the East Africa Delegation, summarized the experience of those present for this historical event:

> We all felt like the first Pentecost gathering, all experiencing an outpouring of the Gifts of the Holy Spirit. Adapting the Scriptures, "we were Ugandans, Kenyans, Germans and Americans, there were inhabitants from Tanzania and India as well as travelers from Rome, yet we hear them speaking in our own tongues of the mighty acts of God."

American sisters missioned in Uganda wrote:

> "Now the mission is part of something bigger and will, hopefully, continue to grow and be a source of proclamation of the kingdom." (Sr. Mary Colette to Sr. Mary Margaret, May 25, 2015)

> May the Spirit course through our minds, bodies, and souls that we may be alive to new whisperings from God in our one mission to proclaim God's goodness to those whom we serve! (Sr. Mary Paulynne to Sr. Mary Margaret, May 24, 2015)

Two months later, the sisters in Covington received an email from one of the Ugandan sisters.

> Even though we are now a delegation i [sic] cannot forget my roots. Before we became a delegation we belonged there. … i [sic] really do feel we are part of this province because i [sic] entered under this province. … We are what we are because of you. It is on this very note that i [sic] take this opportunity to thank all our different Provincial Superiors. … and all other Sisters you are all appreciated. Thank you so much for making us what we are now. (Sr. Mary Juliet to Sr. Mary Carol Baglan, June 13, 2015)

CONCLUSION

At the conclusion of 2015 when the Uganda mission transferred from the sponsorship of the Covington, Kentucky, and Thousand Oaks, California, provinces to becoming part of the East Africa Holy Spirit Delegation, the following were the statistics of the two mission sites in Uganda:

In Buseesa, there were eight sisters: four senior professed sisters and four temporary professed sisters. There were forty-one laymen and women on staff at St. Julie Mission. There were one hundred children attending St. Julie Nursery, two hundred forty-eight students at St. Julie Primary, and one hundred eighty-three students at Notre Dame Academy Secondary.

In Mpala, there were eight sisters: two senior professed sisters and six temporary professed sisters. There were thirty laymen and women on staff at Notre Dame Education Center. There were one hundred eighty-four children enrolled in Notre Dame Nursery School

The establishment and growth of the mission in Uganda has truly been a manifestation of the goodness and provident care of our good God. The preceding pages testify to God's presence and care at every moment. We accepted the invitation of Bishop Deogratias Byabazaire to come to the Hoima Diocese thinking of what we could do for the people especially in the area of education. But we were surprised! How much we have received from the beautiful and faith-filled people of Uganda! So often, they shared even the little they had, and they always shared a smile. They will forever hold a special place in our hearts.

The formation of the East Africa Holy Spirit Delegation coincided with the Twentieth anniversary of the Kentucky and California sisters' arrival in Uganda. In a letter of July 13, 2015, to the sisters in Uganda, Sr. Mary Janet Stamm, one of the first missionaries to Uganda, expressed so well, not just her personal sentiments, but also those of all the sisters in California and Kentucky.

> Dear Sisters,
>
> Happy 20th Anniversary! What many blessings we have received during the past twenty years! I am so grateful to God for calling our Ugandan Mission to birth and for all his many gifts and blessings through these years. Two of the very special graces and gifts that I am grateful for are Jesus in the Blessed Sacrament and secondly the gift of our Uganda sisters. From the very first day we were at our Mission in Buseesa we had Holy Mass and then Jesus took up his residence with us in a poor wooden tabernacle in our storeroom chapel. He moved quite often as the construction progressed but he has always been with us and is to this very day. What a blessing this has been and continues to be for all of us. To see all of you, our Ugandan sisters gives all of us such hope and joy. God is

indeed so very good. We are celebrating with all of you and remembering the good things God has done and thanking him for all that he will yet do for the Holy Spirit Delegation and for SND in East Africa. I thank each of you for all that you have done and continue to do for God and the Ugandan people. May each of you experience God's abundant blessings and continue to be held in his love and care.

With joy, gratitude and many good wishes,

Sr. Janet

Image of Mary in the convent in Buseesa

EPILOGUE

As the East Africa delegation was being formed, Sr. Mary Kristin asked Sr. Mary Ethel (Covington) and Sr. Mary Anncarla (Thousand Oaks) to host a visit for all the national Ugandan sisters who had made vows before the announcement of the delegation. She felt that they had strong ties to Covington and Thousand Oaks, and that such a visit would be welcomed by both sides.

The sisters were to visit in two groups in 2016:

The first group included Sr. Mary Sunday, Sr. Violet Marie, Sr. Anita Marie, and Sr. Mary Juliet. The sisters were scheduled to leave Uganda on May 14 and arrive in the USA on May 15. All were students, had just completed courses at the university and were to returned to Uganda on June 4 in time to begin a new semester.

The second group included Sr. Mary Immaculate, Sr. Mary Annet, Sr. Mary Teopista, Sr. Mary Olive, and Sr. Christine Marie. The sisters departed from Uganda on June 22 and returned to Uganda on July 13.

An unanticipated problem that caused great concern and anxiety was the difficulty the sisters experienced in procuring their visas. Emails from Uganda tracked their progress:

On April 21, Sr. Mary Ethel in Covington received a communication:

> The first two of the sisters from Uganda who were to visit the States in May went to the US Embassy in Uganda for the requisite interviews. We expected this to be entirely routine as it was a simple tourist visa. But their requests for a visa were denied. The official generic letter seems to attribute it to a condition that does not apply.

On May 7, Sr. Mary Ethel wrote:

> Almost miraculously, Sr. Tina was able to get the final two sisters … scheduled for interviews on Tuesday. Pray that this time they are not rejected, and then that they can get the actual visas so they can leave on Friday. It is very tight.

On May 8, from Sr. Mary Ethel:

> I just learned that the two … got approved for their visas an hour ago! Now we just need to pray that the actual paperwork gets processed by Friday.

In the end, the sisters visited the US Embassy on the day of their departure, and after much persistence, finally obtained their visas hours before they boarded the plane for the United States.

IN THE UNITED STATES

While in the United States, the sisters spent time in the Covington and Thousand Oaks provinces and met the sisters of these provinces. They became acquainted with the particular ministries of each of the provinces and visited some local attractions, especially those associated with the provinces' history.

The sisters experienced things the American sisters just take for granted: air conditioning, readily available transportation, the largeness of the provincial centers and grounds, reliable electricity, and running water. One of the Uganda sisters commented that the visit revealed to her how much the missionaries gave up in coming to Uganda.

The sisters traveled to the Chardon province. While in Chardon, the sisters visited the site of St. Mary's Orphanage where the foundress of the Sisters of Notre Dame, Sr. Mary Aloysia, last ministered. They then visited her grave in a nearby cemetery. There were touching moments as the sisters gathered and prayed at each of these special sites. It was obvious that these young sisters had a strong sense of the spiritual heritage of the congregation and recognized Sr. Mary Aloysia's generous response to all God asked of her.

The sisters next visited the Toledo province where they toured the new facility near the Lial Retreat Center. They prayed in the chapel before the crucifix that had once hung in the Annathal Convent in Coesfeld, Germany, many years ago.

Because of the timing of the visit, the sisters were able to meet some of their partners in mission, those who support the Uganda mission. The first group of sisters arrived in Covington in time for the appreciation dinner for Uganda donors. Each sister told her vocation story to the assembled group. The second group participated in Covington's Annual July 4th social, an event that raised funds for the Uganda mission.

One group of sisters visited with the families of the Covington sisters who had or were presently in Uganda.

> "After supper we gathered in our sm. Dining room and the sisters shared with the family members. It was wonderful exchange! They represented all of you so well. We ended about 8:15 when the 4 sang a song and then we joined hands and prayed for God's continued blessings on the Mission. What a happy evening!" (Sr. M. Janet to United States and German sisters in Uganda, May 21, 2016)

In Thousand Oaks, the sisters spent time with the sisters in the provincial center and traveled to the local houses to meet the other sisters. A highlight of the visit was their meeting with one of the first California missionaries to Uganda.

> Sr. Jane Marie welcomed us using Runyoro language. She spoke so many phrases in our local language and we were impressed by how much she could remember after eleven years. She shared so much of her experiences in the early days of the Mission in Uganda. (Sr. Mary Teopista to Sr. Mary Janet, July 9, 2016)

> We had the opportunity to visit one of the famous California missions and walk along the beach of the Pacific Ocean. "We stepped in water and even got our skirts wet by the big waves." (Sr. Mary Teopista to Sr. M Janet, July 7, 2016)

The Uganda visitors especially enjoyed meeting their prayer partners in the provinces and spending time with the older members of the community in the health care centers. The United States sisters commented that the Uganda sisters brought such life and youthful enthusiasm and gave them great hope for the future of Notre Dame in Africa and throughout the world.

On their last evening in Covington, Sr. Mary Juliet spoke a thank you in the name of the Ugandan sisters.

> Dear Sisters, we sang in the song that love is something that you give it away, then it comes right back to you. Indeed, that is what you did. Out of love for us, you gave to us, the first sisters, Srs. Janet and Delrita and the others to come to Uganda. And now here we are right back with you. But we can really say that we are all your fruits, and we are all the work of your hands. It is because of you that we are standing right here.

> Our roots are here and we are glad that we have seen our roots, and this has made us very strong because when you know your roots then you become very strong. And we assure you the Uganda mission will keep growing. We will not let you down.

> Thank you for nurturing us, watering us, pruning us, and making us who we are today. (Transcription of presentation of Sr. Mary Juliet, May 25, 2016)

GLOSSARY

A-Level – Advanced Level: designates the two additional secondary levels (S-5, S-6) after completing O-Level; is a requirement for entrance into the university.

ARU – Association of Religious in Uganda sponsored a hostel for women religious in Kampala

BCDC – Buseesa Community Development Center - A microfinance program that grew to include establishing a primary school, building latrines in the area, and providing occasional health screening, usually with assistance from the United States.

Boda-boda – a motorcycle

Banyoro tribe – predominant tribe in the Kibaale District

Butema brick – brick that is uniquely African. It is several shades of red and orange and is of excellent quality. Produced in Butema.

Bazungu – foreign white people

Cassava – a starch root plant that requires cooking. It can be prepared in a variety of ways.

DEO – District Education Officer

DHO – District Health Officer

DIS – District Inspector of Schools

Ebinyeges – leg rattles worn by boys in Ugandan dances

Empaakos – (pet name) local names bestowed upon each member of the tribe and visitors to show they are one with the people

General Conference – a gathering of the members of the General Council and the provincial superiors, usually to identify the theme of the next General Chapter

General Chapter – an international gathering of representatives from all the provinces in the congregation

General Council – the chief governing body of the Sisters of Notre Dame. It includes the superior general, the assistant, and councilors.

Gomesi – traditional dress of Ugandan women

Ground nuts – peanuts

Head teacher – principal

Jerry cans – twenty-liter plastic containers used to transport or store water

Matooke – a variety of banana that is indigenous to parts of Uganda. These green bananas are used mainly for cooking. Sometimes referred to as plantains.

Matron – a mother away from home. There is one for each dorm building

Mzee – an older person and a title of honor

Mzungu – a white person

Names – The people in the Buseesa area generally have two names: A Christian name and a Ugandan name. Surnames or family names are not used in Uganda.

O-Level – Ordinary Level; designates the first four years of secondary education S-1, S-2, S-3, S-4

PLE – Primary Leaving Exams are national tests administered at the end of P-7. Students must pass these exams to qualify for entrance into secondary school.

Old Boys/Girls – graduates of a school

Posho – corn flour boiled in water until it is thick and pasty

Primary – designates grades one through seven, referred to as P-1, P-2, … P-7

Province – a designated group (usually geographic) of convents under one provincial superior

Provincial Council – the chief governing body of a province. It includes the provincial superior, the assistant, and councilors

Provincial Superior – the sister who serves as the head of a province and the provincial council

Runyoro – tribal language of the people in the Kibaale District

School fees – fees that include tuition, room and board, school uniform, textbooks

Superior General – the sister who serves as the head of the congregation and of the General Council

Sweety – a piece of candy

UCE – Universal Certificate of Education. Exam taken by S-4 students completing the O-Level of secondary education. Passing is required to advance to the next level of education.

Waragi – domestic distilled beverage